LEADING
UNDER
PRESSURE

From Surviving to Thriving Before, During, and After a Crisis

LEADING UNDER PRESSURE

From Surviving to Thriving Before, During, and After a Crisis

ERIKA HAYES JAMES
UNIVERSITY OF VIRGINIA

LYNN PERRY WOOTEN
UNIVERSITY OF MICHIGAN

Routledge
Taylor & Francis Group
New York   London

Routledge
Taylor & Francis Group
270 Madison Avenue
New York, NY 10016

Routledge
Taylor & Francis Group
27 Church Road
Hove, East Sussex BN3 2FA

© 2010 by Taylor and Francis Group, LLC
Routledge is an imprint of Taylor & Francis Group, an Informa business

Printed in the United States of America on acid-free paper
10 9 8 7 6 5 4 3 2

International Standard Book Number: 978-1-84169-790-1 (Hardback) 978-1-84169-791-8 (Paperback)

Library of Congress Cataloging-in-Publication Data

James, Erika H.
    Leading under pressure : from surviving to thriving before, during, and after a crisis / Erika H. James, Lynn Perry Wooten.
        p. cm.
    Includes bibliographical references and index.
    ISBN 978-1-84169-790-1 (hbk. : alk. paper) -- ISBN 978-1-84169-791-8 (pbk. : alk. paper)
    1. Crisis management. 2. Leadership. I. Wooten, Lynn Perry. II. Title.

HD49.J36 2011
658.4'092--dc22   2010018105

**Visit the Taylor & Francis Web site at
http://www.taylorandfrancis.com**

**and the Psychology Press Web site at
http://www.psypress.com**

Dedication

We dedicate this book to our parents, who nurtured us to
be the women we are; our husbands, for their love, wit, and
support; and our children, for inspiring us to keep going.

Contents

PART II: BECOMING A CRISIS LEADER—INDIVIDUAL CAPABILITIES

PART III: ORGANIZATIONAL CAPABILITIES

PART IV: FROM SURVIVING TO THRIVING
UNDER PRESSURE

About the Authors

Erika Hayes James (PhD, University of Michigan) is the Bank of America research associate professor of business administration at the University of Virginia's Darden Graduate School of Business. She has served on the faculties of Tulane University, Emory University, and Harvard University, where she has taught courses in organizational behavior, power and leadership, and crisis leadership. Dr. James's research focuses on leadership, with a particular emphasis on leadership during crises. Her work explores the competencies necessary to lead organizations throughout the life cycle of a business crisis and emphasizes how firm leaders come to realize and manifest opportunities from crises. A secondary research interest is in workplace diversity. Dr. James has explored gender and racial inequities in the workplace, and firm strategic responses to allegations of discrimination. Her research has been published in academic journals such as the *Academy of Management Journal, Strategic Management Journal, Journal of Applied Psychology, Journal of Management Inquiry, Journal of Applied Behavioral Science*, and *Organizational Dynamics*. In addition, her work has been featured in numerous media outlets, including *National Public Radio, The Wall Street Journal, Business Week*, and *The Washington Post*. Dr. James has translated her research into numerous course development materials, and she was the recipient of the Wachovia Award for Excellence in Course Materials (Innovative Case Category) for a computer-based crisis management simulation. She has developed numerous case studies that are used for MBA classes and executive audiences. Dr. James is a member of the editorial board for the *Journal of Management*. She consults in the areas of decision making under pressure, workplace diversity, and building workplace trust.

Lynn Perry Wooten (PhD, Ross School of Business, University of Michigan) is a clinical associate professor of strategy, and management and organizations at the University of Michigan's Ross School of Business. She codirects the Center for Positive Organizational Scholarship and the Executive Leadership Institute. Dr. Wooten teaches corporate strategy, human resource management, leadership, and organizational behavior courses. Her research focuses on how organizations respond, are resilient, and learn from crisis situations. In addition, she studies positive organizing routines and the effectiveness of diversity management programs in organizations. Dr. Wooten's research has been funded by the National Institutes of Health, Sloan Foundation, and Society for Human Resource Management. Her research on executive development and diversity won awards from the Academy of Management and the consulting firm McKinsey and Company, and *The Financial Times* selected her as a Next Generation Business Thinker in Human Resource Management. Dr. Wooten's work has been published in academic journals such as *Academy of Management Journal, Human Resource Management, Journal of Management Inquiry,* and *Organizational Dynamics,* and has been featured in newspapers and industry trade journals and on radio programs. She has also written book chapters, teaching materials, and monographs on workforce diversity, board diversity, crisis leadership, and positive organizing practices. Dr. Wooten is an associate editor of *Human Resource Management* and a consulting editor for the *Journal of Business and Education.* She consults in the areas of strategic human resource management, positive organizing practices, and workforce diversity with both profit and not-for-profit organizations.

Preface

In the time that it took to write this book, the United States and the world experienced tremendous change, and much of that change was marked by crisis. In the United States alone, financial markets all but crashed; companies that once defined America tumbled, or nearly so; a lone gunmen killed 13 military men and women and severely injured 28 others in what was ostensibly one of the safest places in America—the military installation at Fort Hood; and President Obama declared the rapidly spreading H1N1 flu virus to be a national emergency, yet promises of vaccine dissemination were not fulfilled. Many of these events either had global consequences or were sparked from worldwide events. An unfortunate aftermath of all of these events is a lack of public trust in many of America's institutions and the people that lead them.

To say that the global workforce is under pressure may be an understatement. At a macro level, there is the pressure of worldwide competition and the need to operate across the globe. At a more micro level, there is the pressure of individuals or departments to produce more with increasingly fewer resources. Pressure is at once the precipitator and the consequence of crisis. It is ubiquitous, and it is increasingly defining how we function at work. Leaders who can flourish under pressure will be the ones to guide us through these and future turbulent times.

When people have asked us about the type of research that we do, or in what areas of business we teach and consult, we have told them that we are experts in crisis leadership. Naively, we expected managers to engage with us in conversation about why this was an important subject matter and how their organization or organization's leadership could benefit from a deeper understanding of this topic. What we received from executives, however, was one of the following three responses: (1) a dismissive nod of the head followed by a summation of their own organization's business continuity plan (loosely speaking), (2) denial that there was a need for such expertise in their own organizations, or (3) a recounting of how poorly other firms were at crisis management and assurance that their own company would never act in such foolish ways. From the academic community, our crisis leadership ideas were often confused for the study of crisis communication. In fact, there are numerous occasions in which our colleagues (people with whom we have worked for years and who have read and provided feedback on our research) have referred to us as experts in crisis communication. In our minds, crisis communication is just one of several important aspects of leading under pressure.

Committed to our belief that leadership in times of crisis should be a core managerial competency, we refused to be swayed by the reactions of people that did not quite understand, much less buy in to, our notion of crisis leadership. Yet, it was clear that we did not have the language to communicate our message effectively to our audiences, whether the audience was an MBA classroom, corporate executives, directors of government agencies, or leaders of a not-for-profit organization. We were faced with the attitude that crises happen to other people, or that crises were a result of other people's incompetence. Failing to consider that most crises do not discriminate, and that even very competent leaders can find themselves facing a set of undesirable and threatening circumstances, was precisely at the root of the message we wanted to convey. Beyond those two central messages was an even more important one—that crises are about people, and leading an organization before, during, and after a crisis requires continuous focus on the well-being of those individuals. This book is intended to communicate our belief that developing the ability to effectively lead an organization facing immense pressures is no longer an option, nor is it something to be delegated to others. Rather, it is a central aspect of every leader's responsibility to the array of stakeholders that are affected by their decisions. The concepts associated with the ability to lead under pressure, such as decision making, building organizational trust, and organizational learning, should be a required part of management education whether at graduate schools or during professional and executive development engagements. To that end, we offer the ideas, examples, and research presented in the subsequent pages of this book.

Our goal is to help students and business leaders alike deepen their understanding of how we typically respond to threatening situations and to provide food for thought with respect to how one might enact effective leadership behaviors in times of crisis. The book is grounded primarily in academic research. Throughout the book, we integrate the academic discussion with modern examples of crises or crisis handling to illustrate key points. Through an intricate weaving of theoretical, empirical, and practical ideas associated with the concepts of crisis and leadership, we present a comprehensive perspective that we hope will guide the scholarly community toward continued study in crisis leadership, challenge students to prepare themselves for a new leadership form, and provide a road map for students and business leaders to traverse as they continue to navigate the ever-increasing challenges of leading today's organizations.

That said, we want to be clear that our intention in writing this book is to highlight the important role of *leadership* when organizations are under the type of pressure that crises evoke. Unlike the typical crisis management book (which serves an important although altogether different goal), ours does not offer the ABCs of how to handle a crisis. Rather, we offer a framework and set of perspectives of leadership that are particularly relevant when leading under pressure. Clearly developing a business continuity plan before a crisis hits and managing the communication process during a crisis are necessary elements of crisis management. However, these are all tasks to be managed or perhaps even delegated. Leadership, on the other hand, is everyone's responsibility. Finally, to lead under pressure requires a broader mindset and a different set of capabilities than what might be required when one is focused solely on the tactical aspects of crisis handling. We describe this mindset and the requisite leadership capabilities throughout this book.

The book is organized into four parts. Part I serves to introduce the reader to the concept of crisis leadership and differentiate how leadership under pressure differs from general leadership or leadership in times of relative calm. Combined, the two chapters in Part I provide a solid foundation of key terms (e.g., crisis, crisis management, leadership, and so on) and a comprehensive overview of crisis types and general crisis handling strategies. Part II expands the discussion by focusing on the individual capabilities necessary to effectively lead an organization in times of intense pressure. Here, we highlight critical leadership competencies, decision making, and the important role of designing and leading a crisis team. Part III identifies core organizational capabilities that facilitate leadership under pressure. These include an organizational culture or structure characterized by trust and learning, and one that is facile in operating with a global mindset. The final section of the book brings all of the prior information together to outline the circumstances that allow some leaders to perceive crises as potential sources of opportunity (rather than only as a threat). When this happens, the possibility for organizational innovation and positive change increases.

Special Features

Throughout this book, we attempt to shed light on the growing body of research that directly or indirectly is connected to the topic of organizational crises and crisis management. Some of that research reflects our own theorizing and empirical-based studies of the topic. Yet, given the potentially severe implications that crisis events can have on organizations, it would be a disservice not to also address the very practical side of leading under pressure and in times of crisis. Therefore, the chapters, as appropriate, offer two additional resources intended to guide those that lead organizations, big or small, public or private. "Leadership Links" are references to Web-based sources of information from both academic and practitioner communities. They are intended for those readers who would like additional information about the specific topic in the chapter. The "Leader's Hot Seat" poses a set of questions that managers should consider and corresponding answers. These are intended to encourage application of the ideas from the chapter to one's own situation. Finally, several of the chapters include a section called "From Theory to Practice" that serves to connect theoretical-based research with practical implications.

Acknowledgments

It is clearly a team effort to pull off writing a book. We are eternally grateful to the support team that graciously devoted their time, talent, and treasure to this endeavor. Included in this team are the administrations of our respective universities. The Batten Institute and the research committee at the Darden Graduate School of Business, as well as the Ross School of Business at the University of Michigan, provided the funding and support that went into the research and writing of the book. In addition, I, Erika James, am particularly grateful to Dean Robert Bruner at Darden, who granted me a one-year leave of absence during the time that I was writing. The year I was on leave I spent as a visiting faculty member at the Harvard Business School, and I am eternally grateful to my friend and mentor David Thomas, who not only made the visiting appointment possible, but did so in a way that allowed me to pursue writing in the absence of many other professional commitments. The idea to even consider a book on leadership under pressure was sparked by friend, colleague, and mentor Arthur Brief, to whom we are indebted. We are extremely beholden to Christine Davis, who provided exemplary editing (not to mention patience) as we wrote, and rewrote, each chapter. We also thank Joana Young, who came to our aid with respect to helping us graphically depict the key aspects of each chapter. Anne Duffy and Erin Flaherty were our editor and editorial assistant, respectively, at Taylor & Francis. We are grateful for their unending confidence and support. And, to Connie Glover, who was our promoter, cheerleader, motivator, and cover designer—thank you!

Finally, to take on a project of this magnitude requires considerable sacrifice. To our families, Jimmie James, Jordan and Alexandra, and David Wooten, Justin and Jada, thank you for your encouragement, support, and understanding as we spent time away from you to complete this book.

THE MODERN FACE OF LEADERSHIP UNDER PRESSURE

1

Chapter 1

Introduction
Why Crisis Leadership Matters

As we commence the writing of this book and contemplating what contribution we can make to the plethora of books on leadership, and the more recent emergence of books on crisis leadership in particular, the United States has recently gone through one of the most significant confluences of crisis events in its history. The euphemism of "a perfect storm" seems appropriate if not completely accurate. From our vantage point, though, the United States has simultaneously experienced a massive financial crisis, a reputational crisis, and a crisis of trust—the latter of which is largely a function of the two former.

In a two-week period in the fall of 2008, the United States witnessed the shocking collapse of several of its most seemingly stable and secure financial institutions. On September 14 Merrill Lynch entered bankruptcy and was quickly acquired by Bank of America. The next day, Lehman Brothers filed for bankruptcy, was split up, and portions of the former firm were purchased by Barclays. The next week, on September 25, the nation's largest savings and loan association was placed into receivership, ironically on the same day as the firm's 119-year anniversary. The demise of Washington Mutual represented the largest single bank failure in American history. The landslide of financial failures started several months earlier when Bear Stearns, once recognized as the "most admired" securities firm in *Fortune*'s "America's Most Admired Companies" survey, was acquired by JPMorgan Chase for $10 per share, down from the 52-week high of more than $130 per share. Among them, these once stalwart companies had almost 450 years of history, having previously survived other economic downturns, including the Wall Street Crash of 1929.

The causes of what has come to be called simply the financial crisis are too numerous to describe here. Economists, finance gurus, and the federal government will no doubt invest years in trying to identify the appropriate attributions. At the surface, however, it is clear that subprime mortgage lending practices played a major part. Subprime lending refers to the provision of credit to potentially high-risk borrowers, including those who have defaulted on prior loans or who have limited debt experience. When some credit issuers engaged in predatory lending practices, particularly for home mortgages, the result led to massive loan defaults, and lending institutions were forced to write down billions of dollars in losses. At the heart of those losses were Freddie Mac and Fannie Mae, government-backed mortgage lending institutions that survived the financial crisis only with substantial assistance from the U.S. government.

Banks and lending institutions were not the only industries affected by the crisis and in need of federal support. America's largest insurance company, AIG, was close to insolvency before the federal government intervened, granting the company a sizable portion of a $700 billion financial package formally called the Emergency Economic Stabilization Act of 2008, now referred to as simply the "bailout." In the midst of these troubles, America's Big Three automakers (General Motors, Ford, and Chrysler) met with members of Congress to request their own bailout, and they did so more than once. Their initial visit to Capitol Hill resulted in a failed attempt to secure funds and a public relations nightmare for the auto companies when all three executives arrived independently in Washington, D.C., from the Detroit metropolitan area on their corporate jets. The public outcry toward this extravagance suggested that the executives were incapable of fiscal management. It was yet another sign of public mistrust in the institutions, and the leadership, that have been a driving force of the U.S. economy.

In short, it should have been no surprise that during this time period in which some of the giants of the U.S. economy were failing, we saw successive days of hundreds of points lost in the Dow Jones, marked most vividly by a 777-point drop on September 29—the most catastrophic day on U.S. markets in history. Clearly this is a tumultuous time for executives and leaders of every sort. And whether fault lies with a few executives that have severely mismanaged their firms, or with the ratings agencies that have long overvalued financial institutions, or with short-sellers attempting to manipulate the market, or whether this was merely a normal business cycle correcting the excesses of recent years, there is a sense of gloom and panic in the air. There is plenty of blame to go around, and in due time we will eventually learn as much as we need to know about where to attribute fault. Those who are judged responsible will be punished, and the financial events of 2008 will become a discussion for historians. In the meantime, while the experts are hammering through solutions to rescue our economy, Americans are left dealing with an overwhelming lack of trust and confidence in both the private and public sector leaders. The questions we all face are: Can we become a nation of leaders again, capable of leading under pressure and in times of tremendous turbulence? Can we restore trust in our organizations? Can we learn from each other and from history in order to create a better tomorrow? Can we reach across silos within organizations, or across cultural, religious, or economic constraints that divide companies and nations and prevent them from collaborating? The responses to these questions will determine whether we will be crisis leaders or merely managers of the status quo, reacting to the pressure in our environment.

Once considered to be the leaders of business and economic freedom, our reputation in the world has declined precipitously. Foreign investors have taken a substantial role in American business, the U.S. trade deficit and the national debt are at record levels, and the worldwide desire for American goods and services has waned. On top of these economic concerns, the United States has been engaged in a long-term war with Iraq that has in some cases strained our relationship with allies. On other fronts, our primary and secondary educational institutions have become less competitive, and the ability for the nation to adequately care for our elderly and poor has been called into question. Taken together, the financial crisis and the propensity of reputational challenges are enormous burdens.

In addition to the sign of the times described above, the fall of 2008 marked another turn of events in the United States with a historic presidential election—historic in part because the country elected its first African American president. But overshadowing this unprecedented race for the presidency is the daunting task that will face President Obama. He will need to demonstrate extraordinary leadership in order to pull the country out of the doldrums. In some respects, the tasks facing President Obama will require crisis leadership of epoch proportions. But this is not a political book. Rather, it is a book intended to speak to a variety of audiences, including students, scholars, managers, consultants, and others who have a thirst for understanding the essence of leadership as it applies to crisis situations.

So in addressing the question implied by the title of this chapter, crisis leadership matters precisely because crisis events are inevitable. Crisis leadership matters because leaders of organizations and nations *can* make a difference in the extent to which people are affected by a crisis. Crisis leadership matters because in its absence, the stakeholders who are adversely affected by the crisis cannot truly recover from the damaging event. And crisis leadership matters because despite the damage that is caused by a crisis, effective leadership is the one factor that creates the potential for a company to be better off following the crisis than it was before the state of affairs existed.

As scholars of crises, crisis management, and leadership, our observations about crises (current crises as well as crises from times past), and the rippling effect they can have, have assured us of a few things. First, crises are inevitable. Some crises may be avoided, and some may be managed well enough to limit long-term damage, but at the end of the day, every organization and every nation will experience crisis. Second, it is often the handling of a crisis that leads to more damage than the crisis event itself. Third, effective crisis handling involves much more than good communications and public relations. Although these certainly help, rhetoric and positive spin alone will not solve even one of the crises we described above, much less the lot of them. Fourth, learning from crisis is the best hope we have of preventing repeat occurrences. Finally, crisis events *can* create a potential for significant opportunity to be realized for individuals, for organizations, and for countries.

How Crisis Leadership Differs From Leadership in Ordinary Times

The question of whether crisis leadership is different from leadership in ordinary times is a debatable one for sure. In fact, at least one study has concluded that general leadership (leadership in noncrisis situations) is not completely distinct from leadership in a crisis.[1] To this end we can all probably imagine a situation in which someone who was judged to be a fine leader of his or her business was thrust into a crisis and performed as admirably in that situation as he or she did before the crisis. The case of Rudy Giuliani, the former mayor of New York City, offers one prominent example. Although the mayor had his detractors, the idea that he made a positive difference in the lives of most New Yorkers, cleaned up the city streets, and put New York City in a positive trajectory for the future is a commonly held sentiment. Yet, near the end of his tenure, Giuliani was confronted with the most egregious of acts ever faced by a U.S. mayor—the tragedy of 9/11. Within hours of the attacks, we saw images of Mayor Giuliani taking a strong and assertive stance against the aggressors, while at the same time displaying uncharacteristic empathy and emotion toward victims. We witnessed a speedy deployment of city resources and personnel, and we heard unwavering assurance in communicating his plans.

From this example we see someone who displayed effective leadership in times of relative peace *and* in crisis, and thus we could argue that the requisite leadership skills are the same regardless of the circumstances. In other words, if you prove to be a good general leader, then you will be a good leader during a crisis. The need to problem-solve, articulate a vision, and execute a plan, for example, would be expected under any leadership circumstance.

Despite this perspective, we can also just as easily identify someone who is considered to be a solid performer and who has demonstrated leadership skill or leadership potential, only to buckle under the pressure of a crisis. A prominent example is Doug Ivester, former CEO of Coca-Cola. Ivester had been groomed by his predecessor, Roberto Goizueta, to assume the leadership of the company some years in the future. When Goizueta died unexpectedly, Ivester was thrust into the spotlight to lead one of the world's most long-lasting and respected brands. A former accountant, Ivester was known to have been almost obsessively rational and methodical in his roles leading up to CEO. He had worked for Coca-Cola for two decades and in that time had amassed leadership experience in marketing and global affairs, and he had a track record of success at executing the company's strategy.[2] Despite this preparation, Ivester failed at managing the 1999 crisis, in which the Belgian Health Ministry ordered that all Coca-Cola trademarked products be banned from the market and further warned the Belgian community not to buy or drink any Coke products. At issue were hundreds of consumer complaints about an unusual taste and odor coming from the bottled drink. On the heels of mass European fear associated with mad cow disease, Coke was eventually forced into its largest product recall (costing the firm more than $110 million) in the then 113-year firm history. Ivester came across as insensitive and aloof, and failed to move quickly enough, taking more than a week to visit Belgium in person. Even then, he made several public relations gaffes and other missteps that eventually contributed to his forced resignation only two years into the position.

There are other examples of successful leaders who have failed in a crisis, and we will explore those throughout the remainder of the book. But for now, the Ivester case suggests that circumstances and context matters, and that there is indeed a set of skills that may be unique to leadership under pressure. Crises are marked by time constraints, ambiguity, remarkably unusual circumstances, limited or conflicting information, curious onlookers, and a need for immediate and decisive action.[3] Given these pressures, the demands of a leader in crisis can be unique and require a different set of abilities than what would typically be expected during general leadership (i.e., leadership in noncrisis situations).[4] Moreover, where there are overlapping skill requirements, crisis situations promote a hypercontext that calls for extraordinary capability in some of those shared dimensions of leadership.

Defining Crisis Leadership

Our fundamental assumption is that crisis leadership is more than managing corporate communication and public relations (PR) during a crisis. Communication and PR activities are a necessary but insufficient approach to leading an organization through crisis. Crisis leadership even goes beyond the parameters of risk management and legal responsibilities. Indeed, we argue that crisis leadership is about building a foundation of trust not only within an organization, but with a firm's external stakeholders as well. Leaders then use that foundation to prepare their organizations for difficult times, to contain crises when they occur, and most important, to leverage crisis situations as a means for creating organizational change and innovation. This sentiment is precisely what the U.S. Congress asked of the Big Three auto manufacturers. They want the industry's leaders to use their financial woes as a starting point to redesign their business model and to create a new and innovative product line.

Crisis leadership is a frame of mind accompanied by a key set of behaviors. The frame of mind is characterized by openness to new experiences, willingness to learn and take risk, an assumption that all things are possible, and a belief that even in times of crisis people and organizations can emerge better off after the crisis than before. Clearly, crises are traumatic and we don't want to leave a false impression or indicate that there is not real pain and suffering that results from them. Indeed, this can be, and often is, the case. Crisis handlers must address and deal with these circumstances. Our goal with this book, however, is to emphasize that leadership is also about creating possibilities so that organizations can blossom in ways that might not have been predicted in the absence of the pressures that crises evoke.

In sum, the characteristics of crisis leadership may be appropriate for business leaders in all situations, not just during times of crisis—and they are. Displaying these leadership competencies during times of crisis, however, poses a unique challenge. First, leaders in crisis are forced to operate in full public view, with the media and others positioned to report and critique their actions. Second, during a crisis, there is the tendency to want to make the crisis simply go away, resulting in decisions and actions that are oftentimes suboptimal (e.g., cover-ups and deception). These shortcuts can ultimately undermine effective leadership. However, by consciously being attuned to the big picture of a crisis and the opportunities that can be created for the organization as a result of crises, leaders and their organizations can thrive. In short, in today's competitive business environment, developing crisis leadership competencies is mandatory.

Organization of the Chapters

The book is organized into four parts. Part I serves as a foundation for understanding business crises and provides the fundamentals of crisis management. Within Part I, Chapter 2 is a primer on crisis management research. For those readers who are already familiar with this research, we recommend that you proceed to subsequent chapters, where we integrate various leadership constructs with the fundamental tenets of crisis management.

Chapter 2 includes a definition for business crisis and differentiates a crisis from other business problems or challenges. Many scholars agree that a business crisis is a threatening event that may lead to a negative outcome unless swift action is taken. We outline each aspect of a business crisis and offer examples of each. Crises are considered rare, unlike other business problems that occur with more regularity. They are significant, meaning the outcome could be devastating to the firm. In addition, the consequences of a crisis can affect more than just the business, but also stakeholders internal and external to the organization. This can have wide-reaching effects beyond negative publicity.

Chapter 2 also identifies various crisis typologies in order to distinguish among crises, to give a comprehensive overview of them, and to consider their usefulness in preventing and responding to crises. The challenge is to limit the types for the sake of manageability. One typology breaks crises into sudden, which means unexpected situations, and smoldering, or small problems that escalate over time as a result of neglect. Another model explores conventional, unexpected, intractable, and fundamental crises. It is true that typologies have become more complex over time because business crises have become more complicated.

Researchers have identified five stages of the management of a business crisis: signal detection, preparation or prevention, containment or damage control, business recovery, and learning. We describe each phase and ask key questions associated with them to draw managers' attention to the competencies required for leading a business through a crisis.

Part II of the book introduces the individual capabilities that are necessary for leading under pressure. Chapter 3, for example, covers the skills, or competencies, a manager must possess to lead an organization through a crisis. They include planning for, responding to, and learning from the event so that the organization is better off after a crisis than it was before. We use the five phases of a crisis to organize and analyze a set of critical leadership competencies, and we provide examples of their use during various crises. The five phases are (1) signal detection, (2) preparation/prevention, (3) containment/damage control, (4) business recovery, and (5) learning.

In the signal detection phase, recognizing the warning signs of a crisis is important. This is done by making sense of the situation and being able to see others' points of view. During preparation and prevention, it is vital that a leader can influence people to take action by explaining his or her requests and being inspirational. In addition, a leader must be knowledgeable about the business and be able to work across different sectors. And a leader must be creative to confront the unexpected challenges of a crisis. Damage containment includes limiting the financial and other threats to the company's stability. A skilled leader must communicate effectively, and manage public relations to protect the image of the business. In this chapter, we also discuss various methods organizations use to control damage, including the apology and denial. In the process of defending the innocence of the company, its leader may have to take some risks. This goes along with being creative, because maneuvering a crisis will require changing courses and adapting to new situations easily. The recovery phase encompasses carrying on with business while dealing with the damage caused by the crisis. The goal of a company during this stage should be resilience or flexibility. A good leader must encourage collective efficacy so that the organization continues to function and meet its commitments to outside stakeholders. Finally, organizational learning requires that the leader views crisis as a potential source of opportunity. This means he or she must acquire new skills to prevent a future negative event, as well as to promote a future positive event. In this way, a company can actually improve in the face of adversity.

Chapter 4 addresses decision making under pressure, and particularly the issues that affect leaders in the process of identifying problems and solving them. We look at different approaches and their results, and provide real-life examples.

Among the various models of decision making is the rational one, that is, the logical series of steps one takes to reach a decision. First, one defines the problem, then evaluates the situation, analyzes alternatives, and finally reaches a conclusion. This does not take into account that leaders may not have all of the information, or the ability to understand all of it. In addition, a manager has to consider the expectations of stakeholders. As a result of these constraints, an optimal solution is difficult to find.

Another theory of decision making suggests that the more complex a situation becomes, the less likely one is to think logically and be open to important stimuli. Our minds manage data by simplifying it, and the strategies we use to make sense of overwhelming information are called heuristics. In this chapter, we describe different types of heuristics, such as the anchoring heuristic, or the way in which we give preference to information received first. The status quo heuristic is the tendency to play it safe, rather than take risks; the sunk-cost heuristic is a way to justify past choices; and the confirming evidence heuristic is seeking information that supports our own points of view. How a leader frames an issue, as either a threat or an opportunity, also affects his or her decision making. Ethics are relevant during decision making, as well, because organizations must consider what is morally acceptable to stakeholders. A theory on moral intensity includes recognizing an ethical issue, making a moral judgment about it, determining intention, and making an appropriate decision. Our goal in this chapter is to draw attention to the implications of framing issues as threats or opportunities, highlight how moral reasoning affects decision making, and emphasize the limits of our minds, and how those limitations are exacerbated when we experience threat or pressure, as in the case of a crisis.

In Chapter 5 we explore the importance of teams and team leadership in a crisis situation. We discuss the design considerations when building a crisis management team, and how to create an environment in which the crisis team can be responsive, achieve maximum performance, and interact effectively with various stakeholders.

For leaders, composing a successful team requires finding experienced and heterogeneous members. It is helpful when individuals have prior knowledge of a critical event. In addition, each member should contribute something complementary to the group. The leader must identify the purpose of the team and guide it toward the goal without being rigid. Improvisation and flexibility are vital when maneuvering through a crisis. Many crisis teams are ad hoc and lack experience in dealing with significant or crisis events. They often have to learn as they go. As a result, we emphasize in this chapter that team members should be encouraged to seek new knowledge from various places, including outside the group. They can build relationships and network with external stakeholders to develop ideas and gain feedback. To summarize, a successful leader will build a team like a puzzle, so that each piece plays a role and fits the other pieces to make a whole. The team leader will create a vision that others will share and strive toward.

Having discussed the nature of crises and the individual capabilities associated with crisis handling in Parts I and II of the book, Part III illustrates a set of organizational capabilities necessary for leading under pressure. Chapter 6 highlights the fundamental role of trust before, during, and after a crisis. The chapter begins with some definitions of trust, and explores the role of trust between an organization and its stakeholders. More specifically, it details how leaders can successfully emerge from a crisis in an atmosphere of trust.

We describe research identifying four components of trust that appear to be consistent in most definitions: competence, openness, concern, and reliability. It is important for leaders to feel competent and for others to have confidence in them. When leaders are honest and open in the workplace, employees are more likely to believe them during a crisis. Leaders who show concern for employees and the company are especially reassuring during times of crisis. And meeting expectations, or being reliable, exhibits trustworthiness to stakeholders. To these four characteristics, we add a fifth dimension of trust: vulnerability. Many have acknowledged that there is an element of risk involved in trust. Leaders must believe that subordinates will perform to the best of their abilities, even though the possibility exists that they will not. In other words, leadership under pressure may require a willingness to be vulnerable to those that have been entrusted to handle various aspects of the crisis. This willingness is more likely if the organizational culture is generally perceived as trusting. In this case, the work of crisis leaders is to create such a culture before crises occur.

While trust between a leader and stakeholders is built on a long-term relationship, trust among team members during a crisis must occur quickly. One researcher came up with the term *swift trust* to describe trust without the benefit of repeated interaction and assessment. These crisis teams must invoke vulnerability, suspend doubt in the minds of the stakeholders, and accept that they are taking a risk on the outcome of their efforts.

In Chapter 6 not only do we describe different definitions of trust, but we also look at betrayal. The consequences of a violation of trust can be devastating to an organization. Whether it is intentional or unintentional, a betrayal can be a barrier to successfully maneuvering through a crisis.

Finally, we list some ideas for generating trust within an organization. Among these are communicating openly, being honest with oneself and others, and responding to crises in a way that is consistent with the values of the company.

In Chapter 7, we argue that organizational learning can facilitate crisis handling and prevent future crises. We center our discussion around class action lawsuits because they are a particularly ubiquitous type of crisis and therefore provide a rich opportunity for learning how to handle crises across organizations. Class action lawsuits are brought by one or many, and the group that is affected receives compensation for the harm done to them. We believe failures in managing such lawsuits reflect a lack of learning by firms.

In this chapter we focus primarily on discrimination lawsuits. When companies manage diversity well, one by-product is that they are able to limit inequities in the organization that could lead to lawsuits. We describe some perspectives of and barriers to the type of learning that helps avoid these imbalances. For example, one theory states that behavior followed by positive consequences will be repeated, and that behavior followed by negative consequences will end. These patterns represent adaptive learning. In an organization, this means a change in routines, or policies and procedures, will take place. One barrier to organizational learning includes dysfunctional routines. Therefore, if discrimination is a practice, even if it is unconscious, it becomes exacerbated over time. When a crisis occurs, a firm can react in negative ways, such as being defensive. This behavior may include denying the problem and justifying the practice that contributes to the inequity.

Another barrier is when a firm focuses on events in the past, rather than looking at expectations for the future. Because organizations get into the habit of routines, a crisis presents a challenge for which management may not be prepared. With limited experience of a class action lawsuit, a firm cannot call upon past events to guide them through difficult times.

Focusing on the wrong target bars organizational learning as well. In many cases, the emphasis is not on the cause of the crisis, but rather on the resolution of it. Also, without evaluations of performance for the handling of a crisis, a firm may not act as effectively. In other words, the desire for a reward and to avoid punishment motivates learning.

As we close the chapter, we look at failure and how it promotes learning. Failure represents a weak spot where managers can focus their attention. Trial and error involves changing behavior patterns until success is achieved. For example, if leaders heed early warning signals, a crisis may be prevented. And when managers accept failure, they can better identify and analyze the root of the problem.

Chapter 8 addresses globalization and how it affects the management of a crisis. In many cases, instability in one company in one part of the world sends ripples throughout an industry and across nations. How do organizations manage a crisis situation that has an external impact and implications? We present specific cases to illustrate the competencies and tools required to manage a global crisis.

An important leadership skill is a global mindset, which is the ability of an organization to understand the cultural issues surrounding a crisis and coordinate strategies globally as well as locally by managing resources. It is a collective perspective in a company that leads to better articulation of a problem and more effective mobilization.

Also, technology plays an important role in connecting leaders of various organizations to work together to deal with a crisis that spans the globe. Physical access to a region may be impossible, and language barriers and cultural differences can delay or prevent information gathering. Information technology is vital to decision making and crisis handling.

Part IV concludes the book with Chapter 9, which is devoted to the possibility for leaders and their organizations to thrive under pressure. Previous research maintains that leaders perceive crises as either threats or opportunities. Certain emotions are associated with each stimulus. For example, feelings that accompany threats include anger, anxiety, guilt, and depression. These responses can block the way to a positive outcome. Some leaders make a transition from an initial reaction of fear and panic to one of optimism. In Chapter 9, we explore how it is that some leaders see a crisis as an opportunity rather than a threat. We identify factors that contribute to this perspective, such as a leader's ability to reflect and analyze. We note that perceiving value from a postcrisis positive result and believing that a positive outcome is in fact attainable are also important conditions. Thus, the last chapter lists the personal characteristics and situational factors that allow leaders to realize positive outcomes following a crisis, and offers suggestions for how they can create an environment in which this is possible.

Finally, Chapter 9 discusses the manifestations of perceiving opportunity in crisis and offers examples of some success stories. Some ways in which managers recognize a chance for improvement are that they search for the root of the problem, listen to the ideas of everyone involved, address long-term as well as short-term issues, and create an atmosphere of creative problem solving. This chapter culminates our insights on leading in times of crisis and brings together the leadership and organizational capabilities discussed throughout the book to demonstrate how people and firms not only survive but thrive under pressure (Figure 1.1).

Figure 1.1   Leadership Links 1.1

- Center for Positive Organizational Scholarship, Leading in Trying Times
  http://www.bus.umich.edu/FacultyResearch/Research/TryingTimes/default.htm
- Center for Creative Leadership
  http://www.ccl.org/leadership/landing/crisis.aspx

Endnotes

1. Evans, Hammersley, & Robertson, Assessing the role and efficacy of communication strategies in times of crisis, 297–309.
2. Morris, Seller, & Tarpley, *What really happened at Coke?*
3. Pearson & Clair, Reframing crisis management, 59–76.
4. Hadley, Pittinsky, & Zhu, *Measuring the efficacy of leaders to assess information and make decisions in a crisis.*

Chapter 2

A Primer on Crises and Crisis Management

Throughout the late 1990s and well into the 2000s American businesses were characterized largely by crisis and scandal. Among the most notorious business crises was the financial and ethical mismanagement of the Enron Corporation. Enron was originally Northern Natural Gas Company (NNGC) and was founded it 1932 in Omaha, Nebraska. Through a series of reorganizations and acquisitions, NNGC eventually became Enron in 1985, and its CEO at the time, Kenneth Lay, relocated the company headquarters to Houston, Texas. Enron's primary business was the transmission and distribution of electricity and gas throughout the United States. The company also developed, built, and operated pipelines and power plants. Yet, Enron's reputation and wealth were attributed to its ability to market and promote core products and derivatives as financial instruments. Over a period of years, Enron was lauded by *Fortune* magazine as "America's Most Innovative Company," and in 2000 it was named to *Fortune*'s "100 Best Companies to Work for in America." Employees and those familiar with Enron knew it to value opulence and appreciated the firm for its generous pensions and effective management. At its peak, Enron employed more than 22,000 employees and in 2000 claimed revenues in excess of $100 billion.[1]

On the surface, Enron was an American success story. But Enron's success streak came to a notorious end in 2001, when it filed for bankruptcy protection. Over the course of numerous investigations, whistle-blowers, analysts, attorneys, and others revealed a set of irregular accounting practices by the firm that essentially amounted to corporate fraud. Revelations indicated that Enron's assets and profits were inflated at best, or nonexistent at worst. In the wake of these troubles the share price for Enron dropped from over $90 to less than $.50. In addition, some firm leaders were imprisoned; reputations were tarnished; employees lost hundreds of millions of dollars in pension and retirement accounts; and its accounting partner, Arthur Anderson, one of the world's leading accounting practices, was dissolved.

Enron did not stand alone. Around the same time that Enron was collapsing, other prominent firms were ensnarled by accounting or related scandals, including Worldcom, Health South, Adelphia, and Imclone, to name a few of the more public cases. Images on the national news of executives in handcuffs were not uncommon, and newspaper headlines about prominent firms and firm leaders were often negative. The failings of CEOs made the drama of American business at least as compelling as any fictional television series. As a result of the Enron case, the United States entered a period of time in which the predominant sentiment toward business was one of distrust.

Financial scandals are not the only disruptions that have, at one time or another, rocked Corporate America. In fact, throughout history, leaders of firms and their various stakeholders have had to deal with a host of challenges, ranging from the mundane to the severe. Some of the more pedestrian issues might include lawsuits, labor disputes, and product defects. However ordinary or commonplace these challenges may seem, they are problematic nonetheless, and if left unattended or if they become subject to public scrutiny, they may escalate into a crisis situation with the same potential to harm as did Enron's challenges.

Typically, when prompted to think about a crisis, most people's attention turns to large-scale events or catastrophes that threaten human life. These may include the devastation caused by a natural disaster (e.g., 2005 Hurricane Katrina along the Gulf Coast of the United States, or the 2004 tsunami in the Indian Ocean), a plant explosion (e.g., the Bhopal industrial disaster), or a large-scale product recall (e.g., Firestone Tires). Clearly such events require decisive action and leadership of the highest order. Yet all too often executives, politicians, and even crisis management experts fall short in the face of such pressure. Crises create difficult circumstances for anyone affected by them. They are perhaps the most challenging situations that a leader will face in his or her career. Unfortunately, there is precious little formal education or training and, until recently, research on how to lead under the extraordinarily pressure-filled times that crises create.

This chapter will serve as an introduction to business crises. We will define what a business crisis is (distinguishing it from other business "problems") and discuss frameworks for organizing various types of crises. In so doing, we will offer language to differentiate among crises. We will also put business crisis in a historical context and demonstrate how and why crises have evolved as business itself has evolved.

Defining Crisis

Organizations have always been and will likely continue to be vulnerable to crises of some form or another. While each type of crisis poses a unique threat, it helps to understand what differentiates a crisis situation from an unfortunate or unpleasant business challenge. For example, on the surface a train derailment might seem like a crisis. Clearly, the operations of the railroad company are interrupted, cargo or passengers will be delayed in reaching their destination, and resources will be expended in resolving the problem that would not have been necessary had the derailment not occurred. For railroad customers, and the railroad itself, the derailment is certainly a problem and an inconvenience, but is it a business crisis?

Dutton described a business crisis as a type of strategic issue that will likely lead to a negative outcome unless corrective action is taken.[2] She further argued that crises reflect situations that are critically important to an organization, and that they may be distinguished from noncrisis strategic issues because they are accompanied by time pressure and ambiguity. The more important, immediate, and uncertain the issue, the more likely it is to be characterized by the firm as a threat or a crisis.[3] Similar to Dutton,[4] Pearson and Clair defined a crisis as a low-probability, high-impact event that threatens the security and well-being of the public, and is characterized by ambiguity of cause, effect, and means of resolution, and consequently requires decisions to be made swiftly.[5] These, and other definitions of crisis, include three key elements: ambiguity, high stakes, and urgency—all of which help serve to distinguish business crises from other problems or challenges an organization and its leadership may face. In addition to these features, we believe that crises are unique in the infrequency of their occurrence, their reach and magnitude of effect on stakeholders, and the likelihood and impact of publicity.

To more fully appreciate a business crisis, we define it as

> A rare and significant situation that has the potential to become public and bring about highly undesirable outcomes for the firm and its stakeholders, including: injury or death, negative or unwanted publicity, financial or reputational ruin, and enhanced political, governmental, or regulatory scrutiny, therefore requiring immediate corrective action by firm leaders.

Several aspects of our crisis definition are important to highlight (Figure 2.1).

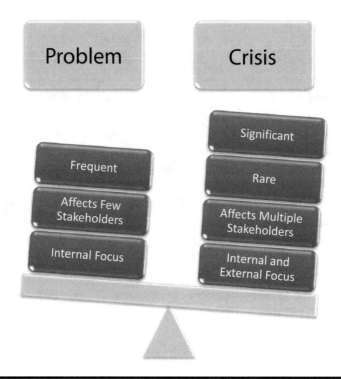

Figure 2.1   Business problem versus crisis.

Rarity

First, crises are rare and unusual events. In other words, what differentiates a crisis situation from a business problem is that problems can be recurring situations to which the firm is vulnerable. As troubling as they may be, delays or cancelled flights in the airline industry due to weather or mechanical breakdowns are generally not considered a crisis by an airline. Not only do weather systems frequently disrupt operations, for example, but also airlines have designed a set of procedures or operations for managing weather delays. Air traffic controllers, flight crews, and customer service representatives follow a standard protocol for dealing with delays and getting passengers to their destinations.

Crises, on the other hand, are abnormal and infrequent, and a firm has little experience or history managing them. As a result, there is typically no well-known or well-rehearsed set of practices for dealing with a crisis. What started as a troubling weather event on February 14, 2007, escalated to crisis status for JetBlue Airways. As a severe winter storm slowly passed through much of the northeastern United States, passengers on JetBlue flights were stranded, and some described it as being "held hostage" on planes at the gate or on the tarmac for upward of 10 hours.[6] During that time, a series of ill-fated decisions by JetBlue's management, in the wake of a storm that proved much more severe than most had predicted, led to a public drama in which passengers and others offered a maelstrom of criticism of the airline. In the end, JetBlue lost passengers who were disgruntled by the airline's poor handling of the situation, what had previously been a very solid reputation in the industry, more than $20 million in revenue in the first quarter of 2007 at a time when the airline and the industry was already suffering, and its founding CEO and chairman, David Neeleman, who was replaced as JetBlue's leader three months after the crisis.

Significance

Second, crises are significant to the long-term health and survival of a firm. The crisis itself or, equally as important, the mismanagement of a crisis situation has the potential of devastating a firm and requiring considerable resources (e.g., time, money, expertise). Examples of some of the more prominent and likely consequences of a crisis are substantial decline in sales or profits, decrease in employee morale, loss of competitive strength, job loss, and individual or firm reputational loss.

In early 2007, Menu Foods, a Streetsville, Ontario, manufacturer of wet pet food, recalled tens of millions of cans of its product when the New York State Food Laboratory discovered the pet food produced by Menu Foods had been contaminated with a chemical that resulted in the deaths or illness of thousands of dogs and cats in North America.[7] The lethal chemical was traced to wheat gluten imported from China, but the massive recall it prompted resulted in devastation in the United States for pet owners, retailers that distribute the private labels of the pet foods manufactured by Menu Foods, and Menu Foods itself. In early 2008 Menu Foods acknowledged that it expects to pay total costs associated with the recall at more than $50 million. In communication to shareholders at the end of the first quarter of 2008, Menu Foods president and chief executive officer Paul Henderson stated that "the recalls that began in the first quarter 2007 seriously affected the Fund's business and financial position in each of the past four quarters," having lost customers representing approximately 37 percent of volume in the first quarter of 2007.[8] The situation faced by Menu Foods was a crisis in that the recall prompted a significant loss in sales and revenue, required financial and business restructuring and other actions that otherwise would not have been necessary, and severely tarnished the firm's reputation with retailers and customers.

Stakeholders

Third, a crisis affects not only the business, but also the stakeholders of that business. Corporate stakeholders generally refer to a person, group, or organization that affects or can be affected by a company's actions. Typical stakeholders include consumers, employees, nearby communities, and even the natural environment.[9] In some cases, the effects of a crisis have consequences beyond geographic boundaries or other immediate bounds and affect stakeholders remotely. For example, the Chernobyl disaster was a nuclear reactor accident in Ukraine that resulted in the release of radioactivity following a power excursion. Although only two people died in the explosion, the radioactive fallout into the atmosphere covered an extensive geographic area and ultimately adversely affected future generations of stakeholders across Eastern, Western, and Northern Europe.[10] More precisely, stakeholders are the individuals and constituencies of a corporation that contribute, either voluntarily or involuntarily, to its wealth-creating capacity and activities, and that are therefore its potential beneficiaries or risk bearers.[11]

The term *stakeholder* can be traced back to a play on the word *stockholder* (a.k.a. shareholder) and was meant to suggest that in addition to those who have a direct financial stake in the firm, there are others whose opinions and needs should be considered in a firm's decision making.[12] According to Freeman, individuals and groups that benefit from or are harmed by, and whose rights may be affected positively or negatively by, a firm's actions, have a stake in that firm. As a result, stakeholders, as well as stockholders, have a right to expect certain actions by firm management.[13] Unfortunately, it is not uncommon for crisis handlers to focus on the needs of the narrow number of stakeholders upon which a firm is resource dependent (e.g., stockholders).[14] Freeman was one of the first to develop the stakeholder concept, distinguishing it from stockholders, and in so doing championing for a more inclusive set of relationships.[15] The stakeholder model, in large part, grew out of Freeman's theorizing.

The stakeholder model is a paradigm of corporate governance that emphasizes the intrinsic value of all of a firm's stakeholders and the significance of their claims on the organization.[16] It further presumes that it is the responsibility of executives and managers to satisfy the needs of multiple stakeholders while simultaneously responding to the interests of shareholders.[17] The stakeholder model is distinguished from the more traditional shareholder model of corporate governance, which emphasizes the corporation as a "shareholder value maximizing entity"[18] that values contractual relationships and assumes that all possible organizational contingencies can be addressed with appropriate contracts. We argue, however, that crisis situations are unlikely to fall neatly within a preconceived contract or negotiated relationship, and in fact, some crises fall outside of the scope of the subset of relationships that can be claimed by share-holders. By contrast, the stakeholder model, with its focus on a broader array of relationships, offers heuristics for how managers might recognize and prioritize stakeholders in a crisis,[19] and can then use this expanded group for problem solving during the crisis.

Figure 2.2 illustrates the common stakeholder groups for a publicly traded organization. The arrows suggest that the relationship between the stakeholder groups (on the periphery of the figure) and the focal agent (the firm) is a recip-rocal one in that the actions by a stakeholder can affect the firm, just as firm actions affect the stakeholder. The ways in which a firm can affect stakeholders are fairly obvious. The JetBlue crisis, in which mismanagement and poor deci-sion making by the firm's leadership following a winter storm negatively affected customers, is one example. What is less transparent or intuitive, however, is how stakeholders affect the firm.

According to the impression management literature, some external stake-holders can have a considerable amount of influence on a firm.[20] Stakeholders have the ability to inflict harm on an organization because of their unique rela-tionship to it,[21] and those who are perceived to be powerful, legitimate, and able to make urgent claims are best positioned to influence a firm. Negative influ-ence can be exerted on a firm during a crisis when stakeholders whose actions in response to a crisis, or the firm's handling of it, stigmatize the firm in a way that further damages the organization and its reputation. In these circumstances, not only must firms deal with resolving the crisis, but they must also deal with managing a tarnished image imposed by stakeholders. As another example,

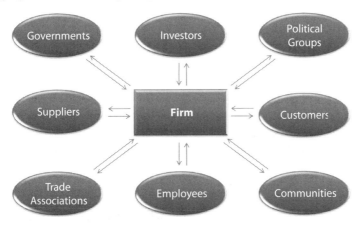

Figure 2.2 Common organizational stakeholders. (Source: Donaldson & Preston, 1995.)

stakeholders may be the sources of a crisis for a firm. In the Menu Foods crisis described above, for example, a Chinese-based supplier of raw material shipped a tainted supply of product to Menu Foods. It was Menu Foods' product, however, that was shipped to customers and initiated the illness and deaths of pets across the country, and it was Menu Foods' reputation and financial well-being that were damaged.

Publicity

Fourth, a crisis can be differentiated from a business problem or challenge in that it is generally, although not always, public. In other words, a business problem is more likely to reach crisis status when the challenge faced by the firm is one that sparks media attention or the attention of prominent or influential stakeholders.[22] When this occurs, not only does firm management have to address the problem at hand, but it must also do so with intense scrutiny from others. More precisely, once a crisis becomes public, top management loses control of the situation, largely because stakeholders and others feel compelled, or are invited by media and others, to respond.

Whether a business problem becomes public is dependent on a number of factors. First is scale or scope. Those issues that are large in scale and have the capacity to affect a substantial number of people, or a noteworthy amount of resources, are more likely to draw public attention than those problems that operate on a smaller scale.[23] Second is the size of the firm itself. Generally, the problems faced by larger and publicly traded firms generate more publicity than similar events faced by smaller, less well-known or private firms. We do not mean to imply that small or privately owned firms do not face crises—they do. Rather, firms that are less well known are less likely to draw media attention to themselves in both the good and the bad times. As a result, when a crisis occurs, smaller firms can more easily focus on resolving the problem, rather than also being distracted by the public scrutiny that can often exacerbate the problem for a firm.

Regardless of whether a crisis receives media or other public attention, both large and small firms must be prepared to respond to their public, or those stakeholders who are immediately affected by the crisis. Addressing the public's concerns and dealing with publicity are separate but related responsibilities. One of the authors sat on the board of directors for a school system. A transition in leadership for one school was poorly managed, and a great deal of conflict erupted within and among parents, faculty and staff, and the board regarding the academic direction the school should take. Heated exchanges occurred at board meetings that were open to the public, and soon the meetings, which prior to the conflict had only been attended by the board and occasionally a guest or two, became increasingly well attended by various community members. As the conflict escalated it received more and more attention. Blogs were created and at one point a local reporter attended a board meeting. The next day the school and its challenges appeared in a prominent part of the local newspaper. This story represents a clear case of a crisis situation in which an organization's public (i.e., its stakeholders) and the public media collided in a way that damaged the reputation of the organization. We believe, however, that effective leadership during a crisis can offset the potential harm that publicity can do. In fact, crisis leaders use both an organization's public and the public media before (through relationship building), during (through honest communication), and after (through learning and resilience) a crisis to create opportunities to be better off following a crisis than before.

Finally, the school board example also illustrates another important aspect of publicity. Generally, organizational challenges become crises when the issue is a controversial one. Controversy invites publicity. As the president of the Institute for Crisis Management (ICM), Larry Smith, claims, what makes something newsworthy is when an event is controversial and counter to what was expected. The example Smith shares is the following: When a dog bites a man, that is not newsworthy—dogs bite. But a man biting a dog is interesting largely because it is counter to what we might expect and so becomes controversial. In the case of the school board, the incoming head of school had proposed some unconventional ideas for the curriculum, and the parents and faculty were uncomfortable with the direction in which she wanted to take the school. Her approach was a controversial one that piqued the interest of multiple stakeholders, including the media.

Categorizing Crisis Types

"If the definitorial starting point [of crisis] is predicated on notions of uncertainty, ambiguity and unpredictability, the typologies approach itself requires careful consideration as any typologizing is the product of selection, ordering and structuring real phenomena, in other words a process of rationalization."[24] Crisis typologies can offer insight into how different organizational threats develop,[25] how stakeholders may be affected, and perhaps most important, how to identify appropriate responses.[26] As noted by one scholar, in addition to these practical purposes, crisis typologies assist in the development of crisis-related research by facilitating an integrative approach to the study of different types of crisis.[27] This is especially important as the nature of business and the reality of the global organizational context changes and diversifies. Unfortunately, it is this reality that makes creating sustainable crisis typologies so difficult. Typologies become obsolete as the future continues to present a significantly different landscape for organizational leaders and scholars than what existed in the past.

That said, crisis typologies serve a critical role for leaders as a means of sense making, a topic we will cover in more detail in Chapter 3, and provide structure in a situation flanked with ambiguity and challenge. For a crisis typology to be useful it must meet four conditions.[28] First, the various crisis categories should be mutually exclusive. The ability to make decisions about or adequately investigate crises is severely hampered when events, either in their totality or some portion thereof, can be interpreted in multiple ways. Second, the typology must be exhaustive, allowing its users to allocate an infinite set of crises to a finite set of classifications. Third, crisis typologies should be as relevant as they are useful, which will aid in the practical purposes of prevention and reaction to crisis situations. Finally, typologies should be pragmatic, limiting the number of classifications to a reasonable and manageable number for leaders and scholars alike. Only when these four conditions are present can we benefit from the categorization of crisis types.

A Brief Review of Crisis Typologies

There are many ways of classifying crisis types, and there are perhaps as many crisis typologies as there are people who have investigated them. As we have indicated, crisis typologies have, by necessity, matured in their sophistication over time. In this section we will present a number of crisis classifications from the most rudimentary to the most comprehensive. Clearly, we are unable to depict every typology, so we offer exemplars of typologies at various stages.

One of the most straightforward and intuitively appealing ways to categorize crisis types uses language from the Institute for Crisis Management (ICM), a crisis consulting and research firm. ICM identified two primary types of crisis situations: sudden crises and smoldering crises.

Sudden crises are significant and unexpected events that disrupt the daily operations of business for some period of time. Natural disasters and other potentially catastrophic events represent typical examples of sudden crises in that they occur suddenly and with limited warning. Other examples include incidences of workplace violence, product tampering, sabotage, technology disruption, executive death, and terrorist attacks. To call the devastation associated with the terrorist attacks on September 11, 2001, a crisis is an understatement for sure, but for some businesses located in New York's World Trade Center and surrounding areas, or for the Pentagon in the metropolitan Washington, D.C., area, the attacks represented a sudden crisis of the highest magnitude. Business leaders in this country could not have conceived that such tragedy was possible, and therefore most were unprepared for it. Employees, customers, and other stakeholders were left in the dark for weeks or longer. Disruptions in technology, including phone lines and computer systems, left many employees not only unable to work, but even unsure of where or when to report.

Smoldering crises are business problems that start out as small, internal problems within a firm, which when they become public to stakeholders can escalate to crisis status as a result of inattention by management. According to the ICM database, nearly three-quarters of all business crises fall in the smoldering crisis category. Consider, for example, the plethora of cases of corporate fraud, mismanagement, labor disputes, and class action lawsuits reported in the news media in the early 2000s. According to Caponigro, smoldering-like crisis situations typically result from the simple day-to-day work performed in an organization and often take the form of management mistakes that have built up over a period of time.[29]

As implied by the sudden/smoldering distinction, at the most basic level crises can be differentiated dichotomously. The distinction between crises that are man-made (e.g., technological) or caused by nature[30] is one of the most common. More recently, Rike has refined these two basic categories to include man-made, natural, and social crises.[31] One of the advantages of a distinction of this sort is the ability to differentiate the *source* of various crises. However, we are finding that this dichotomy is complicated by the near impossibility of separating multiple forms of modern crises that are increasingly linked in one or more ways. Gundel offers global warming as an example, where human beings are both the victims and the cause of the crisis.[32] To say that global warming fits under the natural disaster category is as true as saying that it is a man-made consequence. Yet global warming is not the same type of natural disaster as would be an act of God (e.g., hurricane). As a result, we see the need for further categorical delineation, because the mutual exclusivity condition in this one example is compromised.

Categorizing crises into two broad types, such as sudden or smoldering, or man-made or caused by nature, is a helpful but ultimately insufficient way of distinguishing among a broad array of business threats. To deal with the challenge of mutual exclusivity in distinguishing among crisis types, scholars have offered a wider array of subsets. To their original man-made and natural cause distinctions, Rosenthal and Kouzmin have added mine disasters, oil spills, air disasters, crowd disasters, nuclear crises, and terrorism or chemical explosions.[33] Other organizational scholars have also expanded our understanding of business crises and have attempted to categorize them in more nuanced ways. Mitroff identified seven categories of crises, which are described in Figure 2.3.[34]

These expanded distinctions serve to make the categorization process more efficient because it increases the likelihood that crises belonging to a particular category have common characteristics. That said, it may be difficult to determine the core trait that crises have in common, which is particularly relevant

Economic Related
 • Labor problems, stock market crash, hostile takeovers, changes in trade policy, sharp decline in earnings, loss of major customer account

Informational
 • Tampering with computer records, Y2K, loss of proprietary and confidential information

Physical
 • Loss of key equipment or materials, breakdown of key equipment, explosions, faulty or product design, product failures,

Reputational
 • Slander, gossip, rumors, damage to corporate reputation

Psychopathic Acts
 • Product tampering, kidnapping, terrorism, workplace violence

Natural Disasters
 • Earthquakes, fires, floods, hurricanes

Human Resource
 • Loss of key personnel or executives, rise in workplace accidents, sexual harassment; decline in employee morale

Figure 2.3 Crisis types.

to crisis handlers who are faced with a plethora of possible crisis types and must make real-time decisions about appropriate ways of responding.[35] Thus, we see the advent of crisis typologies that have crisis handling procedures as one of their underlying dimensions or objectives.[36] In addition, we begin to see studies that attempt to match crisis types with crisis response strategies. Coombs and Holladay offered a two-dimensional crisis typology in which external control and intentionality represent orthogonal dimensions, that when crossed form a 2×2 matrix.[37] The external control dimension is subdivided into internal and external control. Internal control represents a crisis that results from action by the organization. Conversely, external control refers to a crisis caused by something or someone outside of the organization. Intentionality, on the other hand, is divided into intentional or unintentional. Intentional refers to a crisis-inducing action that was done on purpose, whereas unintentional means that the crisis-inducing action was not done purposefully. According to Coombs and Holladay, the resulting matrix yields the following for crisis types,[38] the characteristics of which suggest to crisis handlers the best crisis response strategy:

1. Accidents (unintentional and internal)
2. Transgressions (intentional and internal)
3. Faux pas (unintentional and external)
4. Terrorism (intentional and external)

Akin to the Coombs and Holladay typology, Mitroff and colleagues, using survey data from public affairs officers of Fortune 1000 firms, found that crises cluster together in a small number of distinct factors and along two primary dimensions: (1) whether the crisis is internal or external to the organization, and (2) whether the crisis is due primarily to technical or human/organizational factors.[39] The first dimension acknowledges that a crisis may arise from within or internal to the firm or external to it. According to their operational definition, the difference between internally and externally derived crises lies in the perspective of time. Crises that are looked at in the short run are considered to be internal to the organizational environment, whereas those that are looked at from a longer time span are considered external to the organization.[40] Examples of internally derived crises include miscommunication, on-site product tampering, and illegal activities and computer breakdowns, whereas externally derived crises include natural disasters, hostile takeovers, executive kidnapping, or labor strikes.

The second distinction in their typology is between those crises that are caused by technical or economic failings (e.g., product defects, systems failure, and bankruptcy) and those caused by people/organizational/social breakdowns (e.g., workplace violence, sabotage, and rumors). Mitroff and colleagues position the dimensions along vertical and horizontal continuums to suggest that crises may be more or less internally/externally derived, or may be more or less people/technical focused.[41] In short, according to this delineation of crises, the defining categories are not necessarily discrete classifications.

As yet another example, Marcus and Goodman, in their work on how corporate crises affect investor reactions and stock market returns, offered another crisis typology.[42] They posit that crises differ in at least two respects: (1) their effect on potential victims and (2) their origin or source. Using these distinctions, they identified three types of crisis. *Accidents* are one-time unintentional and unfortunate events that occur unexpectedly and have clearly identifiable victims and cause. *Scandals,* on the other hand, are disgraceful occurrences that compromise the perpetrators' reputation. Scandals have less clearly identifiable victims than accidents and their cause is often ambiguous. Finally, they identify *product safety and health incidents* as situations that over a period of time or with repeated occurrences have the potential to create mass suffering. According to Marcus and Goodman, product safety and health incidents are between accidents and scandals in terms of victim identification and cause identification.[43]

Following the terrorist attacks of 9/11, the attention to crisis management on a worldwide scale has increased, and a new crisis category has emerged. *Abnormal* crises result from deliberate evil action.[44] By contrast, *normal* crises are the consequence of ill-structured technological systems, to which any organization using hazardous technology is susceptible.[45] Although normal accidents can themselves be catastrophic, abnormal crises are particularly horrific in their intentionality and severe pain and suffering caused by another human being.

Finally, there is a crisis typology that is at once intended to keep pace with the changing organizational environment and introduce features that facilitate in the proactive or reactive measures that must be carried out to avoid or combat crises.[46] This typology attempts to address the shortcomings of crisis classification systems of earlier times while meeting the criteria that a typology should include categories that are mutually exclusive, exhaustive, relevant, and pragmatic. The first dimension of this typology answers the question of whether a crisis is *predictable*—the answer to which aids in the prevention stage of a crisis. A crisis is predictable "if place, time, or in particular the manner of its occurrence are knowable to at least a third competent party and the probability of occurrence is not to be neglected."[47] To be considered predictable, a specific crisis event must be known to be possible, *and* the probability of occurrence should exceed a threshold value. A manager in a manufacturing facility, for example, should know that equipment malfunction is possible (therefore satisfying the knowable criteria) and can assess from historical record the frequency with which breakdowns have occurred over a specified period of time. If the frequency of this possible event can be considered more than "rare," then the crisis is most likely a predictable one.

The second identifying feature of crises is their *influence possibility*, which serves to aid crisis handlers in both their proactive (prevention) and reactive (response) handling of the crisis.[48] A crisis can be influenced if responses to stem the tide or to reduce damages by antagonizing the causes of a crisis are known and possible to execute.[49] It is important to note that the degree of difficulty in influencing a crisis can vary dramatically and over time. For example, it may take much more effort and resources to control or end a plant explosion than it would to squelch a workplace rumor.

Using predictability and influence possibility as the primary classification system, Gundel established a four-area matrix of crisis types, where crises may be easy or hard to predict and easy or hard to influence.[50] The crises categories that emerge from this typology are conventional crises, unexpected crises, intractable crises, and fundamental crises:

- *Conventional crises* are predictable and have well-known influence possibilities. The prototypical example of a conventional crisis is the massive failing of a technological system because such events can be anticipated and, with proper planning, averted or minimized.
- *Unexpected crises* have influence possibility but are unpredictable events compared to conventional crises. Their unpredictable nature suggests that

they may be impossible to prepare for or prevent. Weick's depiction of the Mann Gulch forest fires is an example of an unexpected crisis.[51,52] In this case, 13 firefighters, including 12 smoke jumpers who were parachuted into a forest fire in the Helena National Forest in Montana, were killed in part because the fire raged in unexpected and unpredictable ways. Despite the firefighters' experience in forestry and forest fires, their expertise was no match for the speed and erratic directions that this fire took.

■ *Intractable crises* can be predicted, but the ability to influence their occurrence or outcome is extremely limited, making them potentially more dangerous or devastating for stakeholders. Intractable crises can be both man-made and natural. The Bhopal disaster represents a technological or man-made event that could have been predicted, but once started was nearly impossible to affect. Similarly, the 2004 tsunami in the Indian Ocean is by all accounts an event that could conceivably have been anticipated but impossible to control.

■ *Fundamental crises* constitute the final crisis type in this matrix. Fundamental crises represent the most dangerous class of crises in that they are both unpredictable and impossible to influence.[53] Together these features suggest that leaders facing fundamental crises can never achieve preparedness or sufficient responsiveness. The terrorist attack of 9/11 would fall into this crisis category.[54]

In sum, as organizations continue to increase in complexity, so too do the crisis types to which they may be vulnerable. Thus, in the evolution of the study of crisis and crisis management, organizational scholars have increasingly argued for and attempted to define more sophisticated crisis typologies and engaged in more fine-grained analysis of crisis events.[55] As part of that examination, scholars have considered such factors such as (1) the source or origin of the crisis, (2) stakeholders affected by the crisis, (3) crisis resolution strategies, and (4) preventative measures to avoid crises altogether.[56]

Assigning Responsibility for a Crisis

A discussion on crisis and crisis management would not be complete without some attention given to the assignment of responsibility (a.k.a. blame) for a crisis. In the theoretical development of crisis research, attribution theory from social psychology has come to play an important role. In its simplest form, attribution theory is a framework for explaining the cause of events, and crises are events for which people seek causes and make attributions. In so doing, they make judgments about the level of organizational responsibility for a given crisis once the cause has been determined.[57] Research has shown that there are at least three factors people consider when making an attribution.[58] First is the stability of an event in which the frequency of the event's cause is assessed. Those that occur frequently are seen as stable, whereas those that are less frequent are considered unstable. Second, control reflects whether an event's cause is controllable, by either the organization (internal control) or agents outside the organization (external control). Finally, attributions may be determined by locus, or if the event's cause is connected to the intentions of a particular actor or connected to the situation.

In crisis, as in other situations, the judgments that people make about the stability, control, and locus of an event in turn affect one's feelings toward an agent, whether it be an individual or organizational actor.[59] In other words, people determine the extent to which an organization or its members should be held responsible for a crisis once they have determined the cause of the crisis.[60] Crises that are deemed to be stable (there is a long history of the event within the firm), have low external control (the cause cannot reasonably be attributed to actors or influences outside the organization), and be a strong internal locus (the act was intentional, and by inference could have been prevented) are generally considered to have a high level of organizational responsibility. Conversely, attributions about organizational responsibility are less likely to occur when the cause of the crisis is judged to be unstable (a rare or unusual occurrence), have strong external control (outside agents were influential in the event's occurrence), and have a weak internal locus (the act was unintentional). Under these circumstances, the organization may be perceived to be a victim of circumstances rather than the responsible agent.[61]

Generally speaking, stakeholders respond much more antagonistically to a firm in crisis when the firm itself is perceived to be at fault or responsible for the crisis. Consequently, on average, these organizations tend to suffer much more reputational damage than do firms that are not perceived to be responsible. There are exceptions, however, and the exceptions often have more to do with the crisis handling than with the crisis itself. Consider the attack on the World Trade Center on September 11, 2001. Clearly the crisis was one in which the firms within the towers were not responsible. In fact, much was made in the press about those companies being a victim of the attacks, and the world's sympathy was directed toward those organizations. Yet, as time passed, and the crisis management practices became public, the public's sympathy began to dissipate when some firms were judged to be insufficiently sensitive to the needs of its various stakeholders as they tried to rebuild their business. In these cases, a crisis for which an attribution of responsibility was not initially ascribed to an organization resulted in firms having some fault for the hardships experienced by stakeholders.

Phases of Crisis Management

Crises are complicated events. Although many crises seem to happen instantaneously, in truth they unfold over a period of time. Researchers have established a minimum of five phases through which business crises pass.[62] These phases provide some insight into effective management practices during times of crisis. In Chapter 3, we will use this framework in order to showcase a model of leadership competencies necessary for managers to lead under pressure. But for now, let us first understand the foundation of crisis management upon which this book will build.

Phase 1: Signal Detection

While these are less evident in many sudden crisis situations (e.g., natural disaster), most other types of crisis have a number of early warning signs that lead an enlightened manager to know something is wrong. Unfortunately, these warning signals often go unheeded for several reasons. First, there may be an illusion of invulnerability leading to an attitude or perspective that "bad things happen to other people." Second, in times of calm and, in particular, in times of crisis people are subject to ego defense mechanisms, such as denial, that allow leaders to preserve a pristine image of themselves and their organizations even in light of information or evidence to the contrary.[63] Last, and even more troubling, is a failure in signal detection precisely because it is the decision making and behavior of organizational leaders that are contributing to the pending crisis. This is an all too common occurrence as represented by data from the Institute of Crisis Management indicating that over 50% of all crises are sparked by management activity.

Phase 2: Preparation/Prevention

The preparation and prevention phase is one in which managers engage in activities to plan for or avert a crisis. These activities may include developing crisis policies and procedures, identifying a crisis response team, performing crisis drills, and more. As Pearson and Mitroff caution, the preparation and prevention stage of crisis management should not imply that the goal for managers is to prevent all crises.[64] This would be impossible. But with some realistic planning and expectations, managers will be better positioned to prevent some crises and better able to manage those that are unavoidable.

Phase 3: Containment/Damage Control

Containment and damage control tend to preoccupy management time and attention when crises occur. Indeed, it is these activities that people associate with crisis management, and an important step toward the next phase: business recovery. The goal of the containment/damage control phase is to limit the reputational, financial, and other threats to firm survival in light of the crisis. This is achieved, for example, by activities that limit the encroachment of a localized crisis into otherwise unaffected parts of the business or the environment.[65]

Phase 4: Business Recovery

One of the ultimate goals of any crisis situation is to get back to "business as usual." In our own research of firms involved in class action discrimination lawsuits,[66] we found that executives are constantly trying to reassure stakeholders that, despite the disruption, business affairs are operating smoothly or will be returning to normal soon. In the business recovery stage, crisis handlers should have a set of short- and long-term initiatives designed to return the business to normal operations.

Phase 5: Learning

Organizational learning is the process of acquiring, interpreting, acting on, and disseminating new information throughout the firm. When it comes to managing crisis situations, however, firm leadership runs the risk of adopting a reactive and defensive posture that prevents learning.[67] Firms taking a learning stance would still be subject to the earlier crisis phases *and* would be enhanced by an explicit attempt to understand the underlying organizational factors contributing to the crisis. Then they could leverage this insight to facilitate fundamental change in firm systems and procedures (Figure 2.4).[68]

Figure 2.4   Phases of crisis management.

Summary

Understanding the phases of a business crisis and the dimensions upon which crises are categorized, and the ability to distinguish between a business challenge and a true crisis are fundamental and necessary precursors to developing the leadership competency to successfully lead organizations in turbulent times. What we have offered in this chapter is essentially the basics of crisis and crisis management. From this base, subsequent chapters will introduce you to ideas and practices that will help in the transition from "just getting by" when times are at their most challenging to thriving personally, professionally, and organizationally. Table 2.1 identifies key questions associated with each phase that

Table 2.1   Questions to Consider at Each Crisis Phase

Crisis Phase	Questions Leaders Ask
Phase 1: Signal detection	• What are the organization's vulnerable areas?
	• How can the organization's vulnerable areas result in a crisis?
	• What situations and practices does the organization ignore that may lead to a crisis?
	• Does the organization acknowledge things that may be uncomfortable to confront?
	• How do the organization's systems and policies contribute to potential crisis situations?
Phase 2: Preparation/ prevention	• Has leadership created a plan for reacting to crises?
	• Has the organization allocated appropriate resources for crisis prevention?
	• Will the organization's infrastructure facilitate or hinder the resolution of a crisis?
	• Has the organization's culture developed a readiness mentality for responding to crisis?
Phase 3: Containment/ damage control	• Is the organization positioned to implement a strategy for limiting damage during a crisis?
	• How does the organization control crisis-related information?

(continued)

Table 2.1   Questions to Consider at Each Crisis Phase (continued)

Crisis Phase	Questions Leaders Ask
Phase 3: Containment/ damage control (continued)	• Who are the stakeholders with whom the organization needs to be concerned, and what do we need to do to satisfy them?
	• What message should the organization communicate to stakeholders, and how should it communicate it?
• Phase 4: Business recovery	• What are the organization's short- and long-term recovery plans after the crisis?
	• What critical activities must leadership be engaged in to recover from the crisis?
	• What metrics will we use to evaluate the performance of our business recovery strategy?
	• How will leadership communicate the end results of the business recovery phase?
• Phase 5: Learning	• What did the organization learn from the crisis?
	• Did leadership reflect on past mistakes and behaviors?
	• Has the organization engaged in a change of behavior to prevent future crises?
	• Has the organization developed a memory to prevent future crises?

Figure 2.5   Leadership Links 2.1

- Crisis Management
  http://managementhelp.org/crisis/crisis.htm
- Seven Dimensions of Crisis Communication Management
  http://www.e911.com/monos/A001.html
- Institute for Crisis Management
  www.crisisexperts.com
- Crisis Leadership: Making a Difference When Disaster Strikes
  http://www.ccl.org/leadership/enewsletter/2008/JANissue.aspx
- Stepping Into the Void
  http://crisisleadership.blogspot.com/

leaders may want to consider in preparation for becoming crisis leaders rather than crisis managers. We use these phases as a backdrop to focus leaders' attention more explicitly on the knowledge, skills, and abilities (a.k.a. competencies) needed to holistically address business crises (Figure 2.5).

Endnotes

1. McLean & Elkind, *The smartest guys in the room*.
2. Dutton, The processing of crisis and non-crisis strategic issues, 501–517.
3. Billings, Milburn, & Schaalman, A model of crisis perception, 300–316.
4. Dutton, The processing of crisis and non-crisis strategic issues, 501–517.
5. Pearson & Clair, Reframing crisis management, 59–76.
6. *CBS News Interactive*, JetBlue attempts to calm passenger furor.
7. *Orlando Sentinel*, Maker of contaminated pet food settles with pet owners.
8. Menu Foods, *Menu Foods income fund announces 2008 first quarter results*.
9. Mitroff, Pearson, & Harrington, *The essential guide to managing corporate crises*.
10. Shrivastava, Mitroff, Hiller, & Miglani, Understanding industrial crises, 285–303.
11. Post, Preston, & Sachs, *Redefining the corporation*.
12. Goodpaster, Business ethics and stakeholder analysis, 53–73.
13. Freeman, *Strategic management*.
14. James & Wooten, Leadership as (un)usual, 141–152; Brockner & James, Toward an understanding of when executives see crisis as opportunity, 94–116.
15. Freeman, *Strategic management*.
16. Donaldson & Preston, The stakeholder theory of the corporation, 65–91.
17. Clarkson, Defining, evaluating, and managing corporate social performance, 331–358; Goodpaster, Business ethics and stakeholder analysis, 53–73.
18. Sundaram & Inkpen, The corporate objective revisited, 350–363.
19. Freeman, The politics of stakeholder theory, 409–421.
20. Gardiner & Martinko, Impression management in organizations, 321–338; Ginzel, Kramer, & Sutton, Organizational impression management as reciprocal influence process.
21. Savage et al., Strategies for assessing and managing organizational stakeholders, 61–75.
22. Shrivastava et al., Understanding industrial crises, 285–303.
23. Ibid.
24. Pollard & Hotho, Crises, scenarios and the strategic management process, 723.
25. Gundel, Towards a new typology of crises, 106–115.
26. Pearson & Mitroff, From crisis prone to crisis prepared, 48–59.
27. Gundel, Towards a new typology of crises, 106–115.
28. Ibid.
29. Caponigro, *The crisis counselor*.
30. Rosenthal & Kouzmin, Crises and crisis management, 277–304.
31. Rike, Preared or not...That is the vital question, 25–32.
32. Gundel, Towards a new typology of crises, 106–115.

33. Rosenthal & Kouzmin, Crises and crisis management, 277–304.

34. Mitroff, Think like a sociopath, act like a saint, 42–53.

35. Gundel, Towards a new typology of crises, 106–115.

36. Allen & Caillouet, Legitimation endeavors, 44–63; Benoit, *Accounts, excuses, and apologies*; Hobbs, Treachery by any other name, 323–346.

37. Coombs & Holladay, Communication and attributions in a crisis, 279–295.

38. Ibid.

39. Mitroff, Pauchant, & Shrivastava, Conceptual and empirical issues in the development of a general theory of crisis management, 83–107.

40. Ibid.

41. Ibid.

42. Marcus & Goodman, Victims and shareholders, 281–305.

43. Ibid.

44. Mitroff & Aspaslan, Preparing for evil, 109–115.

45. Perrow, *Normal accidents*.

46. Gundel, Towards a new typology of crises, 106–115.

47. Ibid.

48. Ibid.

49. Ibid.

50. Ibid.

51. Weick, The collapse of sensemaking in organizations, 628–652.

52. Ibid.

53. Gundel, Towards a new typology of crises, 106–115.

54. Ibid.

55. Marcus & Goodman, Victims and shareholders, 281–305; Pearson & Mitroff, From crisis prone to crisis prepared, 48–59.

56. Marcus & Goodman, Victims and shareholders, 281–305; Shrivastava, Crisis theory/practice, 23–42; Dubrovski, Management mistakes as causes of corporate crises, 333–354.

57. Coombs & Holladay, Communication and attributions in a crisis, 279–295.

58. McAuley, Duncan, & Russell, Measuring causal attributions, 566–573.

59. Weiner, An attributional theory of achievement motivation and emotion, 548–573.

60. Coombs & Holladay, Communication and attributions in a crisis, 279–295.

61. Ibid.

62. Pearson & Mitroff, From crisis prone to crisis prepared, 48–59.

63. Wooten & James, When firms fail to learn, 23–33.

64. Pearson & Mitroff, From crisis prone to crisis prepared, 48–59.

65. Ibid.

66. James & Wooten, Diversity crisis, 1103–1118.

67. Brockner & James, Toward an understanding of when executives see crisis as opportunity, 94–115.

68. Wooten & James, When firms fail to learn, 23–33.

BECOMING A CRISIS LEADER— INDIVIDUAL CAPABILITIES

Chapter 3

Critical Leadership Competencies Before, During, and After a Crisis*

Most executives are not prepared to handle a crisis. They generally have neither the formal training nor the experience that would allow them to develop the knowledge, skills, abilities, and traits, or more simply the competencies, to engage in crisis leadership. In the book *Outliers*[1] Malcolm Gladwell describes what makes people outliers, whether it be in sports, academics, or the business arena. In attempting to understand those who appear to be truly gifted (e.g., Tiger Woods, Jack Welch) one thing that Gladwell uncovered may seem contrary to how most of us have come to perceive excellence—that talent is not necessarily innate. Although there is a place for natural talent, Gladwell argues not only do external factors matter but, more important, that people work at excellence. He goes on to offer numerous examples of people who have toiled at their chosen craft in relative obscurity before becoming the "overnight" sensation that the world knows them to be. In fact, Gladwell argues that, on aver-

---

* Many of the crisis leadership competencies, and associated examples, described in this chapter were drawn from earlier research that we conducted. See Wooten & James, Linking crisis management and leadership competencies, 352–379.

39

age, outliers spend 10,000 hours perfecting their skill. Now, imagine needing to have 10,000 hours of crisis handling before one becomes an expert in crisis leadership. Although we certainly hope that such extensive practice will never be required, it does raise the question of just what competencies leaders need to engage in crisis leadership.

Crisis leadership entails a complex set of competencies that leaders must adopt if they are to lead an organization through the various crisis phases and into a successful recovery.[2] When these competencies exist within a firm's leadership, the likelihood of a firm becoming resilient after a crisis is greatly enhanced. In short, crisis leadership demands an integration of knowledge, skills, abilities, and traits that allow a leader to plan for, respond to, and learn from crisis events. In its most ambitious form, crisis leadership is also about handling a crisis in such a way that the firm is better off after a crisis than it was before,[3] but we will return to this idea in Chapter 9.

Although plenty has been written on how to manage a crisis, we know relatively little about the competencies associated with that activity. In their research, crisis scholars Pearson and Clair[4] described the four Cs of crisis management. They argue that leaders need to be mindful of the four Cs: the *cause* of crises, crises *consequences*, *cautionary* measures for preventing crises, and *coping* mechanisms for responding to crises. To these, we add a fifth C—*competencies* needed for leading throughout the crisis life cycle. It is the competency of a leader or of a leadership team to analyze and act before, during, and after a crisis that ultimately determines the extent to which the organization recovers.

Linking Leadership Competencies and Crisis Management

Leadership has been described as a collective phenomenon whereby many people contribute to the organization and influence its activity.[5] In that light, leadership is dynamic, and necessary roles evolve over time as the circumstances dictate. In the most extreme cases, leadership's influence can extend beyond the organization's boundaries.[6] Crises are extreme events, and an important indicator of effective crisis leadership is the ability to positively influence the vast number of stakeholders who are affected by the crisis. Crisis leadership, then, requires a core set of competencies that allow people to determine an appropriate course of action and then to execute that action. Moreover, effective crisis handling requires that leaders develop these competencies not only for and in themselves, but promote their development in those they are leading. More directly, leaders must take responsibility for orchestrating a work environment that infuses a competency-based approach to crisis management.[7] Such an approach highlights knowledge, skills, and abilities—all characteristics that are within the control of the leader and, as such, can change or be developed over time. In this regard, we are sympathetic to Gladwell's proposition that a significant part of what makes someone an outlier (and in our case a superb crisis leader) is his or her willingness to work at developing the necessary competencies.

In the remainder of this chapter, we identify, analyze, and provide examples of a set of critical crisis leadership competencies, and organize them by the crisis phase in which their display is most relevant. Doing so provides a road map for decision makers, and a conceptual structure upon which researchers can build. Recall from Chapter 2 that the five phases of a crisis are (1) signal detection, (2) preparation/prevention, (3) containment/damage control, (4) business recovery, and (5) learning.[8] In the phases of signal detection and crisis prevention, the competencies we will discuss focus on how organizations can eliminate vulnerabilities to a crisis and minimize their weaknesses based on early warnings. For the damage control phase, we identify operation-oriented competencies that help to contain a crisis. Last, for the business recovery and learning phases, the crisis leadership competencies focus on rebuilding the organization and creating knowledge.

It is important to note that leading under the pressure that a crisis imposes is exceptionally difficult, and examples of situations in which critical crisis leadership competencies were displayed can be rare. Likewise, true crisis leadership can mean that a crisis was averted, or that the crisis was handled in such a way that its impact was lessened and therefore the crisis and its handling were less worthy of attention. As a result, there are generally fewer noteworthy examples of true crisis leadership and the competencies associated with it. That said, some of our examples of crisis leadership competencies may be negative examples, or examples of what not to do. Negative examples, or what some might even call failures, however, can be as powerful a learning tool as positive examples, and thus we include them here.[9]

Critical Competencies at Each Crisis Phase

Signal Detection

Signal detection is the stage in a crisis in which leaders should, but do not always, sense early warning signals (red flags) that suggest the possibility of a crisis. On April 16, 2007, Seung-Hui Cho, a student at Virginia Polytechnic Institute and State University (Virginia Tech), commenced two separate attacks on the university campus in Blacksburg, Virginia. Cho's shooting rampage resulted in the deaths of 32 students and faculty, the wounding of many others, and his own suicide. The Virginia Tech massacre, as it has come to be known, was the deadliest school shooting in U.S. history. Virginia Tech was both praised and criticized for its handling of the crisis. One of the harshest criticisms came from the Virginia Tech Review Panel, a state-appointed task force responsible for reviewing the case. The conclusion from their report was that school officials did not do enough to prevent the attack. For many, what made this conclusion particularly egregious is that some Virginia Tech faculty and staff had information and concerns about Cho long before the shooting took place. For example, as described in the review panel's report, school officials were aware of but, because of federal privacy laws, did not report a history of anxiety-related problems. In addition, the report detailed incidents of aberrant behavior by Cho in his junior year at Virginia Tech. Some of Cho's former professors had judged his writing and classroom demeanor as disturbing,[10] and he had been investigated by the university for stalking female students. Finally, in 2005, Cho had been declared mentally ill by a Virginia special justice. In short, there were numerous signals that something might be dangerously amiss. With this as a backdrop, we turn to the critical competencies that are necessary in the signal detection stage of a crisis.

Sense Making

Sense making is the act of turning circumstances into a situation that can be comprehended explicitly in words and that serves as a "springboard into action."[11] Stated differently, sense making represents an attempt to create order and make sense, retrospectively, of what occurs. It is driven by a desire to make things appear rational to ourselves and to others. Yet sense making is influenced by context. We read contextual information into the stimuli or circumstance that we are confronting; how we interpret that context influences how we make order or make sense of what we are facing. When confronted by something unusual, something we do not understand, or for which we have no reference, we grab hold of data that will force the anomaly into something we can comprehend, or upon which we can make decisions or take action. The warning signals that could, theoretically, inform us that a crisis is pending are themselves unusual enough that our mind finds a way to put them in a context or circumstance we understand. Unfortunately, for new stimuli (as crises generally are), we tend not to have a framework that allows us to make sense of new events, and as a result, we run the risk of ignoring the stimuli altogether.

According to scholar Karl Weick and colleagues, the process of sense making addresses three fundamental questions: How does something come to be an event? What does the event mean? What should I do relative to the event?[12] The ability to be attuned to each of these questions and organize the answers in a way that leads to credible action during the signal detection phase is a defining

competency during this precrisis stage. Sense making should help in the predict-
ing and potentially preventing of a crisis. If, for example, the Virginia Tech officials
had questioned more explicitly why a student's behavior would become increasingly aberrant and aggressive, they may have reached a set of conclusions that
would have propelled them into alternative courses of action. In this case, relevant
sense-making questions might be: Is Cho's behavior typical of other college students? What are the possible consequences of such behavior for other students,
for the victim, for the organization? Am I comfortable with these consequences?
What action can or should I take in light of this behavior? Asking these questions
is an important first step in the sense-making process. Consider the following
diagram (Figure 3.1) of what sense making around Cho's behavior might look like
from the vantage point of a faculty or staff member at Virginia Tech. Note that one
does not have to necessarily predict a specific crisis event from one or more trig-
gering events. Rather, the process of engaging in sense making brings to the fore
an obvious conclusion—nothing good will likely result from Cho's behavior. It
also paves the way for identifying concrete steps that can be taken. In the absence
of sense making, it becomes all too easy to live in the realm of generality, wishful
thinking, and faulty assumptions—a pattern of thinking that prohibits us from
being mindful of warning signals or red flags of possible danger.

Sense making is not easy, and sense making during a crisis is even more difficult.[13] Ironically, the very act of trying to understand one or more stimuli can

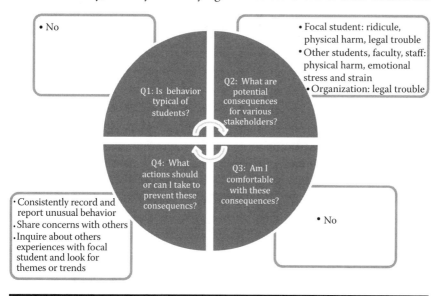

Figure 3.1   Example: Sense-making questions for the Virginia Tech shooting.

intensify the stimuli in adverse ways. In the case of the Virginia Tech shooting, as increasing attention was given to Cho's aberrant behavior, the more disturbed and agitated he became. So the trade-off can be a complicated one. On the one hand, you can ignore the signals and hope for the best. This strategy requires very little investment and frees up time and other resources for conducting traditional business. Yet if the worst-case scenario comes to pass, leaders find themselves consumed with managing a crisis. On the other hand, one can engage in sense making at the first sign of a problem. This approach requires an investment of time and resources up front, but could potentially thwart a full-fledged crisis from occurring. In the minds of most, however, the early investment in sense making, and the actions that result from it, may seem like overkill in light of an "unlikely" event. This conclusion may be true, but an important aspect of the sense-making competency is the ability to not only make sense of discrete events, but also to make sense of a series of events that, on the surface, may seem unrelated.

Perspective Taking

Perspective taking refers to the ability to consider another person's or group's point of view,[14] and can lead to a merging between one's self and someone else in such a way that there is greater understanding. Perspective taking has been linked positively to one's social competence and self-esteem,[15] cognitive functioning,[16] and moral reasoning,[17] and negatively to social aggression[18] and stereotyped thinking.[19] Perhaps most germane for the purposes of crisis leadership, though, is that the act of considering how someone is affected by his or her situation yields an empathic response.[20] What better time for a leader to take the perspective of various stakeholders and to demonstrate empathy than during a crisis? In fact, during a crisis, one of the core responsibilities of a leader is that of ensuring the well-being of those affected by the crisis. Perspective taking allows leaders to better understand and empathize with others, and, in turn, act in the best interest of stakeholders.

Perspective taking is especially relevant during the signal detection stage of crisis. Failing to consider the implications of seemingly inconsequential events, or warning signs, can be interpreted as being insensitive to how others in the organization experience those events. What may seem insignificant to a leader who is fairly distant from the daily operations of the organization may in fact be quite significant to employees or customers who experience the event. Furthermore, without the proper attention by the leader, the event continues to occur and over time will grow in intensity until it becomes a full-fledged crisis.

Most leaders are quite skilled at perspective taking. One could argue that to achieve a leadership position (as traditionally measured by title, status, or hierarchy), perspective taking is a necessary component in managing one's career in a way that allows for upward mobility. Failure to take the perspective of one's boss, for example, would adversely affect his or her ability to deliver the type of work that generates strong performance evaluations and promotions. Yet our observations tell us that perspective taking is a differentiating factor between people who demonstrate true crisis leadership versus those who focus primarily on the damage control activities of crisis management. In particular, people engaged in crisis management tend to have a more narrow range of stakeholders for whom they engage in perspective taking, whereas, we have argued, crisis leaders take the views of multiple stakeholders.[21] The pull against multiple-stakeholder perspective taking is a strong one. Crisis handlers are influenced by a number of factors, some internal and some external to the organization. Chief among them, however, is the need to respond to stakeholders that have power over the firm. For public organizations, shareholders represent one such group. In recent years, we have seen laser-like focus by firm leaders on shareholders, while the attention directed to other stakeholders, including customers and employees, suffered in the wake. In the midst of a crisis, shareholders, important stakeholders indeed, may not necessarily be the most in need of empathy and constructive action, yet power dynamics that exist between firm leadership and shareholders can heavily influence who gets management's attention.

The Firestone product recall in 2000 offers a relevant example of the dangers of narrow perspective taking during the signal detection stage of a crisis. Considered to be perhaps the most deadly auto safety crisis in American history, the National Highway Transportation Safety Administration issued a letter to the leadership of Firestone and Ford Motor Company requesting information about the high incident rate of tire failure on Ford Explorer SUVs. Ford's data confirmed unusually high failure rates, and even more troubling, it concluded that when the tires fail, the vehicle often rolls over, killing the occupants.[22] On August 9, 2000, both Ford and Firestone agreed to a recall of several tire models. Before reaching this stage, however, there were numerous signs of a pending crisis that went ignored or undetected by the leadership of both companies.[23] One such warning signal was a memo about supplier quality problems, reports of accidents, complaints about the vehicles in overseas markets, and reports from their own risk management department. In addition to their failure to heed these important warning signals, firm leaders seemed to have had a narrow target group in mind when considering action steps for what eventually became the product recall crisis. It appears as if firm leaders had taken the perspective of shareholders, rather than also considering how the impact of faulty tires affected other stakeholder groups, including, for example, their customers—some of whom in the end became victims. Had firm leaders taken the perspective of their customers, and the public writ large, they likely would have had a more empathic response in deciding how to manage the crisis. As it stood, however, during the signal detection phase of the crisis, Firestone's leadership focused on the data (rather than also considering the concerns of and implications for customers) and interpreted the data as being of acceptable risk.[24] In this case it is easy to infer that the decision makers were largely concerned with shareholder reaction to the crisis rather than also the perspective of the consumer and end user. In the absence of assuming a more inclusive perspective-taking stance, Firestone was heavily criticized in the media for its slow and unemotional response.

Preparation/Prevention

Stage 2 of crisis management is preparation and prevention. It is during this stage that crisis handlers begin preparing for or averting the crisis that had been foreshadowed in the signal detection stage. For organizations such as the Red Cross, whose primary mission is to prepare for and prevent the escalation of crisis events, the activities and competencies for this crisis stage are well known. For almost every other organization, however, prevention and preparation activities can be a challenge. Despite all of the controversy that surrounds it, Wal-Mart is one example of a firm that in some ways seems to have mastered crisis preparation and prevention. In fact, they are often at the forefront of firms that are able to prepare for natural disasters, such as a hurricane. One journalist has described Wal-Mart as an emergency relief standard bearer after having witnessed the chain's incredibly speedy and well-coordinated effort to get supplies to the Gulf Coast region in anticipation of Hurricane Katrina in 2005.[25] Years later, in the efforts to prepare for Hurricane Gustav in 2008, Wal-Mart personnel scoured Mississippi and Louisiana in search of empty store facilities that could be used as shelters, developed business continuity plans that would allow the retail chains to operate immediately after the storm passed, and contacted state government agencies to secure transportation credentials that would allow Wal-Mart trucks to carry generators and other supplies into anticipated damage zones.[26] Clearly, these activities would not prevent the storm, but they would lessen the severity of some of the deleterious consequences that natural disasters cause, and they would allow the affected communities to prepare for the storm in thoughtful and appropriate ways. Although these exact activities may not be relevant in every pending crisis, the larger point is that some preparation and prevention activities commence in advance of a crisis. There are several relevant crisis leadership competencies that are associated with this crisis stage.

Influence

In times of crisis, leaders are exceptionally dependent upon their workers, and even people or groups outside of their direct control, to follow directions and provide information that will facilitate decision making and action taking. More than this, however, leaders will need to call on others to do things that are not a part of their standard operating procedures. Yet, when people are feeling threatened, they become less receptive to trying new things and become more likely to constrict information flow.[27] As a result, an important part of the leader's job, and one of the most important determinants of his or her success, is the ability to influence or convince others.[28] The Wal-Mart example highlights an important leadership competency during a crisis—the ability to influence.

An early empirical study examining the use of influence in organizations sought to uncover how people influence colleagues.[29] The authors first identified a range of influence tactics that people used at work by analyzing the written descriptions of managers. Specifically, the managers in the study were asked the following: "Describe an incident in which you actually succeeded in getting your boss, a co-worker, or a subordinate to do something you wanted." In their descriptions, respondents were asked to write about what they wanted from the target, what they did, whether there was resistance from the target, and what further influence tactics were used in response to the resistance. Fourteen influence categories emerged from the data analysis. Examples of some of these categories are personal negative actions (e.g., chastise the target, express anger), exchange (e.g., invoke past favors or offer to make a sacrifice), persistence (e.g., repeat requests or reminders), reward (e.g., verbal reinforcement), demand (e.g., invoke rules), and coalition building (e.g., obtain support from others). Drawing on the managerial leadership literature, a subsequent study refined this set of original influence tactics and to it added inspirational appeals (e.g., emotional requests that appeal to one's values) and consultation (involving others in the decision-making process).[30]

Although the influence categories described in the research above are commonly used in organizations, we do not advocate many of them with respect to crisis leadership, either because they do not represent the aspects of leadership we espouse or because they are inappropriate during a crisis. Negative actions and making demands, for example, connote a leadership based on threats rather than leadership that inspires collaboration and attempts to bring out the best in people. Coalition building, although an important part of collaborative leadership, may take more time than we would expect a leader to reasonably have during a crisis.

Among the influence categories identified in prior research, there are two that we believe are particularly relevant to crisis leadership. First, is explaining the rationale for why you are attempting to influence the target. *Rationality* or *rational persuasion* is generally the most widely used influence tactic. Influence behaviors that characterize rationality include presenting information in support of one's point of view, explaining the reason for the request, using logic, and demonstrating competence in the request. During a crisis, leaders need to show that they are competent, calm, and in control of the situation. They clearly will need the help of others in resolving the crisis, and they are more likely to get that help if they appear to act rationally and responsibly. Sharing information about the crisis allows people to better understand the threats faced by the organization and draws them into wanting to help. In the absence of this information, people may dismiss or underestimate the severity of the situation and the need for their participation. Similarly, to influence someone's behavior during a crisis the leader needs to logically articulate his or her concerns, the impact of the crisis, and what specifically he or she is requesting people to do.

The second highly relevant influence tactic is the use of inspirational appeals. Crisis events are emotionally charged. People that are affected by them and people that must lead organizations through them experience the gamut of emotions throughout the crisis life cycle. Therefore, leaders will be well served if they are able to tap into the emotions of those whom they are leading. Examples of inspirational appeals are using emotional or symbolic language; speaking to personal or organizational values, a sense of justice, or organizational loyalty; and appealing to the desire to excel or overcome a challenge.[31] Inspirational appeals tap into the emotions that people are already experiencing during a crisis and can provide an important lever for motivating desired behavior.

In the Wal-Mart example, influence played a significant role in their ability to mobilize employees and convince organizations outside of their jurisdiction to take action in ways that were atypical. With Hurricane Gustav bearing down, Wal-Mart employees were fearful about what would happen to their own homes and families, and we have to believe that those self-interests were competing significantly with the needs of their employer. Yet, what we witnessed were leaders who were able to influence employees in such a way that the employees' concerns became secondary to the needs of the organization. Leaders demonstrated a capacity to calmly and rationally communicate what they needed from employees in a way that mobilized them to work for the organization and not only for themselves. In addition, Wal-Mart leaders were able to influence government agencies, not widely believed to be the most flexible of organizations, to make allowances and changes to their procedures in ways that would better prepare the community for the pending storm. One could argue that influence is actually easier in times of crisis. After all, people are desperate for the crisis to end and ostensibly would do anything to bring about the end. Yet, in reality what we see when people are experiencing threat is the tendency to fall back on routines and what is known rather than to consider new and creative ways of problem solving. The ability to influence through rational argument and inspirational appeals helps to convince people to experiment and seek new ways of doing things, and therefore becomes a critical crisis leadership competency.

To this point, we have been talking about influence as a bottom-down strategy. In other words, we have described it is a tactic directed toward a target at a lower level in the organization. When it comes to crisis management, however, it is often lower-level employees who have critical crisis-related information, or who observed warning signs and recognized a pending crisis. The challenge for this group is to influence upward. The term *issue selling* is the label used to characterize a set of behaviors used by middle managers to direct top management's attention to and understanding of important issues that otherwise might not reach the radar screen of top management.[32] Issue selling can play a vital role in the transition between the signal detection phase of a crisis and the preparation and prevention phase.

Central to issue selling is the ability to be persuasive and influential to set or change the strategic direction of a firm, and such behaviors are particularly significant in circumstances or environments that are atypical (e.g., highly competitive or high velocity),[33] including environments where there is pressure for rapid and high-quality decision processes. By definition, organizations on the verge of a crisis represent one such environment in which issue selling would be appropriate. For example, mid-level employees may need to convince their leaders that the recurrence of small but unusual activities or events is something that requires action or, at the very least, more explicit investigation. Yet, doing so can seem like an uphill battle. Given the unlikely occurrence of a crisis and the plethora of more immediate and tangible issues that a firm usually faces, activities associated with crisis preparation and prevention are rarely seen as pressing concerns among key decision makers. For firm leaders to pay attention to crisis preparation, it will require a change agent that is skillful in issue selling.

Organizational Agility

Crisis leaders who are competent at managing organizational agility have a thorough knowledge of all aspects of the business and can work across organizational functions, departments, or silos to accomplish a task. Organizational agility requires the integration of the structural, technological, and human aspects of an organization, and as a result, leaders must be both knowledgeable and flexible to make connections across these three domains.[34] In a case study examining the human resources management strategy for fostering organizational agility in employees, one firm identified attributes and behaviors associated with being organizationally agile.[35] One of the most germane behaviors as it relates to crisis management is the ability to anticipate and identify potential threats and to minimize the probable effects of those threats. In preparing or planning for a crisis, the ability to be organizationally agile is critical because although a crisis event may initially affect one aspect of the business, ultimately the entire organization may be affected. In the crisis preparation and prevention stage, a crisis leader must consider the organization in its entirety. Moreover, to the extent that a crisis leader understands all aspects of the organization and is able to span organizational boundaries to get things done, the more comprehensive a crisis plan is likely to be.

Using another Wal-Mart example, Wal-Mart demonstrated organizational agility in its preparation and management of the Hurricane Katrina crisis. Before Katrina hit land, Wal-Mart marshaled its extensive distribution network to stock its stores with the necessary supplies that are normally purchased during a natural disaster. As a result, it was able to serve the Gulf Coast region better than other companies or federal agencies. Its efficiency, in contrast to government bodies that did not react until days after the hurricane, was the result of a CEO who used his previous logistics experience to manage stores during Hurricane Katrina and was able to assemble a cross-functional emergency operations center designed to quickly bring together people from different groups in Wal-Mart to make decisions and set priorities for tasks.

Creativity

Defining the concept of creativity has been a long-standing debate in the field of psychology. The debate centered on whether creativity is a process, a personal characteristic, or a product. The debate was also sparked over attempts to identify objective criteria by which to evaluate creativity.[36] Although the debate lingers, one prominent creativity scholar has attempted to reconcile the debate by arguing that a conceptual way to think about creativity is that it is subjective and we must abandon the hope of defining creativity by objective measures. She defines creativity as follows:

> Creativity can be regarded as the quality of products or responses judged to be creative by appropriate observers, and it can also be regarded as the process by which something so judged is produced.[37]

In the workplace, creativity most often refers to the production of new or useful ideas, products, services, processes, or procedures. Within the crisis leadership domain, the ability to think and act creatively is a necessary skill because, as we have said, crisis events cannot be adequately managed with routine or traditional thought patterns or with routine problem solving. Conventional wisdom might suggest that competence in creativity is most relevant for damage control and containment activities. After all, one would need to think creatively to identify and execute solutions that would resolve the crisis. While we do not discount the importance of creativity in that phase, we also believe that creativity is equally necessary during the crisis preparation and prevention phase. By engaging the creativity competency during the planning and prevention stage of a crisis, one could conceivably prevent the crisis altogether or limit its impact.

The ability to think creatively about how a firm is vulnerable to a crisis and then to plan for multiple contingencies requires an ability to brainstorm and imagine in ways that go beyond the traditional thinking about corporate concerns. In addition to brainstorming about the potential types of crises that a firm may be susceptible to, the most competent crisis leaders will identify full-fledged scenarios of possible crisis events. A part of that scenario planning is the ability to project the trajectory of the warning signals to anticipate precisely how these small and seemingly inconsequential events may manifest in more significant ways. Those scenarios then would be used as the foundation for preparing the organization for how to respond should an actual crisis occur.

Containment/Damage Control

The third stage of crisis management is containment and damage control. The goal of crisis containment and damage control is to limit the reputational, financial, safety, and other threats to firm survival. Crisis handlers are working diligently during this stage to bring the crisis to an end as quickly as possible to limit the negative publicity to the organization, and because doing so will allow leaders to move into the business recovery phase (Stage 4). It is the containment and damage control stage that is generally the most vivid in the minds of people who are experiencing a crisis precisely because so much of management's time and attention is focused on the unfolding crisis. Moreover, damage control is often the most vivid stage for observers of a crisis in large part because of the ubiquitous nature of various forms of media that bring to our attention crisis events.

As we write this chapter President Obama is facing one of the most severe economic crises in recent history. Intentional use of various media outlets has, for the first time, allowed the public to have virtually a front-row seat in the ongoing nature of the crisis and in the political and business attempts to resolve it. Not only has the current presidential administration used traditional television and print media to provide transparency as it attempts to rescue the nation's economy, but it has solicited the public's involvement in the recovery process through the use of the Internet. The underlying theme of these actions is that communication is a central component to the damage control process. In fact, the effectiveness of one's communication can be the defining feature of whether a crisis is perceived as having been handled successfully or unsuccessfully. Thus, communicating effectively is a critical crisis leadership competency.

Communicating Effectively

An important function of a leader is not only to manage the performance of the group or organization that he or she is leading, but also to manage the perceptions of its performance. When an organization is threatened, either by its own doing or as a result of some external force, its ability to perform is weakened and the organization becomes vulnerable to negative publicity. During these times, effectively managing not only the performance of employees and others dealing with the crisis but also the organization's image is critical. The competency most closely identified with crisis handling is the ability to communicate well. Often, the type of communication observed during a crisis event is one that is rooted in the public relations tradition and attempts to position the organization or the crisis it is facing in relatively favorable terms. In other words, crisis communication is used to positively shape the stakeholders' perceptions of the crisis and the organization.[38] Many large and public organizations retain a staff of public relations or communication personnel, or hire public relations specialists when such service is required. Yet, the ability and willingness to communicate with stakeholders during a crisis is as much the responsibility of leaders as it is that of communication experts. During the damage control phase of a crisis, crisis leaders will identify and connect with key organizational personnel, provide or solicit necessary information and instruction, and attempt to restore calm or provide reassurance to affected constituents. Depending on the type of crisis, leaders also may need to be persuasive, confident, or empathic in their messaging.

In early crisis communication research the focus was on understanding rhetorical approaches to image restoration. Crises, after all, are image-damaging events. To counteract the reputational threat that crises pose, leaders must convey information and feelings that resonate positively with relevant audiences. Such rhetoric comes in the form of accounts, or "statements made by a social actor to explain unanticipated or untoward behavior."[39] Two general types of accounts emerged from earlier research. *Excuses* represent an account in which the communicator admits that the event or behavior is bad or wrong, but denies full responsibility for it. *Justifications*, conversely, are accounts in which the communicator accepts responsibility, but denies any negative or pejorative association with it.[40] For each type of account, scholars have identified subcategories including, for example, accident-based excuses (e.g., "we had to perform an emergency landing in the water because both of our engines failed when struck by birds") and denial of injury-based justifications (e.g., "it was unfortunate that we had to land in the water, but at least everyone survived").

In addition to the forms of communication described thus far, other scholars, including Goffman and Schonbach,[41] have written extensively about various forms of accounts in response to face-threatening events or behavior. Their work forms the foundation of the impression management field. Impression management refers to the process by which one tries to control the perceptions that other people form of him of her with the goal of preserving his or her self-image. According to Goffman, people attempt to establish and maintain impressions that are congruent with the image they want to convey to various audiences.[42] One of the most prominent types of face-saving accounts that came from Goffman's research was the apology. He argued that a complete apology consists of five elements: an expression of regret, acknowledgment of expected behavior, repudiation of the behavior or event, promise to behave correctly in the future, and atonement and compensation. In recent years we have seen the apology used by prominent sports figures (Los Angeles Laker's Koby Bryant), clergy (Colorado evangelical preacher Ted Haggard), and political figures (former U.S. senator and presidential candidate John Edwards) following revelations that they have engaged in extramarital affairs. Likewise, business leaders have apologized so often recently that there is now a term for it—the CEO apology. Interestingly, the sincerity of these public admissions and apologies has been called into question by the media and others. The public backlash may be a result of apology overload given the number of high-profile incidents requiring an apology in a relatively short time frame. Alternatively, the actions by these leaders came at a point in U.S. history that is characterized by a great deal of mistrust of all forms of leadership, and such behavior by these men (and some women) simply added insult to injury.

Schlenker contributed to the knowledge base of accounts with his work on predicaments or "situations in which events have undesirable implications for the identity-relevant images actors have claimed or desire to claim in front of real or imagined audiences."[43] In addition to the forms of accounts described above, Schlenker identified *defenses of innocence* as another type of account used for face-saving purposes. Defenses of innocence are used primarily to deny the culpability of the transgressor; either the event did not happen or the person or organization was not responsible for it. A company spokesperson will often use this type of account when communicating with media following a crisis for which the firm is perceived to be responsible. In a study examining the communication patterns of firms following allegations of discrimination, for example, the data showed that in 90% of the cases, firms adopted a denial or defense of innocence stance.[44] Prototypical responses by firms in the study's sample include: "We deny that our chain engaged in any unlawful discriminatory practice" or "We are confident that there has been no discriminatory conduct."

Whereas the research on accounts described thus far was initially developed in response to negative behavior by an individual, other scholars have explicitly examined the accounts used in response to organizational wrongdoing.[45] This body of work has come to be known as organizational impression management, and such communication tactics are particularly relevant in times of crisis or controversy when an organization's legitimacy is challenged or threatened.[46] It is precisely during the damage control phase of a crisis that the media's portrayal of the organization, and in turn the public's perception of the organization, may be most diminished.[47] Consequently, verbal accounts come to play an important role in communicating messages that will influence audience reaction to the organization. Thus, just as is the case for individuals, rhetoric and social accounts at the organizational level are used by crisis handlers to shift negative attention away from the firm and shift it toward positive aspects of the organization. Elsbach studied controversial events of two organizations and found that in the process of trying to garner organizational legitimacy following these events, organizational spokespersons used defenses of innocence and justifications to portray the events and the organizations in a positive light.[48] These organizational impression management tactics are believed to attenuate the negative aspects of an event and accentuate any positive aspects that can be attributed to either the event or the organization.

Although some forms of rhetoric can work to an organization's advantage during a crisis, it is not a foregone conclusion that impression management tactics will always enhance an organization's image. Moreover, not all rhetoric is appropriate for all crisis types. Part of the responsibility of a crisis leader is to discern the type of message that will facilitate a favorable impression and create legitimacy for the organization at its darkest hour. Scholars have identified social accounts that convey *mediating messages* as being particularly effective during some crises. Mediating messages are accounts that (1) convey rationality (e.g., neutrality, consistency, and logicality) or (2) communicate understanding and consideration of stakeholders' views (e.g., timeliness, respect, and bilateral communication). Conveying rationality and being sensitive to stakeholders can lead to crisis handlers being viewed as competent, expert, and credible in the handling of the crisis; however, the effectiveness of each mediating message is context dependent.[49] Rational messages appear to be most effective for unforeseeable crises or events that were externally caused and therefore beyond the organization's control. Such events include natural disasters, oil spills,[50] and financial downturns.[51] In these cases, the crisis leader can claim legitimacy in the face of the crisis precisely because there was nothing the organization could have done to prevent the crisis event, and any other organization in the same set of circumstances would have fallen victim to the same event. On the other hand, research shows that accounts conveying stakeholder consideration and understanding are viewed to be most effective following crisis events that are more predictable and foreseeable. In these cases, the organization can anticipate the repercussions of a crisis event and can be proactive in conveying empathy with those who will likely be affected by it. As Elsbach points out, the appropriateness of these messages for various crisis types may also depend on the severity of the crisis. For crisis events in which stakeholders may be severely affected, consideration accounts may be appropriate regardless of whether the crisis event was foreseeable.[52]

The situational crisis communication theory (SCCT) further makes our point that various forms of rhetoric or accounts may be more or less appropriate for various crisis types.[53] SCCT attempts to match the crisis response (social account or rhetoric) with the crisis type for the purposes of best protecting the organization's reputation or image. In determining the most effective crisis response, four factors appear to be most relevant. First is the extent to which stakeholders believe the organization was able to control the crisis event. Second is the amount of responsibility attributed to the organization for the crisis event. Although organizational control and crisis responsibility are highly correlated constructs,[54] research suggests that the level of crisis responsibility is a uniquely important factor in the potential threat to an organization's image, and therefore should be considered distinct from organizational control[55] as a predictor of image threat. Third, crisis handlers must consider the severity of the crisis. Severity refers to the amount of human, financial, and environmental harm that the crisis is likely to inflict. The final factor to be considered in determining the most effective crisis response is the organization's performance history. Performance history refers to a firm's past actions or conduct, especially as it relates to its crisis and crisis handling history.[56] In an empirical investigation of crisis responses, one study revealed the significance of performance history with respect to diversity crises on current crisis response strategies for class action discrimination lawsuits. The data revealed that firms that had a prior history of discrimination were uniquely more likely to adopt accommodative responses than firms that had no history of discrimination or firms that were perceived to have resolved past discrimination positively.[57] Firms experiencing their initial encounter with a diversity crisis, on the other hand, were far more likely to adopt denial-based rhetoric.

According to the SCCT, the relationships among perceived organizational control, crisis responsibility, crisis severity, and performance history are important. Perceptions of organizational control positively influence perceived organizational responsibility for the crisis. Crisis severity and performance history, alternatively, both serve to moderate the relationship between organizational control and crisis responsibility. For example, the more severe the crisis is believed to be, the more stakeholders will attribute greater responsibility to the organization. The communication-related responsibility of the crisis leader, then, is to ultimately identify the response (e.g., verbal account, rhetoric, or impression management technique) most amenable to the complex set of relationships that exists for a given crisis.

Noted crisis communication expert Timothy Coombs synthesized prior research on crisis response strategies into a list of eight: (1) attack on the accuser,

(2) denial, (3) excuse, (4) victimization, (5) justification, (6) ingratiation, (7) corrective action, and (8) full apology. Coombs argued that crisis handlers can order these response strategies along a continuum that assesses the extent to which they must consider the needs of the organization (defensive strategies) relative to the needs of the potential victims of the crisis (accommodative strategies).[58] He also argues that the most effective crisis response strategies are those in which crisis handlers have matched the crisis response to the level of crisis responsibility. For crises in which there is perceived to be a great deal of crisis responsibility (e.g., organizational misdeeds or wrongdoing), the more effective response strategies are accommodative (e.g., corrective action or apologies) to the needs of affected stakeholders. For natural disasters, rumors, and other crisis types for which little attribution of organizational responsibility is likely to be made, response strategies can be more instructive (e.g., informing people how to protect themselves) or defensive (e.g., denial) (Figure 3.2).[59]

As we conclude our discussion of the importance of communicating effectively during the damage control phase we want to underscore that communication is not only about strategically determining and executing appropriate messages. What also helps to elevate a leader's competency in communicating effectively during a crisis is his or her ability to connect emotionally and psychologically with an audience. This may involve displaying one's vulnerability and one's capacity to be empathic to a wide variety of stakeholders. Moreover,

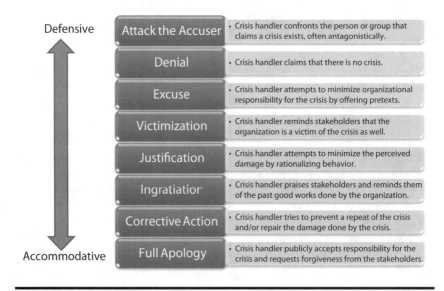

Figure 3.2 Crisis response strategies.

knowing the precise message that will resonate with stakeholders and then conveying that message at the right time is critical. Appearing reactionary rather than proactive in one's messaging can undermine even the most strategically astute and well-intentioned communication. In short, a truly gifted crisis leader will have the capacity to convey strength and inspire confidence, while simultaneously connecting to the emotional needs of people. To pull this off, a leader must be trusted; trust is a topic to which we will return in Chapter 6.

Risk Taking

Over the years, psychologists have conducted a vast amount of research on the role of personality on leadership effectiveness.[60] They have concluded from this research that good leaders demonstrate a particular constellation of personality traits. The *Big Five Personality Traits* are perhaps the most prominent and comprehensively examined categorization of human personality. Known as simply the Big Five, the personality traits are organized into five classes: neuroticism, extraversion, openness to experience, agreeableness, and conscientiousness. Organizational psychologists have examined these traits with respect to effective leader performance and found that the trait openness to experience has emerged as the strongest predictor of leadership effectiveness. Research has also suggested that risk taking is linked to the Big Five trait of openness to experience and, moreover, that risk taking is an important aspect of leadership and creativity (a crisis leadership competency we identified earlier).[61] For example, leaders must be willing and capable of changing courses and thinking broadly and unconventionally when needed.[62] Crisis situations present one such circumstance in which risk taking is particularly relevant. Crisis situations are inherently risky. They represent new challenges for which crisis handlers are not only generally unprepared, but also have little to no prior experience from which to draw ideas on how to resolve the crisis. Consequently, the ability to contain a crisis requires leaders who are able to identify and execute novel approaches to problem solving in a very limited period of time and under situations of extreme uncertainty. In short, leaders who are able to adapt quickly to the new and changing environment and who can be open to trying new things should be more effective at containing the damage than crisis handlers who are not strong in this dimension (Figure 3.3).

In the research on strategic issues, scholars have theorized about how organizations respond to threatening or crisis situations. The threat-rigidity model suggests that organizational decision makers tend to become more conservative and restrictive in their information sharing when experiencing a threat.[63] When less information is shared, decision makers in turn have less information upon which to draw ideas for problem solving. Likewise, by restricting information

Figure 3.3 Crisis phases.

flow, decision makers are likely to narrow the scope of organizational activity and rely increasingly on well-learned or habitual behavior. To varying degrees, each of these responses moves the organization away from risk taking by limiting the range of possible response options. To be clear, we do not advocate for unnecessary risk, but to the extent that risk taking is associated with creative thinking and innovation, the tendency to be risk averse may hinder the organization's ability to develop novel ways for containing the crisis.

When Martha Stewart Omnimedia (MSO) was confronted with the financial scandal of its CEO and corporate icon, Martha Stewart, the board took great risk by completely reconceptualizing the business. From its inception, the MSO brand was indistinguishable from Martha Stewart. She was the face of the company, both literally and figuratively. Because Martha Stewart was so closely associated with MSO, the insider trading scandal threatened to tarnish the reputations of both the woman and the brand. The board adopted a high-risk damage control strategy by removing Martha Stewart from all of the media-related aspects of the business. Her face would no longer garnish the magazine or book covers; she was removed from the once visible CEO position; her television shows were taken off the air; and her name was de-emphasized on products. There was considerable debate about whether the firm would survive with this new branding strategy. Although some could argue that the firm was left with no other choice given the negative publicity that the scandal generated, for an organization whose strategy and brand had been so closely intertwined with its founder, there was considerable reason to doubt whether the company would survive the dissociation. But because of the board's willingness to adopt a new strategy in the midst of a crisis, MSO has not only survived but spawned new products that likely would not have come to fruition had it not been for the willingness by its leaders to take risks.

Business Recovery

Stage 4 of crisis management is business recovery. When a crisis hits, organizations must be able to carry on with their business in the midst of the crisis while simultaneously planning for how they will recover from the damage the crisis caused. Revenue stream and reputation are the two aspects of the organization most in jeopardy during and following a crisis. If these are irrecoverably damaged it becomes virtually impossible for the organization to survive. Yet, the chances that some organizations will not survive a major crisis, or will at the very least struggle to regain precrisis operating status and financial security, are not insignificant. Consider these chilling facts. In 1996 a terrorist group orchestrated a bomb attack in Manchester, England. More than 40% of companies that were affected by the attack went out of business—for good.[64] Following the terrorist attacks of September 11, 90% of relief funds went to small businesses, indicating the magnitude of the damage done to this aspect of New York City's economy. Granted, terrorist attacks of this magnitude have historically been exceptionally rare. That said, by definition, crises of all types are rare events, but they nevertheless require forethought and planning to continue operations during and after the crisis. So what does this mean for leadership? It means that crisis handlers not only must engage in continuity planning (determining human, financial, and technology resources needed to keep the organization running), but will also actively pursue organizational resilience. In fact, we argue that one of the defining characteristics that determines whether a firm will successfully adjust and thrive under pressure-laden situations or will teeter on the brink of failure is resilience. Thus, the ability to be resilient and promote resiliency in the organization is a critical competency of the business recovery stage.

Promoting Resilience

Initial reactions to adverse events are typically negative. We feel sorrow following the death of a loved one, anger after someone has betrayed us, or fear when a natural disaster strikes. According to psychological research, there are at least four potential consequences to these negative responses.[65] The first is that the target of adversity will experience a continued downward spiral in which the initial emotion is compounded until the target succumbs.[66] A second, and slightly less deleterious outcome, is that the target survives but is somehow diminished or weakened by the trauma. Third, the target may return to baseline or the same level of functioning that existed before the trauma. Last, the target may surpass the baseline and actually thrive despite the adversity.[67] We will return to the notion of thriving following crisis events in Chapter 9. For now, the remainder of this section is concerned primarily with the third possible consequence—resilience. Not only is resilience the least that crisis handlers should be striving for amidst a crisis, but it most aptly characterizes the goal of the business recovery stage of crisis management.

More than this, however, promoting resilience can have a positive effect for the organization and for those specifically responsible for handling a crisis. Following an initial challenge or threat, if a person or group has been encouraged in resilience, then when subsequent adverse events (of the same sort or possibly of a different sort altogether) threaten the organization, those same people over time become desensitized to traumatic events.[68] In other words, whereas an initial crisis can provoke panic, anxiety, fear, or defensiveness, a person's response to future occurrences is less severe if he or she has been encouraged in the ways of resilience following the initial crisis. Under these conditions, to the extent that negative emotions do occur following subsequent adversities, people who had previously been encouraged toward resilience are able to move beyond the negative emotions that typically accompany crises and toward productive behavior more quickly. We are not suggesting that promoting resilience will necessarily lead to higher or better functioning, but rather, it will facilitate a resistance to deleterious emotional responses to future threats so that they experience subsequent threats less acutely and are able to recover from them more efficiently.

The literature on resilience is vast and it spans across a number of disciplines. Some of the psychological research on resilience characterizes it as a personal characteristic or as a set of personality traits that come to portray an individual as sturdy, resourceful, and flexible in the face of uncertainty and threat.[69] Other research characterizes resilience as a dynamic process.[70] According to Sutcliffe and Vogus,[71] in the organizational theory literature the idea of resilience as *adaptability* has become popular. The implications of resilience for organizational functioning in general, and crisis management in particular, are clear in Wildavesky's argument that to be resilient is to be vitally prepared for adversity, "without knowing in advance what one will be called to act upon."[72] In one of the most clear and succinct definitions, Carver defines resilience as "the capacity to recover from a downturn to a former state of relative well being."[73] A noteworthy implication from this definition is that resiliency is a process—one that involves transition from one psychological or physical state to another. Metaphorically, resilience is easy to imagine. Consider, for example, viscoelastic foam (a.k.a. memory foam), a material that was originally designed by NASA to help astronauts absorb enormous G-forces at liftoff and reentry. Today, memory foam has become a familiar material used in mattress and pillow technology. The claimed benefits of memory foam are that not only does it absorb the impact of the human body (as do most mattresses or pillows), but also it goes back to normal shape once pressure is removed from the foam. In other words, the material is resilient. You see evidence of the resiliency when you push firmly on the foam (add pressure or stress as in a crisis or other adverse event) and release—there is a physical movement from the indentation produced by your hand back to the original state. This image reinforces the procedural nature of resilience over the trait perspective, which would argue that resilience is static.

From an organizational perspective, the trait characterization of resilience is particularly troublesome because of the implication that a person either is able to overcome adversity or is not. If perceived as not being resilient, then he or she may self-impose restrictions on their contribution to problem solving or will not be included by others in the problem-solving process.[74] For our purposes, we believe in learned capability and argue that a person's inherent resilience capacity can positively adjust. We further believe that it is the intentional act of positively adjusting one's resilience during pressure-laden situations, as well as the competency to influence others to become resilient, that distinguishes poor or average crisis handlers from strong crisis leaders.

The ability to promote resilience in an organization that is under pressure or experiencing a crisis is a critical leadership competency. Consider the alternative. When in crisis, people panic and experience a host of negative emotions. It is the leader's responsibility to try to manage those emotions in such a way that helps followers deal with the situation and continue to function so that the organization itself is able to continue meeting its overall objectives and commitments to customers. Crisis handlers who are able to promote resilience do so by encouraging two underlying factors: competence and efficacy.[75] Carol Dweck's work on competence and learning orientation has shown a positive relationship between a person's willingness or tendency to seek out new and challenging learning opportunities and resilience. Specifically, these individuals are more willing to tackle failures, persist during difficult times, and particularly germane to crisis handling, derive insightful and creative solutions under adverse conditions.[76] Likewise, research on groups and teams has found a similar connection between competence and resilience. Teams that are led to acquire new skills, master a variety of situations, and improve competence are more likely to positively adjust under pressure.[77] Sutcliffe and Vogus argue that this positive adjustment occurs because groups who have "honed their competencies are more likely to register and handle the complexity of dynamic decision environments and may be more motivated to persist in the face of obstacles and adversities."[78]

In addition to competence, collective efficacy is another factor believed to promote resilience. Self-efficacy, a term coined and made popular by noted psychologist Albert Bandura, is the belief that one is capable of performing to a certain standard and succeeding in specific situations. Collective efficacy, in turn, is a group's shared belief that together they can organize and successfully execute on a course of action. Furthermore, collective efficacy has been shown to have a positive effect on performance under pressure,[79] and this effect was found in research where efficacy developed naturally in the group and where efficacy was created experimentally.[80] Yet, leaders do not have to merely hope that a team, particularly a crisis team (a subject to which we will return in Chapter 5), will develop collective efficacy. There are a number of things that are well within leaders' control to encourage efficacy, and in so doing promote resilience. Scholars have suggested that building a team that is diverse in knowledge and experience plays a considerable role in collective efficacy. Teams feel secure and confident, for example, in their ability to problem solve in challenging situations when they know they can draw upon the vast expertise of other group members. Similarly, structuring a group in such a way that it is able to be flexible in the *content* of its work (e.g., provide the group with a variety of tasks) and in the *process* by which the work is completed is another factor that contributes to collective efficacy and resilience.

Learning

The previous four crisis phases (signal detection, preparation and prevention, containment and damage control, and business recovery) largely address leadership responsibilities and requisite competencies at the outset and during a crisis. As we have discussed, effective crisis handling in these stages can bring an organization back to at least a precrisis level. Unfortunately, all too often leaders assume that crisis handling stops after the business recovery phase. Consequently, although the organization may have resumed effective operations, salvaged its reputation, and resolved the financial concerns that the crisis imposed, without engaging in postcrisis learning and reflection the firm remains susceptible to similar threats in the future. After all, crises are more likely to be perceived by crisis handlers as potential sources of opportunity, rather than only as threats (a subject to which we return in Chapter 11), when organizational decision makers adopt a learning orientation and use prior experience to develop new routines and behaviors that ultimately change the way the organization operates. Crises can be a catalyst that produces individual and organizational learning.[81] The best leaders recognize this and are purposeful and skillful in finding the learning opportunities inherent in every crisis situation.

In the early to mid-2000s, Americans watched as one company after another battled corporate scandal, many of which involved accounting irregularities and fraud. One such firm, Tyco International, became the poster child of corporate greed and irresponsibility. Tyco's chairman, Dennis Kozlowski, and chief financial officer, Mark Swartz, were accused of essentially stealing $600 million from the firm in the form of unauthorized bonuses, and were also found guilty of falsifying business documents, conspiracy, and inflating the stock price. In a graphic display of the inappropriate use of corporate funds, television media blasted images of a toga-clad birthday party that Kozlowski threw for his wife. The party was a $2 million lavish affair that took place on the island of Sardinia and was paid for by Tyco. In 2005 Kozlowski and Swartz were sentenced to up to 25 years of jail time in state prison. Tyco was sentenced to pay upward of $2 billion to a class of defrauded shareholders. The company's financial stability and reputation were in shambles. Despite this crisis, the new leadership worked hard at learning how to instill high standards of business practices into Tyco's corporate culture after the scandal. They engaged in a reflective process that began with the top management team conducting a root cause analysis of the organization's past mistakes. In addition, they evaluated and adopted best practices from other companies, and as a result of their learning drafted a list of 25 governance practices and a guide to ethical conduct that is used for employee and board training. Tyco's actions following the crisis are a prime example of the learning phase of crisis management and speak to the importance of a leader adopting a learning orientation. Below, we briefly introduce the concept of individual learning and the role that this competency plays in leading under pressure. In Chapter 9, we discuss learning as an organizational capability.

Individual Learning Orientation

In their work on how leaders come to see and manifest opportunity in crisis, Brockner and James propose that one's individual learning orientation is crucial to that process.[82] Moreover, they argue that one's individual learning orientation must work in tandem with the organization's overall learning orientation to realize potential opportunities. Two such opportunities that are germane to the learning phase of crisis management are (1) the opportunity to reduce the frequency, likelihood, or impact of a future negative event; and (2) the opportunity to enhance the frequency, likelihood, or impact of a future positive event. At its core, learning generally involves the process of acquiring new information and implementing a change in behavior as a result. The relationship between learning and behavior change is a powerful one and is central to individual learning theories in psychology.[83] Carol Dweck's work on individual learning proposes, for example, states that people have tendencies toward one of two types of achievement. Those with a *learning orientation* strive to develop competence by acquiring new skills and mastering new situations.[76] These individuals are motivated by the learning process and by the opportunities for growth and development that it provides. Alternatively, people with a *performance orientation* are motivated to learn primarily to gain favorable judgments of their competence or to avoid unfavorable judgments.[84]

Tendencies toward either learning or performance orientation have been shown to predict differential patterns of emotional and behavioral responses to threats[85]—a finding particularly germane to our objective of identifying critical crisis leadership competencies. Individuals who are prone toward a learning orientation elicit more adaptive responses to adverse conditions, including not being easily discouraged by challenges, or using challenging situations as a reason to pursue new knowledge.[86] These findings support the thesis that crisis handlers that have or develop a learning orientation will in fact engage in reflection and learning subsequent to the initial emotional and behavioral responses to crises. Doing so will facilitate the organization's ability to learn from the crisis and prevent or lessen the damage resulting from a similar situation in the future.

Summary

The human resource function of a firm understands that competencies are a critical element of the talent of the organization. Competencies help the firm identify the talent to be brought into the organization. They are used to distinguish performance, for the purposes of development and reward, and serve to guide behavior. Under ordinary, or noncrisis, circumstances employees may rely on a core set of competencies that have fostered their successful contribution to the firm. The competencies that are required during a crisis can be, but are often not, the same ones that are utilized in a typical day.

In this chapter, we have highlighted a set of knowledge, skills, abilities, and behaviors that are germane to each crisis phase. We caution leaders from believing that their highest performing employees in times of peace will necessarily be the same employees to rise to the top during a crisis. While this may be true in some cases, assuming so may yield undesirable consequences. Recall our example in Chapter 1 where Coca-Cola's former CEO Doug Ivester had been lauded as a supremely competent leader, but severely mismanaged the crisis in

Belgium, which led to an extensive recall of the product due to health concerns. Likewise, it can be dangerous to assume that an average performer cannot rise to the occasion and prove to be a gifted crisis leader. Perhaps there has been little opportunity to utilize creativity, engage in risk taking, or be resilient on a day-to-day basis, but under pressure leadership requiring these and other competencies can come from people from whom you may least expect it. Being clear on what competencies to look for in your employees and even how to develop competence in those areas will serve the organization well before, during, and after a crisis (Figures 3.4 and 3.5).

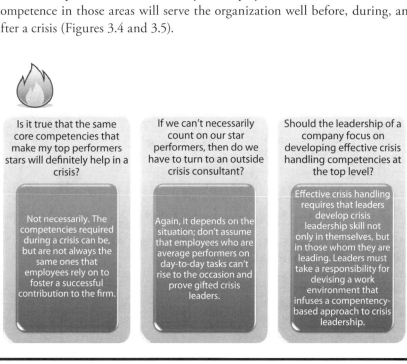

Is it true that the same core competencies that make my top performers stars will definitely help in a crisis?

Not necessarily. The competencies required during a crisis can be, but are not always the same ones that employees rely on to foster a successful contribution to the firm.

If we can't necessarily count on our star performers, then do we have to turn to an outside crisis consultant?

Again, it depends on the situation; don't assume that employees who are average performers on day-to-day tasks can't rise to the occasion and prove gifted crisis leaders.

Should the leadership of a company focus on developing effective crisis handling competencies at the top level?

Effective crisis handling requires that leaders develop crisis leadership skill not only in themselves, but in those whom they are leading. Leaders must take a responsibility for devising a work environment that infuses a compentency-based approach to crisis leadership.

Figure 3.4   Leader's hot seat.

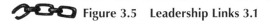 **Figure 3.5   Leadership Links 3.1**

- Crisis Decision Making
  http://www.varaces.org/racesadv/DecisionMakinghandout.pdf
- Leadership Through Crisis
  http://www.mckinseyquarterly.com/Organization/Talent/Leadership_through_the_crisis_and_after_McKinsey_Global_Survey_results_2457

Endnotes

1. Gladwell, *Outliers.*
2. Bolman & Deal, *Reframing organizations.*
3. Brockner & James, Toward an understanding of when executives see crisis as opportunity, 94–115.
4. Pearson & Clair, Reframing crisis management, 59–76.
5. Spreitzer & Quinn, *A company of leaders.*
6. Denis, Lamothe, & Langley, The dynamics of collective leadership and strategic change in pluralistic organizations, 809–837.
7. Bass, *Leadership and performance beyond expectations.*
8. Pearson & Mitroff, From crisis prone to crisis prepared, 48–59.
9. Sitkin, Learning through failure, 231–266.
10. Johnson, *College gunman disturbed teachers, classmates.*
11. Weick, Sutcliffe, & Obstfeld, Organizing and the process of sense making, 409–421.
12. Ibid.
13. Weick, Enacted sensemaking in crisis situations, 305–317.
14. Galinsky & Moskowitz, Perspective-taking, 708–724.
15. Davis, Measuring individual differences in empathy, 113–126.
16. Piaget, *The moral judgment of the child.*
17. Kohlberg, Moral stages and moralization, 31–53.
18. Richardson et al., Empathy as a cognitive inhibitor of interpersonal aggression, 275–289.
19. Galinsky & Moskowitz, Perspective-taking, 708–724.
20. Batson, *The altruism question.*
21. James & Wooten, Leadership as (un)usual, 141–152.
22. Legal Information Center, Overview of the recall.
23. Simision, Lundegaard, Shirouzu, & Heller, Blowout, A1.
24. Heller & White, Ford Motor Co. is investigating reports about failures of Firestone truck tires, A6.
25. Zimmerman, Wal-Mart's emergency-relief team girds for Hurricane Gustav, A3.
26. Ibid.
27. Staw, Sandelands, & Dutton, Threat-rigidity effects in organizational behavior, 501–524.
28. Yukl & Falbe, Influence tactics and objectives in upward, downward, and lateral influence attempts, 132–140.
29. Kipnis, Schmidt, & Wilkinson, Intraorganizational influence tactics, 440–452.
30. Yukl & Falbe, Influence tactics and objectives in upward, downward, and lateral influence attempts, 132–140.
31. Ibid.
32. Dutton & Ashford, Selling issues to top management, 397–428.
33. Dutton, Ashford, O'Neil, Hayes, & Wierba, Reading the wind, 407–423.
34. Crocitto & Youssef, The human side of organizational agility, 388–397.
35. Shafer, Dyer, Kilty, Amos, & Ericksen, Crafting a human resource strategy to foster organizational agility, 197–208.

36. Amabile, The social psychology of creativity, 357–376.
37. Amabile, Social psychology of creativity, 1001.
38. Coombs, *Ongoing crisis communication*.
39. Scott & Lyman, Accounts, 46.
40. Ibid., 46–62.
41. Goffman, Remedial interchanges, 95–187; Schonbach, A category system for account phases, 195–200.
42. Goffman, *The presentation of self in everyday life*.
43. Schlenker, *Impression management*, 137.
44. James & Wooten, Diversity crises, 1103–1118.
45. Elsbach, Managing organizational legitimacy in the California cattle industry, 57–88; Elsbach & Kramer, Members' responses to organizational identity threats, 442–476; Sutton & Callahan, The stigma of bankruptcy, 405–436.
46. Chen & Meindl, The construction of leadership images in the popular press, 521–551.
47. Marcus & Goodman, Victims and shareholders, 281–305.
48. Elsbach, Managing organizational legitimacy in the California cattle industry, 57–88.
49. Elsbach, The architecture of legitimacy.
50. Marcus & Goodman, Victims and shareholders, 281–305.
51. Bettman & Witz, Attributions in the board room, 165–183.
52. Elsbach, The architecture of legitimacy.
53. Coombs & Holladay, Helping crisis managers protect reputational assets, 165–186.
54. Ibid., 167.
55. Coombs & Schmidt, An empirical analysis of image restoration, 163–178.
56. Coombs & Holladay, Helping crisis managers protect reputational assets, 165–186.
57. James & Wooten, Diversity crisis, 1103–1118.
58. Marcus & Goodman, Victims and shareholders, 281–305.
59. Coombs & Schmidt, An empirical analysis of image restoration, 163–178.
60. Zacaro, Trait-based perspectives of leadership, 6–16.
61. Morgan, *Imaginization*.
62. Eagly & Carli, *Through the labyrinth*.
63. Staw, Sandelands, & Dutton, Threat-rigidity effects in organizational behavior, 501–524.
64. Curtin, Hayman, & Husein, *Managing a crisis*.
65. Carver, Resilience and thriving, 245–266.
66. Aldwin, *Stress, coping, and development*.
67. Carver, Resilience and thriving, 246.
68. Ibid., 248.
69. Luther, Cicchetti, & Becker, The construct of resilience, 543–562.
70. Masten, Resilience in individual development, 3–25.
71. Sutcliffe & Vogus, Organizing for resilience, 94–110.
72. Wildavesky, *Searching for safety*, 70.
73. Carver, Resilience and thriving, 247–248.

74. Luthar, Cicchetti, & Becker, The construct of resilience, 543–562.

75. Sutcliffe & Vogus, Organizing for resilience, 101.

76. Dweck, C., Motivation.

77. Bunderson & Sutcliffe, Why some teams emphasize learning more than others, 49–84.

78. Sutcliffe & Vogus, Organizing for resilience, 101.

79. Bandura, *Self-efficacy*.

80. Wood & Bandura, Social cognitive theory of organizational management, 361–384.

81. Sitkin, Learning through failure, 231–266.

82. Brockner & James, Toward an understanding of when executives see crisis as opportunity, 97.

83. See, for example, Skinner, *Contingencies of reinforcement*.

84. Diener & Dweck, An analysis of learned helplessness, 451–462.

85. Dweck, Self-theories.

86. Cron, Slocum, VandeWalle, & Fu, The role of goal orientation, negative emotions, and goal setting when initial performance falls short of one's performance goal, 55–80.

Chapter 4

Decision Making for the Crisis Leader

Although not a typical organization, or a "leader" in the traditional sense of the word, perhaps one of the most striking examples of successful handling of a crisis was the emergency landing of US Airways flight 1549, also known as the "Miracle on the Hudson." On January 15, 2009, shortly after takeoff, flight 1549 left New York's LaGuardia airport headed for Charlotte, North Carolina. Within minutes the plane, under the direction of Captain Chesley "Sully" Sullenberger, struck a flock of birds, debilitating the plane's two engines. With moments to make a series of potentially life or death decisions, Captain Sullenberger opted to land the plane on the Hudson River rather than attempt to make it back to the airport. With the words "brace for impact because we're going down," Captain Sullenberger safely landed the jet in the Hudson River, where the plane stayed afloat long enough for all 155 passengers to be rescued from the water. Clearly, the pilot's ability to make quick decisions under pressure was a competency that allowed the passengers and crew to survive the emergency landing and prevent a dire situation from becoming a catastrophe.

In Chapter 3, we identified a host of critical crisis leadership competencies as they relate to each of the five stages of a crisis. Clearly, decision making is one such competency. Because decision making, and in particular the ability to make decisions under pressure, is germane to every aspect of crisis management, we have reserved an entire chapter to its discussion. We hope that readers will begin to develop or enhance their own decision-making capability so that organizations can reap the same benefit from effective decision making as the passengers of US Airways flight 1549.

In this chapter, we focus primarily on the decision-making process. We highlight the challenges that accompany decision making in crisis situations and present the research on the cognitive biases and motivations that affect the decision-making process. Before doing so, however, we feel it is important to start with a discussion on the decisions themselves and precisely the types of issues with which managers struggle in the course of their daily work.

Modern-Day Decisions

Recently one of the authors was asked by a professional executive education firm to conduct a seminar for middle- to high-level executives across a variety of industries. The seminar was to focus on the topic of decision making. I asked for clarification and some context to better understand the motivation for this particular topic. He explained that in recent years he has received an increasing number of requests from his client organizations for workshops that would provide practical advice and solutions for managers that perceive themselves to be under constant pressure at work. He elaborated by saying that managers are complaining about not having adequate time or resources to accomplish what is expected of them, and that they are asked to make decisions for which they are unprepared, and for which they lack authority, information, support, and other resources. This description is consistent with the findings of a seminal study of managerial behavior by Henry Mintzberg more than 30 years ago.[1] In the book *The Nature of Managerial Work*, Mintzberg describes findings that suggest that managers struggle with making decisions, especially those that require systematic data analysis. Interestingly, the language that this client used in describing the challenges managers face when making decisions (e.g., feeling unprepared, having limited information or inadequate time) resembles the same characteristics that are used to describe crises (see Chapter 2). So, in their minds, the decision-making process is akin to managing a crisis. Furthermore, they are uncomfortable shouldering this responsibility because they perceive it to be beyond the scope of their responsibility and competency.

In preparing for the workshop that the author would eventually conduct on decision making, she invited participants to send examples of the types of decisions they found to be challenging. Below are some of the verbatim examples provided by the workshop participants. Although we may not elevate these descriptions to the same crisis status that Captain Sullenberger faced as he attempted to land a plane with no functioning engines, the descriptions represent crisis-like situations in the minds of these managers.

Manager A: I was in a closed-door one-on-one meeting with a probation-ary employee (newly hired) discussing performance. The meeting actually had been scheduled twice before, the prior week, but due to operational issues was cancelled both times. I have placed a high value on reviewing new employee's performance 90 days into their job and it was important to me that the meet-ing occurred on this third attempt. The meeting had just started when another employee knocked on the door stating that an employee's spouse was on the phone and was in some state of crisis and required my immediate attention. Apparently the woman in crisis had just been admitted to the hospital with a potentially serious health concern. She was very upset and emotional. Her request to me was that I get her husband home immediately. Her husband was on a boat in an offshore and remote location. He also had dropped his cell into the harbor, and so contacting him would be a challenge. I consider my decision under pressure to be this: Do I cancel the meeting a third time and immediately start working on the crisis situation at hand, or proceed with my meeting first? With the sensitive nature of the employee's crisis, it would have to be handled by "senior management" and my supervisor was on his day off.

Manager B: I am a technology lead, but find myself being held entirely account-able for all aspects of delivering projects. These projects lack organizational support from critical business areas. To make matters worse, the funding for these projects is tentative. My entire unit could be gone in a few months' time and I'll be the person delivering the message to my group. The necessity to deliver the projects forces me to make decisions well out of the scope of my knowledge. So, not only are these decisions made under pressure, but many of them are decisions I should not be making in the first place.

Manager C: I work in policies and procedures for a major U.S. airline. The decisions I make affect airport operations and our customers travel experience at hundreds of airports. I normally have to poll many stakeholders when mak-ing decisions, and this tends to slow the process down and delay operations (planes flying). However, hasty decisions frequently miss some elements and adversely affect one or more of our key stakeholders. My biggest challenges are (1) identifying all relevant stakeholders, (2) flexing between working collabora-tively and working unilaterally, (3) reaching a final decision before operations are disrupted . . . potentially causing another crisis.

As illustrated in the examples above, many managers perceive that a sig-nificant part of their time is spent "fighting fires" that, if left unattended, could escalate into large-scale crisis situations. They are frustrated by the ambiguity that they face and feel encumbered by competing priorities. In short, making decisions is hard, and yet the vast majority of their time is spent making deci-sions. The contact at the executive education firm lamented the fact that his client organizations did not appear to be spending adequate time thinking pro-actively and strategically about key business decisions. As a result, employees spend more time than necessary responding and reacting to situations and, in so doing, feel overwhelmed by the pressure.

This executive is not alone in how he characterized his client organizations. Since that consulting engagement we continue to see an increasing frustration in managers' ability to make effective decisions, and this challenge is exacerbated as firms are facing increasing pressure and economic insecurity. Moreover, we found that managers tend to resonate with the decision-making-under-pressure language and easily make the connection between effective and ineffective decision making and crisis handling.

A Primer on Decisions and Decision Making

Put simply, decision making is the process by which one identifies problems and tries to solve them.[2] At one level, our inclusion of a chapter on decision making is a disservice to scholars who have devoted their professional life to the study of decisions and decision making.[3] There are entire fields of study, journals, and professional associations (across multiple disciplines) whose objective is to contribute to our knowledge base of the decision-making process. Our goal here is not to play in that field in terms of new theorizing about decision making, but rather to highlight some of the prominent decision-making perspectives, and use this information to illustrate decision making in the context of crisis leadership. The remainder of this chapter will unfold in the following way: (1) provide an introduction to some of the most common approaches to decision making, (2) introduce decision making biases that can adversely affect judgment during a crisis, and (3) establish the importance of ethics in the decision-making process.

Rational Approaches to Decision Making

The process of decision making requires first and foremost that a judgment be made among a set of options. Each of us engages in decision making hundreds of times a day, and the judgments we make range from the mundane (e.g., what to wear on any given day) to the extraordinary (e.g., whether to accept an expatriate assignment at work). Although there are a variety of decision-making approaches, the rational decision-making model is perhaps the most intuitive and easily recognizable. By rational, we mean that the process of deciding among alternatives is "logically expected to lead to the optimal result, given an accurate assessment of the decision maker's values and risk preferences."[4] Using the rational decision-making process one navigates cognitively and methodically through a series of steps or stages.

Defining the Problem

On the surface, "the problem" may seem obvious, and accordingly this step of decision making would be a fairly easy one. Unfortunately, situations that are clearly black and white are rare in organizational settings. Consider the examples we provided at the start of this chapter. In each of those cases, the decision to pursue one course of action generally means making undesirable or less satisfying choices. For the manager debating between holding an overdue performance appraisal for a subordinate and attempting to contact an employee in a remote location when he learns that the employee's spouse has a medical emergency, there is clearly a trade-off to be made. Both circumstances are clearly important, and prioritizing one over another poses a dilemma. Another objective in the problem-solving stage is to segregate the root issues from the surface issues to clearly specify the core problem, not merely a symptom or some other superficial aspect of a deeper set of issues. For example, perhaps the underlying issue for this manager is that the organization's values are ambiguous, and therefore prioritizing between options that are both regarded as important becomes more complicated. Taking this step should clarify priorities and values, make salient the relevant issue, and help focus attention and resources.

Determining and Weighing Evaluation Criteria

This step is perhaps the most overlooked stage in the decision-making process. The time pressures in most organizations are such that managers are in the mode of fire: aim, ready; rather than ready, aim, fire. As a result, when confronted with a problem or difficult decision, the tendency is to immediately think of solutions and start responding (or reacting) without proper analysis of the situation and the desired outcome. Recently, I observed a colleague teaching a case study that I have taught many times before. Generally, an initial question to the class is whether to promote a rogue but highly successful employee. This question generates great classroom debate as the students have very strong opinions one way or the other. In the class that I observed, the instructor started it with a different question. Rather than asking if the protagonist should be promoted, she asked what criteria one would use to determine whether the protagonist should be promoted. This simple twist on the question initiated a very different type of discussion—one that I would argue was richer and generated more analytical rigor. The emotion in the room was muted relative to what I had been accustomed to, but the quality of the conversation was heightened. The same thing happens in organizations. We are drawn immediately to the outcome, to the decision, and we fail to adequately consider what it is we hope to achieve with our decision. Without the analysis, a desired outcome is as much a matter of chance as it is anything else. Thinking critically about what one hopes to achieve from the problem-solving effort and then identifying and prioritizing a set of metrics or other criteria that guide one's thinking should more consistently lead to effective decision making.

Generating Alternatives

Almost without exception people engaged in decision making will identify multiple alternatives to the problem they face. If too much time is spent on this activity, however, managers can become inundated with information and struggle with sorting out the relevant from the irrelevant considerations. This situation generally leads to what is commonly referred to as the analysis-paralysis syndrome and inhibits effective decision making. According to a leading decision-making scholar, Max Bazerman, an optimal search for alternatives is one in which a decision maker considers alternatives up to the point at which the additional benefit from the new information is equal to or less than the costs incurred by seeking additional alternatives.[5]

Evaluating the Alternatives

Before a final decision can be reached, a decision maker must consider the extent to which the various alternatives generated in the previous step meet the evaluation criteria described above. In the process of evaluating alternatives, the decision maker must identify and consider the consequences that can result from each alternative. The challenge here is that some alternatives may appear more or less attractive than others because of external pressure on the decision maker to make a decision quickly or make a decision that favors one constituent over others. If such extraneous factors were not a part of the original evaluation criteria, then the rational decision-making process is potentially undermined. For example, one may have in fact performed adequate analysis on the problem at hand, but then ultimately make a decision because of influence from a significant stakeholder who was not a part of the original analysis.

Reach a Decision

In the final step, the decision maker processes the information gathered from the previous steps and calculates the ideal option. Variables in the calculation include at a minimum the anticipated outcome from each alternative, the assigned weight for each alternative, and the assigned weight for each criteria for those alternatives.

Benjamin Franklin, one of America's founding fathers, was a skilled businessman, scientist, philosopher, musician, and more. He was also known to engage in a simple and rational method of decision making that he called moral or prudential algebra. His approach could arguably be among the first articulations of rational decision making. In the following eighteenth-century letter to British theologian Joseph Priestly, Franklin describes his decision-making algorithm[6]:

Dear Sir,

In the affair of so much importance to you, wherein you ask my advice, I cannot, for want of sufficient premises, advise you what to determine, but if you please I will tell you how. When those difficult cases occur, they are difficult, chiefly because while we have them under consideration, all the reasons pro and con are not present to the mind at the same time; but sometimes one set present themselves, and at other times another, the first being out of sight. Hence the various purposes or inclinations that alternatively prevail, and the uncertainty that perplexes us. To get over this, my way is to divide half a sheet of paper by a line into two columns; writing over the one Pro, and over the other Con. Then, during three or four days consideration, I put down under the different heads short hints of the different motives, that at different times occur to me, for or against the measure. When I have thus got them all together in one view, I endeavor to estimate their respective weights; and where I find two, one on each side, that seem equal, I strike them both out. If I find a reason pro equal to some two reasons con, I strike out the three. If I judge some two reasons con, equal to three reasons pro, I strike out the five; and thus proceeding I find at length where the balance lies; and if, after a day or two of further consideration, nothing new that is of importance occurs on either side, I come to a determination accordingly. And, though the weight of the reasons cannot be taken with the precision of algebraic quantities, yet when each is thus considered, separately and comparatively, and the whole lies before me, I think I can judge better, and am less liable to make a rash step, and in fact I have found great advantage from this kind of equation, and what might be called moral or prudential algebra.

Wishing sincerely that you may determine for the best, I am ever, my dear friend, yours most affectionately.

B. Franklin

Constraints to the Rational Decision-Making Process

Although decision makers *think* they engage in rational decision making when confronted with a choice, *actually* engaging in rational decision making is difficult. The rational decision-making model assumes a number of factors that are hard to satisfy, and consequently prescribes how decisions should be made rather than how they are actually made. It assumes, for example, that people have *access to complete information* upon which to base the final decision. The assumption of complete information can be called into question along every stage of the decision-making process, not just the final step. Does one ever truly have all of the information necessary to identify the true nature of the problem to be solved, much less to identify the most optimal solution? Is one really capable of considering the needs and expectations of all of the various stakeholders who will be affected by the outcome of the decision in determining the appropriate evaluation criteria and how those criteria should be weighted? Can one ever really think of all of the possible alternatives for a decision? The answer to each of these is no.

Not only are decision makers constrained by access to information, but they also have *cognitive limits* on the amount of information that they can reasonably be expected to process at any one time.[7] So even if we did have all of the possible information about a particular dilemma, we would still be limited by our own intelligence and brain functioning in making sense of it in a meaningful way. The rational decision-making model assumes *unlimited time and resources*, precisely the conditions that most people argue are lacking. In addition to insufficient information, limited cognitive capability, and inadequate time and resources, the rational approach to decision making does not explicitly consider that most people function interdependently. In organizational settings we frequently rely on and are accountable to others, and therefore are generally unable to operate with *unilateral authority*. Weighing and identifying evaluation criteria, determining alternatives, evaluating options, and so on, happen within a context in which input from key constituents (i.e., bosses, peers, suppliers, customers, and the like) is a central part of the process. As a result, decision making is affected by the needs and desires, values and expectations of others. As one example, in a study we conducted on how firms respond to class action discrimination lawsuits, the findings revealed that when external stakeholder groups (in this case prominent civil rights groups) publicly voiced their frustration with the firm and its alleged indiscretions toward minority employees, their initial decisions for responding to the allegations changed from a denial-based and defensive posture to one of acknowledgment and cooperation.[8] In this case, the decision for how to respond to the discriminatory charges was heavily influenced by an authoritative constituent.

Similarly, the organizational context plays an important role. Every firm has its own culture, norms, and values. Employees are socialized into operating within those organizational parameters, and decision making is likely to be as influenced by the organization's culture as by personal values and belief systems. Yet the rational model does not explicitly articulate the extent to which organizational culture is a factor in decision making. Finally, most of us have an *emotional investment* in the decisions we make. The more a decision involves a project or people that we care about, the more likely it is that emotions will influence the decision-making process.

As a result of each of the constraints described above, decision making becomes less rational than the model might suggest and, therefore, presents an interesting challenge for those who must lead during a crisis. As bystanders voyeuristically watch another's handling of a crisis situation, they will no doubt find many opportunities for criticism and disagreement with his or her decisions. We argue that the observers own decision-making frame follows the perfect and rational model of how decisions should be made (and the subsequent perfect and rational outcomes that such a process should yield). In reality, however, the decision making for the crisis handler is much more limited, given the constraints just described, and therefore imperfect in both process and outcome, providing a window of opportunity for criticism by a relatively naive observer (Figure 4.1).

Bounded Rationality

Credited as being responsible for the concept of organizational decision making, Herbert Simon recognized that true rational decision making is virtually impossible precisely because of the set of limitations described above.[9] Simon writes, "The human being striving for rationality and restricted within the limits of his knowledge has developed some working procedures that partially overcome

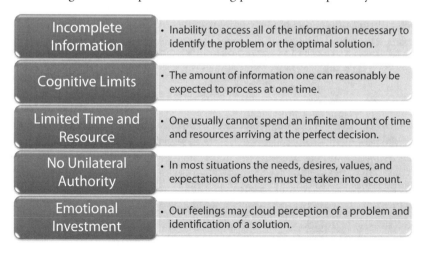

Figure 4.1   Constraints to rational decision making.

these difficulties. These procedures consist in assuming that he can isolate from the rest of the world a closed system containing a limited number of variables and a limited range of consequences."[10] Simon coined the construct *bounded rationality* and suggested that constraints to rationality limit people's ability to solve complex problems and process information. More specifically, as the complexity of a situation increases our capacity to think logically and rationally diminishes—our rationality is therefore bounded, preventing us from making the most optimal decisions.[11] The implications of bounded rationality are particularly noteworthy in a crisis. By their very nature crises are complex problems that require immediate attention and action. Crisis handlers are pulled in multiple directions as everything becomes escalated to emergency status. On top of this, stakeholders, the media, and others are watching and judging the crisis handlers' performance. The assessment of the crisis handlers' decision making is based on a rational model in which the pressures and constraints experienced by the actual crisis decision makers are not felt by those voyeuristically observing the unfolding crisis. In other words, bounded rationality does not apply to those of us watching a crisis and evaluating its management, but it is a very real limitation for crisis handlers.

Bounded Awareness

Related to bounded rationality is bounded awareness, or the failure to perceive and process information that is easily available to decision makers.[12] Bounded rationality and bounded awareness are similar in the defining construct of boundedness or limitation—mental processes are constrained in such a way that normal functioning becomes virtually impossible. They differ in that bounded rationality deals with our ability to make sense of, process, and use information, whereas bounded awareness deals with our ability to take in information. When our awareness is bounded we are prevented from focusing on easily observable and relevant data. As a result, we literally see some accessible and perceivable information while failing to see other such data—data considered to be out of focus for the decision maker.[13] Decision-making scholars Chugh and Bazerman are intentional in using the word *failure* in describing bounded awareness, as they believe bounded awareness to represent costly errors, especially in times of crisis. The failure to which they refer represents a misalignment between the information needed for high-quality decision making and the information that is ultimately included in the decision maker's consciousness. The gap between these two leads to suboptimal decision making.

Interesting connections have been made with respect to bounded awareness regarding the ways in which people *actually* miss data present in their visual field and the way in which they are *metaphorically* blind to critical information needed for effective decision making.[14] In a cleverly designed experimental study Simons and Chabris asked subjects to watch a videotape of six people passing a basketball to one another in an irregular and dynamic pattern.[15] While watching the video, subjects were also asked to count the number of times the ball was passed from player to player. Of the nearly 200 observations, subjects noticed a piece of inconsistent information (the appearance of a woman with an umbrella or a person wearing a gorilla costume during the video clip) in only 54% of them. Subjects simply did not see the incongruent and unexpected stimuli. These authors theorize that when the demands on our attention are high and our cognitive faculties are being taxed (e.g., focused on the number of times the ball is passed), we are more susceptible to bounded awareness (e.g., failure to see the gorilla). Crisis handling and decision making under pressure are among the most cognitively taxing activities leaders will engage in, and during crises it is likely that leaders will be blind to relevant stimuli.

Bounded awareness occurs at various crisis phases. In the signal detection stage, for example, crisis handlers may fail to see or seek relevant information about their environment. This failure has implications for the crisis leadership competency sense making. Failing to recognize important red flags that would alert leaders to a pending problem will surely impair their ability to make sense of their environment and take appropriate action. Bounded awareness can also adversely affect crisis leadership competencies during the preparation and pre-vention stage. Failure to take in key information can limit a leader's ability to influence others to take crisis planning seriously because their arguments for doing so will not be grounded in complete or accurate data. Likewise, recall that creativity is a critical competency during preparation and prevention. Incomplete information can adversely affect one's ability to identify creative solutions for crisis prevention. In later crisis phases, bounded awareness might impede a crisis handler's ability to learn from a crisis because the *relevance* of the information he or she has is outside of his or her awareness.

Coping With the Limitations of the Rational Decision-Making Model

So how are decisions actually made? In their seminal work, March and Simon suggested that individuals *satisfice* or strive to achieve an acceptable solution or decision rather than an optimal one.[16] People will consider a subset of the pos-sible alternatives and choose one that meets a minimal or satisfactory standard of acceptability.[17] For example, during the process of budget planning, individual managers will submit requests for the funds needed to achieve departmental goals. Generally these requests exceed the available organizational resources, so decisions must be made regarding whose budgets to cut and by how much. The negotiated decision is a result of satisficing where the individual managers settle for an amount less than originally requested (suboptimal) but sufficient enough to achieve at least the minimal goals of their department.

Following on the heels of March and Simon, Kahneman and Tversky developed prospect theory and later cumulative prospect theory, which describe an alternative approach to decision making.[18] Prospect theory is particularly relevant to the decision making that occurs when one is faced with risk or uncertainty. According to the theory, people frame the outcome of a decision as a gain or a loss relative to a certain reference point (e.g., the status quo). Further, people tend to have different tolerance levels for gains versus losses relative to the chosen referent, and express greater concern over potential losses than they do pleasure for potential gain. Prospect theory also points out a tendency for people to overestimate extreme but unlikely events (e.g., crises), and underestimate mundane or average events. Taken together, we can infer that people facing high-risk decisions, or decisions clouded with uncertainty, will believe them to be more impactful than they really are, and in attempting to deal with decisions will err on minimizing the damage or the loss rather than trying to achieve some gain. In considering the reality of decision-making constraints and the tenets of both prospect theory and bounded rationality it becomes clear that rational decision making is almost an oxymoron. We simply do not have the cognitive capacity to make decisions in such a manner. In the next section, we identify even more precisely several cognitive biases that affect decision making.

Factors That Affect Judgment and Decision Making

Heuristics

Following the work of March and Simon, Tversky and Kahneman introduced a set of ideas about the way in which our judgment is influenced in the course of decision making.[19] They suggested that people are heavily influenced by the efficiency with which our brains function. In particular, our minds simplify information and data. We in turn base our analysis and make decisions on this truncated information. These simplifying strategies, or heuristics, serve an important purpose. They help us manage and make sense of data that otherwise would overwhelm us. Bazerman has described heuristics as "standard rules that implicitly direct our judgment . . . and serve as mechanisms for coping with the complex environment surrounding our decisions."[20] In most cases, heuristics are helpful. They can help managers facing dilemmas like the ones we described at the outset of the chapter, where there is too much information to sort through in too little time. However, because we are not consciously aware of the way in which heuristics affect our judgment, their utility can quickly become dysfunctional and can lead to severe errors in judgment and decision making. Their danger lies in their invisibility, and when we fail to recognize them, we fall into dangerous decision-making traps.[21] We are particularly susceptible to the dangers of heuristics when we are under pressure, as in crisis situations.

We use heuristics on a daily basis. At the grocery store we squeeze and smell the peaches to determine their ripeness because we know that if there is inadequate give to the touch or no scent to the smell, then they are not ready to be eaten. When playing blackjack the rule of thumb is to hold on 17. When driving we have a sense about how much over the speed limit we can safely drive before we risk getting a speeding ticket. These and similar examples may be idiosyncratic to each individual. For example, I will drive 10 mph or less over the speed limit, but my husband will not travel more than 5 mph over the speed limit. There are, however, universal heuristics that seem to be generalizable across the population.[22] We discuss four of the more universal heuristics below.

Anchoring Heuristic

Managers frequently base decisions on the information they have been provided. In fact, most organizational decision-making structures and reporting relationships are set up in such a way that subordinates gather information, analyze it, and present it in a condensed form that can be easily interpreted and used for decision making by the manager. Executive summaries and PowerPoint presentations are two common examples of this type of information sharing. Oftentimes, only the most relevant and favorable (as determined by the subordinate) information is presented; superfluous and unfavorable information is discarded. Yet in the act of sorting through and weeding out seemingly unnecessary information, the manager becomes anchored around the filtered data with which he or she is presented. To illustrate this point to MBA students or executive audiences we might ask them a question like the following: "Is the annual average temperature in Kalamazoo, Michigan, on July 6 warmer than 72 °F?" Since we are not in Kalamazoo at the time, and generally no one in the group is from Kalamazoo, no one really knows for sure, but inevitably the group will be split fairly evenly with half of them believing that the average temperature is generally warmer. I then ask specific individuals in the group, "What is your best estimate of the average temperature in Kalamazoo on July 6?" Again, the respondent does not have the answer, but is required to make a decision with no, or at least limited, data upon which to base his or her judgment. Or so he or she believes.

The anchoring heuristic is the tendency to give disproportionate weight to information received first. Initial impressions, estimates, or data anchor subsequent thoughts and judgments. In the temperature example, students were anchored by the initial question referring to 72 °F. In other words, after settling on a decision about the average temperature being more or less than 72 °F, their subsequent best estimate of the temperature in Kalamazoo is determined in relationship to the 72 °F anchor they were given. In comparison to students who were not previously anchored, students who are initially anchored around a specific temperature tend to have less variance in their specific estimate answers, and the variance that does exist tends to be determined in relation to the anchoring value.

During a crisis, crisis handlers are frequently anchored by the information they receive from various experts. A firm's legal counsel, their human resources executive, or even a whistle-blower, is generally one of the first people to provide information that ultimately serves to anchor the recipient of the information. Oftentimes the information or guidance about an unfolding crisis is solicited by the crisis handler, in which case the handler has unintentionally predetermined the framing for how he or she will be anchored. Clearly, an attorney will offer expert legal advice, whereas a public relations specialist will offer input on communication strategy. Depending on to whom one turns for information, a manager will likely be anchored in very specific ways. Our primary concern with anchoring is that the initial information that the manager receives will set him or her down a particular path, and one that may or may not be relevant or appropriate. In other words, different anchors can yield different decisions for the same problem.[23] By virtue of these experts being specialists in a particular domain, they tend to have a more narrow perspective of the broader organizational issues and considerations. They offer specific advice as it pertains to their area of expertise, but it is ultimately the manager's responsibility to put that information in context. What we have seen, however, is that managers or crisis handlers may abdicate decision-making responsibility to these experts, precisely because they are experts, or allow the expert opinion to anchor their decision making in a way that narrows or constrains their thinking, when what is actually needed is a broadening of ideas.

To limit the extent to which one becomes anchored or abdicates decision making to experts, we suggest that managers should solicit information from a variety of sources. Not only might legal counsel be relevant during a crisis, but so might information about communication strategy, human resources policy, research and development, and more. By gathering multiple sources of information one is less likely to be anchored by a particular piece of data. Similarly, thinking about the problem and possible solutions to it on one's own before consulting others will allow managers to be more reflective about the information they ultimately receive from others. Moreover, because the manager presumably has the best overall perspective about the organization, he or she can take the expert's opinion and position it within a broader context as a result of his or her initial thinking about the problem. Finally, we encourage managers to view problems from multiple perspectives. In our teaching on decision making we will often use a disguised case that depicts a situation in which owners of a race car must decide whether to race in an upcoming event despite having had multiple previous engine failures.[24] The owners' career in racing is on the line and the outcome of their decision to race or not could bankrupt them or allow them to purchase a second car and continue on to the next season. As we unfold information to students or executive audiences they become anchored around a particular piece of data that is presented in the first set of information. Despite receiving additional subsequent data that might be even more relevant to their decision making, students are narrowly focused on what they received initially and the vast majority of the groups' decisions hinge on that initial data. Had they more carefully considered subsequent information they would have realized that the data they were anchored on were among the more irrelevant pieces of information and the decision that that information would suggest would be catastrophic.

Status Quo Heuristic

For one of the authors, a favorite pastime was to use a computer-based financial tool to create graphs and charts to track annual spending (sad but true). She would spend hours poring through data to determine precisely how much was spent in every possible category in a given year (e.g., groceries, dining out, clothes, charitable contributions, membership fees, utilities, etc.). Eventually, she realized that each year not only did the spending categories remain relatively stable, but that the percentage of income spent on each of those categories was stable as well. She discovered that her behaviors tended to perpetuate the status quo, or demonstrate bias toward keeping things the same year after year. Her most fundamental needs and desires didn't change on an annual basis (e.g., home, clothing, food, transportation, entertainment), nor did her values or the way in which she prioritized those values. So in retrospect she should have anticipated fairly stable spending habits. This tendency to perpetuate the status quo is common in every facet of life. It is rooted in a desire to avoid change, and thereby protect our ego from potential criticism or regret by doing something differently. As Hammond and his colleagues state, "Sticking with the status quo represents, in most cases, the safer course because it puts us at less psychological risk."[25] The tendency toward status quo is so strong that even when one is presented with multiple options, he or she is more inclined to stick with the status quo, presumably because having to decide among multiple options is more labor-intensive than deciding between one or two options.

For managers the status quo can mean that they will have a tendency to seek routine practices and procedures for both ordinary circumstances and for those that are exceptional. Likewise, they may mimic what they have seen others do in response to similar situations. This kind of benchmarking can certainly be functional in some aspects of organizational life, but think about what distinguishes crises from other management challenges. Namely, crises are not routine events, but rather, they are atypical and infrequent occurrences for which there is generally no prior decision-making rubric. Consider, for example, the current economic crisis plaguing the United States. The economic downturn has been compared to the Great Depression of the 1930s and 1940s and is characterized by the stock market plummeting, unemployment reaching all-time highs, and profits of our great manufacturing industries plunging. If we focus only on the ways in which the two circumstances are similar, then we might well be served by implementing some of the same mechanisms that helped lift the economy back then. Yet despite these similarities, the times and circumstances are very different. Our economy is a global one now, technology has fundamentally changed the way business is conducted, and information transmission, a service economy, and environmental concerns have become our central focus. In light of these differences, the usefulness of the strategies employed during the Great Depression is extremely limited. We are on unchartered territory and the leadership in the federal government and in our corporations will have to find new ways of handling the crisis. There is no adequate status quo upon which to rely, and any effort to employ the same strategies as in the past will surely fail.

For those who prefer to think about the current financial situation in a more quantitative fashion we state it this way: Our economic circumstance is such that we can no longer find solutions by attempting to solve for X as in an algebraic equation. Ordinarily, we would have at least one known or quantifiable variable that would make the calculus possible. However, in our present circumstances every conceivable variable in the equation is an unknown. Therefore, we must conceive of fundamentally new ways of problem solving. The resignation of General Motors CEO Rick Wagoner may be among the most prominent examples of our point. Following a submission of plans to Congress for how the company would restructure in an effort to solicit additional federal funds, President Obama rejected the ailing company's turnaround plan. He subsequently encouraged Wagoner's resignation, essentially stating that the plans did not go far enough in creating a car company of the future and that the old ways of doing business for the automotive industry were no longer appropriate or acceptable. Perhaps we could have predicted the difficulty that GM would have in rethinking its business. As the status quo becomes increasingly entrenched in the psyche of employees, managers, suppliers, and customers, the ability to break away from the infrastructure that exists becomes harder. Having failed to seize the occasion when change would have been expected, management finds itself stuck with the status quo.[26]

For those who want to minimize the effect of the status quo heuristic, Hammond and colleagues offer the following advice. First, keep the overarching objective front and center in your mind as you attempt to make decisions and engage in problem-solving activities regarding crisis situations. Handling a crisis is hard work and it becomes all too easy to fall back on what we know or what we've done in the past. Forcing yourself to answer whether those previous actions will actually resolve the current dilemma can go a long way in helping to make new opportunities or alternatives clear. Second, consider whether you would use the status quo option if it were not the status quo. Again, status quo is comfortable, it is easy, but it is not always the best or only option. In fact, we will go so far as to say that in a crisis situation status quo is quite likely the absolutely wrong option to pursue precisely because it is unlikely that past options are relevant for the current unusual circumstances. Third, avoid the tendency to exaggerate the cost (time and effort) involved in adopting strategies or making decisions that are different from the status quo. Everything about handling a crisis is challenging. Decision making under those circumstances is certainly no exception, and a crisis is no time to try to take the easy way out. As we will describe more fully in Chapter 9, crises may be the perfect opportunity to fundamentally change the way decisions have been made in the past and create an opening for new and innovative ideas to emerge.

Sunk-Cost Heuristic

Individual and group decision making alike are susceptible to the phenomenon of sunk costs. The tendency to make decisions in a way that justifies past choices, or sunk costs, including choices regarding investments of time or money that are now irrecoverable, is a ubiquitous experience. Let's be honest: We have all called a customer service number, been placed on hold, and simply waited for a human being to come on the line. After a couple of minutes you say to yourself that this is wasting your time and you really should hang up and try again later (presumably when you have more time). Instead, however, you begin to negotiate with yourself, saying things like "three more minutes and then I'm hanging up." Inevitably those 3 minutes will pass, and so will another 5 or 15 minutes. But by now, you have put so much time in to the call you convince yourself that your turn is bound to come at any second. So you continue to wait, all the while reasoning that to hang up now would really confirm that you have wasted your time. Yet in reality, what you have experienced is the sunk-cost trap.

For a more organizationally relevant example, consider the R&D team that has been charged with developing a new product. They make an initial investment of human and financial capital into the project and their initial efforts fail to live up to expectations. So the team goes back to management to ask for additional time, money, and perhaps manpower to continue the project—because after all, "they are really close." Over time additional requests for resources continue and in reality the project is no closer to being finished, ready, or up to code as it was after the initial request. But throwing the towel in just does not feel like the right thing to do, given how much effort has already been expended. We justify additional expenditures despite not seeing any return on earlier investments.

So even if we know intellectually that sunk costs are immaterial to subsequent decisions, why are we susceptible to this decision-making bias? In large part we are prone to the sunk-cost heuristic because our initial choices of investments of time, money, or human effort are inextricably linked to our ego. After all, for the R&D team, the project to which they devoted their efforts and perhaps sacrificed other aspects of their life to complete can be interpreted as a reflection of themselves—their capabilities. To surrender the project would suggest that they have failed, that they were wrong. Thus, in order to save face, they (we) rationalize future investments to avoid perceived failure. The 2008 U.S. economic crisis potentially presents a good example of sunk costs. The Obama administration was being criticized by some as continuing to throw good money after bad at U.S. banks, insurance companies, the automotive industry, and as some have accused, just about anyone else who wants a hand out. It is perhaps too early to tell the consequences of the federal bailout plan, but already we are seeing the groundwork being laid for future "investments" in the same companies that have already received billions of dollars. In this way, the sunk-cost heuristic is intertwined with status quo. Decisions are being made to follow the same course of action as has been used previously. By not considering other options decision makers run the risk of continuing to pursue a bad course of action.

To counter the sunk-cost trap managers are encouraged to seek out the opinions of those who were not involved in the initial decisions. By doing so, they are more likely to get a fresh perspective on what has become an old problem. Moreover, by soliciting the opinions of those independent from the dilemma you limit the exposure to the danger posed by being too closely aligned to the problem and therefore being subjected to the trappings of one's ego. A second managerial option is to broaden one's consideration of stakeholders to the problem. This is a point to which we will return in Chapter 9. But suffice it to say, thinking about the implications of decisions on a wide array of constituents may motivate managers to consider alternative and potentially better uses of their investments. Finally, as hard as this may seem, managers must remind themselves and those with whom they work that even the most talented of workers will make errors in judgment. This in and of itself is not the problem. Rather, perpetuating those errors by doing more of the same is what they should seek to avoid. This requires careful attention to normative behaviors, politics, and organizational policies. Managers and HR systems may inadvertently reward and punish the outcomes of the decisions and disregard the quality of the decision-making process.

Confirming Evidence

More than perhaps any other, the confirming evidence heuristic will likely resonate with most readers. It is simply the tendency to seek out information that supports our existing instinct or point of view while avoiding information that contradicts it. Like with the sunk-cost heuristic, soliciting confirmatory information is also largely about preserving our ego. We want to be right just as much as we want to avoid being wrong, as is a primary motivation behind the sunk-cost heuristic. Consequently, we set ourselves up for success by narrowing the set of people, resources, and other sources of data to those that we feel reasonably confident will support our perspective. The car racing case study that we described earlier in this chapter beautifully represents this point. In deciding whether to participate in the final race of the season, despite unexplained engine failure, the owners both subtly and unconsciously ask for information that supports their desire to race. This includes discounting data provided by the mechanic that conflicts with their desired choice and even diminishing the relevance of the mechanic's qualifications.

Interestingly, it is not only an individual's predilections that make him or her susceptible to confirming evidence. There are many organizational systems that support and perpetuate this tendency. Consider, for example, a typical hiring process in a firm. One piece of data that decision makers rely on when deciding among potential employees is letters of recommendation. Generally speaking, candidates know that they will be expected to supply reference letters to the hiring firm, so whom do they ask to write a letter on their behalf? These are people who themselves have made the decision to hire the person and presumably will confirm their assessment of themselves. People that may have a less favorable view of the candidate are unlikely to be asked for their opinion. In the end, the hiring organization is getting a biased external perspective of the candidate.

During a crisis, a natural tendency is to react, make decisions, and adopt behaviors even before we know what it is we really want to achieve from our actions or decisions. Because leaders are in unchartered territory, they become susceptible to the confirming evidence bias precisely because they may be desperate for confirmation that the decisions being made are the correct ones. In these circumstances, leaders may unconsciously solicit information and interpret data in a way that reinforces their thinking, even if that thinking is wrong. Moreover, perceived or actual time pressure that accompanies a crisis can become a justification for failing to seek a wide array of opinions or perspectives.

So what is a leader to do to offset the tendency to seek confirming information? First, recognize that your own reasoning and decision making may in fact be correct, but that it will be in your best interest to test your logic with others. This can be achieved in a number of ways. First, solicit perspectives from a variety of sources. This is particularly true if you are seeking input from subordinates. Recognize that if your organization represents a culture or has a track record of shooting the messenger, being penalized for bad news, or providing information or opinions that contradict those of a superior, then you are likely to only receive information that confirms your point of view. Peers, supervisors, and others may be more willing to challenge your assumptions and encourage you to think about the problem in new and different ways. Second, force yourself to examine all of the data with which you are presented with equal rigor and challenge yourself to be receptive to all of the data.[27] Pause and reflect when you find yourself being dismissive of some information and accepting of others. Third, specifically identify someone to challenge your point of view. Ask him or her to play the devil's advocate and counter or question your assumptions. Finally, perhaps most difficult of all, reflect on your underlying motives in your decision making and crisis handling. Are you motivated by time and want to reach a decision quickly? Are you motivated by fear? Are you motivated by your ego and wanting to prove a point? Or are you motivated by wanting to find the best possible solution—one that will attempt to satisfy many relevant stakeholders. By thoughtfully examining your motivations you will be more open to seeking the opinions of others and may become more mindful of perspectives that may confirm or disconfirm your own assessment.

Framing

How an issue, or any other appropriate substitute (e.g., situation, dilemma, problem, crisis), is framed in the minds of decision makers can serve as the springboard for how it is ultimately resolved. By and large, issues are framed either as threats or as opportunities. Similar to the characteristics of a crisis, the framing of a situation either as a threat or as an opportunity reflects a sense of urgency and challenge and is associated with high stakes.[28] For organizational decision makers, framing an issue as a threat or as an opportunity is of considerable import, especially for determining subsequent activity and firm performance.[29] As decision makers filter and interpret incoming information (à la the various biases described above), they make judgments about this information that inform them as to whether the firm should direct its activity to the internal or external environment in response to the issue it is facing. Internally directed actions are aimed primarily at adapting the organization to the pressures of the environment. These are actions that leaders can have direct control over and are generally perceived to be low-risk changes (e.g., changing organizational structure, implementing new policies and procedures, reducing costs). Externally directed actions, by contrast, are aimed at modifying the environment (e.g., developing new markets). These actions are more risky because leaders have less control over them and generally require considerable investment and resources with no guarantee of return.

Considerable research has not only confirmed a threat/opportunity framing dichotomy,[30] but it has indicated that people typically have a bias toward interpreting negative events primarily as threats—either to themselves or to the organization. In reality, however, issues are merely ambiguous environmental stimuli.[31] They have no inherent value and only become good (opportunity) or bad (threat) once they have been interpreted as such. Issues that are interpreted as threats are believed to result in loss. Moreover, managers are less likely to believe they have control over threats,[32] and consequently may become despondent and reactionary in their handling of them.[33] In highly uncertain environments where the outcomes of a decision are ambiguous, threat-rigidity arguments claim that leaders will attempt to offset the negativity associated with threats, by taking action in areas in which there is perceived greater organizational control.[34] Generally, these are domains that are internal to the organization, such as cost cutting, budget tightening, and information restriction.[35] In addition, because threats highlight the riskiness of a situation, decision makers may be inclined to respond in risk-averse ways.[36] Consider, for example, a typical first response to an actual or anticipated downturn in a firm's financial performance. When interpreted as a threat, many company leaders will move quickly to cut costs by cutting overhead (downsizing), a domain in which managers have ultimate control. They can take comfort in the fact that action was taken in response to the dilemma. But whether such action reflects crisis leadership is debatable. We suggest that it may not. In responding to the issue only from a threat frame, corresponding threat responses exclude the types of actions that may be considered when approaching the same issue from an opportunity frame. In other words, these leaders may have bound their awareness in such a way that prohibits them from seeing through the opportunity lens.

Opportunity framing is represented by the interpretation of an issue as a possible or likely gain, and is perceived to be something over which the decision maker can exert control. Opportunities make gain and achievement rather than loss and failure salient, and therefore decision makers may tend toward more risk-seeking behavior. The financially dire circumstances currently facing the Big Three U.S. automakers (General Motors, Chrysler, and Ford) can readily be interpreted exclusively from a threat frame. After all, it is challenging to imagine climbing out of the very deep hole that these companies are in. Yet, opportunity frames exist even under these circumstances. For example, there is the opportunity to reinvent the companies from a traditional auto manufacturing industry into another organizational form that uses the human capital (e.g., knowledge, skills, abilities) of the existing labor force in new and innovative ways. The Obama administration's push toward green technology may be one such opportunity. Clearly making this type of adjustment is not easy, and we certainly do not mean to diminish the challenges associated with a transition of this magnitude. We simply offer this as an extreme example of how decision making and the outcomes of those decisions may differ when environmental stimuli are perceived as an opportunity rather than only as a threat.

By way of another example, we offer Kodak's story. Kodak is an iconic firm with more than 120 years of history in manufacturing and retail sales of film to consumers. Yet in the early to mid-1990s, the very product that built Kodak's reputation was becoming obsolete. Digital technology was taking over, and although film technology was as good as ever, the interest and use of film waned dramatically as the market for digital technology grew. Analysts and others predicted that Kodak would not survive. But thanks to some innovative leaders that approached the situation with an opportunity lens, Kodak has risen from the ashes. How did Kodak do this? Layoffs and plant closings were part of the restoration effort, but they were not the only part. Simultaneously, they were also acquiring new businesses that would help propel them into the digital technology space and refocus their efforts on offering digital imaging and printing products and services. They also transitioned away from the consumer market and moved more toward business-to-business marketing strategies. It may seem unusual that a firm that is hemorrhaging money might spend upwards of $3 billion on purchasing new companies, but that is precisely the type of externally focused behavior that often accompanies an opportunity framing of a problem. Opportunity frames can serve to expand leaders' minds in a way that allows them to pursue alternatives that were not even considered from a threat frame. In talking about the new and improved Kodak, then newly appointed chief business development officer Jeffrey Hayzlett said, "In part of the transformation, each group was focused on the things it did well. And so, we needed to bring in someone who took a more holistic and broader view. . . ."[37] Hayzlett has been credited as having the perspective that would help Kodak imagine what was possible, despite the threats, and lead the organization in executing a strategy that would make it a market leader in digital technology. Had he and his team approached their problems only from a threat frame, it is unlikely that they would have considered much less attempted these fairly aggressive tactics.

Another illustration of an opportunity frame in decision making is provided by Herb Chambers, owner of the largest number of car dealerships in New England. Chambers or his dealerships are regularly featured in local and national news outlets for consistently outperforming the competition across 28 automotive brands, including Mercedes-Benz, Audi, Buick, BMW, Chevrolet, Jeep, Lexus, Toyota, and others. In 2007 his dealerships totaled $1.7 billion in sales and have received more JD Power awards than any other auto dealer in the northeast region of the United States. But 2008 and 2009 proved to be very challenging times. Sales dropped 6% in 2008 and in the first quarter of 2009 were down more than 20%. So what does Chambers do? While competitors are implementing gimmicks to offload inventory he is looking to buy additional dealerships. When asked recently by a National Public Radio reporter how he can afford to do this in the current economy, he stated that he is looking to the long term: "The economic crisis will eventually end and when it does, I want to be ready with dealerships and cars available for customers."[38] The way in which Chambers framed or interpreted the difficulty in his business, and the decision to be aggressive in pursuing new opportunities at a time when others are looking inward to stay afloat, is another sound example of the difference in opportunity versus threat framing. To be fair, though, Chambers may have an advantage over his competitors. Namely, relative to other dealership owners, the Chambers automotive group is resource rich. It has slack resources that prove to be helpful in providing organizations capabilities to act in ways that may not be possible for organizations with limited resources.[39]

In short, framing an issue as an opportunity will put the decision maker on a very different response path during crisis handling than will a threat frame. We do not exclusively advocate opportunity frames, however. After all, some events are extremely tragic, and handling them from a threat frame, where the focus should be primarily on damage control activity initially, may be the only viable option. Consider the devastating events like the 6.3 magnitude earthquake that struck the central region of Italy on April 6, 2009. After four days the death toll was at 289 and rising. Clearly, one cannot consider the opportunities to be gained from such a tragedy at a time when focused attention must be on search and rescue or recovery efforts, public safety, and other damage control behaviors. Leaders' attention should be focused internally on the people and businesses in the region. In this and other truly devastating events, conservative and internally focused actions are an appropriate response. What we argue, however, is that in many cases, crisis situations can eventually be identified as both a threat and an opportunity, and the best leaders are those that can interpret situations from both frames. We will devote considerably more attention to the topic of manifesting opportunity from crisis in Chapter 9 (Figure 4.2).[40]

> **Anchoring**
> • Basing decisions on the information initially presented.

> **Status Quo**
> • Bias toward keeping things the same.

> **Sunk-Cost**
> • Tendency to make decisions in a way that justifies past choices, particularly choices regarding investments of time or money.

> **Confirming Evidence**
> • Tendency to seek out information that supports our existing point of view and to avoid information that contradicts it.

> **Framing**
> • The context in which an issue is presented (positively/negatively, threat/opportunity).

Figure 4.2   Heuristics: Unconscious biases that affect decision making.

Ethical Decision Making

In light of various financial scandals (e.g., Bernard Madoff Ponzi scheme, Enron, Martha Stewart) and other crisis events, and the commonly held perspective that these crises were largely due to questionable practices and behaviors, a chapter on decision making would be incomplete without at least a cursory discussion of ethical decision making.[41] Ethical decision making is relevant to organizations when managers of their own volition make decisions or take actions that have the potential to harm or benefit others.[42] An ethical decision is defined as one that is both legal and morally acceptable to the larger community. By contrast, unethical decisions are either illegal or morally unacceptable to the larger community.[43] Effective crisis leaders not only understand the distinction between the ethical and unethical decisions, but are intentional about their decision making so that their decisions are legally and morally above reproach and that they inflict the least amount of harm possible on stakeholders.

There has been a steady increase in the attention that management scholars have given to the issue of ethical decision making in the past 30 years.[44] Some of this research has provided a review of the literature, while other research has offered models of ethical decision making. A much smaller subset of ethical decision-making research has attempted empirical investigation of the topic. As management scholar Linda Trevino reasoned, the lack of empirical attention may be a result of the delicate and complex nature of the topic, and the unwillingness of managers to allow their ethics to be directly observed and measured.[45] To this point, more than a decade ago I worked for a Fortune 100 financial services firm on a competency-modeling project for the firm's middle- and senior-level managers. When asked about the various leadership skills and abilities that were needed to perform successfully, a theme around morals and ethics emerged. In the design of the competency model, we included this theme and ultimately labeled it integrity and ethics. Interestingly, however, as drafts of the model were sent to senior executives for review and revision the integrity and ethics category disappeared. When we asked the executives why they felt the category should not be included, they reasoned that there was no way to measure a person's ethics—they either have them or they do not—and you cannot assign behaviors to ethics. This rationale supports another one of Trevino's assertions about management's beliefs—that ethics is a matter of subjective preference about which no objective evaluations can be made.

Although the body of research on ethical decision making is growing, the reality of its utility in Corporate America continues to outpace research. Ethical dilemmas are ubiquitous in organizational life where environments are characterized by uncertainty and where "multiple stakeholders, interests, and values are in conflict and laws are unclear."[46] Managers are called upon to use their own discretion or their best judgment in circumstances where they feel woefully unprepared (see again the concerns expressed by Managers A, B, and C at the outset of this chapter). Under these conditions, the influences of cognitive biases become exacerbated and our cognitive capabilities (e.g., awareness and rationality) are further reduced. As a result, we open the door for decision making that can be characterized as faulty and potentially unethical as managers gravitate toward quick and short-term focused solutions that may not be in the best interest of the organization.

An analysis of the ethical decision-making research suggests that there are two prevailing assumptions about what contributes to ethical or unethical decision making and behavior: the role of the individual or the role of situational factors. At the individual level variables such as a person's knowledge, values, attitudes, and intentions have been offered as factors that affect decision making.[47] Much of the research examining how the individual affects decision making is rooted largely in Kohlberg's model of moral development.[48] This theory addresses how people reason during the decision-making process, how they justify a moral choice, and that knowledge, values, attitudes, and intentions are a part of the reasoning process. Kohlberg's theory does not address the outcome of a decision, but rather the thought process that goes into the decision. It is concerned with social judgments of people and prescriptive judgments of what is right and wrong. Moreover, the model defines three broad levels of moral development, with each level having two stages through which people pass in the same sequence as they mature from childhood to adulthood.[49]

Stages 1 and 2, broadly labeled the preconventional level, are marked by a person's concern with concrete consequences (e.g., rewards and punishments) of his or her decisions or actions. Thus, at Stage 1 of the preconventional level a person might choose to obey the law to avoid punishment. Stage 2 of this level is characterized by a person choosing to follow a set of rules for instrumental gain; it is in his or her best interest to do so. The conventional level houses Stages 3 and 4, and is concerned with doing what is right to meet the expectations of others or a set of social norms. Specifically, at Stage 3 one is motivated to fulfill the expectations of a significant other (parent, spouse, boss), whereas in Stage 4 the person is concerned with conforming to the norms of a broader society. Kohlberg believes that most adults operate at this conventional level. In the final level, labeled principled, a person is mindful of universal norms, laws, and expectations but sees beyond them to make decisions about what is right in light of a set of values and principles. At this level, a person would act in accordance with his or her ethical principles even if doing so might violate formal rules of law.

As Trevino points out, Kohlberg's model of cognitive moral development has made a tremendous contribution to the field of business ethics research.[50] It not only provides an empirically validated construct of moral judgment, but also defines stages that can be used as a basis for understanding and explaining why managers make the decisions they do when confronted with ambiguous or ethically challenging dilemmas. Moreover, the stage definitions have face validity, or are intuitive enough that one need not have a background in ethics or philosophy to be able to understand and apply them. However, Kohlberg's model is limited to a cognitive assessment of decision making, focusing exclusively on how people *think* about a situation. It does not consider behavior or what people actually do when confronted with ethical issues. Although it assumes that thought and action are correlated given our drive for consistency between the two, some researchers have argued that moral judgment alone is a necessary but insufficient condition for behaving ethically.[51]

In addition to individual-level considerations, situational factors such as the organizational context can also affect ethical decision making. For example, Trevino's model proposes a theory in which situational factors interact with individual characteristics. She identified elements of one's immediate job context and characteristics of the work as relevant situational variables. In another model, significant others and opportunity to behave unethically were identified as key situational factors.[52] The opportunity to behave unethically is related to the existence of professional codes, corporate policy, and rewards and punishments, all of which are indicative of an organization's culture.[53] Likewise, socialization processes, environmental influences, and hierarchical relationships combine in a way to "stack the deck" against ethical behavior.[54] In one of the more comprehensive models of ethical decision making a group of researchers catalog more than 20 environmental factors (work, personal, professional, governmental, legal, and social) and individual attributes that affect ethical decision making.[55]

A criticism of the research that has focused on the influence of either individual or situational factors, or some interaction of the two domains, is that it fails to address the issue itself over which decision makers grapple. In fact, some scholars have noted that when ethical dilemmas arise, the consensus regarding proper decision making will likely change as the issue changes.[56] For example, most people would not endorse embezzling company funds, but there is considerable research to suggest that employee misconduct related to theft (e.g., bringing home office supplies or padding expense accounts) is ubiquitous.[57] Although the behaviors differ in scale and in consequence to the organization and to the decision maker, they both represent employee theft. Yet prior research did not fully capture the expectation that people might make different choices because of differences in characteristics like scale or consequence associated with the form that the issue takes. As one study found, corporate managers use different modes of moral reasoning for different types of moral issues.[58] Thus, it is reasonable to conclude that issues associated with crisis handling, or that the decision making associated with issues that might contribute to a crisis would be rationalized differently than issues of less significance.

To address this research void, Jones argues that we must consider the characteristics of what he calls the moral issue and presents a model in which the issue itself can affect ethical decision making and behavior.[59] Drawing on theory from social psychology, Jones coined the term *moral intensity* to reflect six characteristics of an issue that he argues are related positively to ethical decision making. *Magnitude of consequences* is defined as the sum of the harms (or benefits) done to victims (or beneficiaries) of the decision in question. After two recent surgical procedures resulted in adverse consequences (including the death of one patient), Massachusetts General Hospital decided to suspend its pediatric cardiac surgery unit, reasoning that the potential for harm (subsequent patient injury or death) was too high to continue performing surgery until investigations were undertaken to determine the cause of the problem. In this case, the magnitude of the consequences contributed to the hospital's decision to suspend surgeries. *Social consensus* is the degree of social agreement that a proposed decision or action is either evil or good. Jones offers an example of workplace discrimination to illustrate this construct. He says, for example, that it is commonly believed that the evil associated with discriminating against minority job applicants has greater social consequence than the evil associated with refusing to act affirmatively on behalf of minority applicants. *Probability of effect* is the combined function of the probability that the issue in question will actually take place and that the issue will actually cause the harm (benefit) predicted. When Firestone made the decision to continue to manufacture and sell a particular tire despite data showing that the tire was known to cause blowouts on some vehicles under certain conditions, executives may have reasoned that the probability of effect was so small as to make the risk worthwhile.

Jones defines *temporal immediacy* as the length of time between the present and the onset of consequences of the issue in question. In this case, a shorter length of time implies greater immediacy, whereas a longer time frame is associated with less immediacy or consequence. As economists have communicated, people tend to discount the impact of events that occur in the future. Similarly, the greater the distance between the decision and its consequence being realized, the less likely people are to believe that the consequence is a result of the decision. It may be for this reason that the Ponzi scheme pulled off by Bernard Madoff succeeded for so many years. Madoff had led clients to believe that he had been investing their money for decades when in reality he was doing nothing more than pocketing the money for personal gain. Yet, it is probable that Madoff reasoned that the likelihood of being caught was remote, and in the event that his scheme was ultimately revealed, it would happen so far into the future that psychologically the future consequences of his decisions were discounted.

The concept of distance is related to Jones's fifth characterization of moral intensity. *Proximity* is the feeling of social, cultural, psychological, or physical closeness that the decision maker has for victims or beneficiaries of the decision or action. Generally people care more about others that are close to them in some way than they do about people that are more distant. Consequently, we tend to make different decisions when we think our decisions will adversely affect someone we care about than we might if those decisions affect someone whom we do not know or is in some other way distant from us. Jones offers the infamous Milgram experiments as an example of the proximity attribute of an ethical issue.[60] In 1974 Milgram designed a series of experiments whereby subjects (called "teachers" in the experiment) were ordered by the researcher to administer increasingly powerful electric shocks to a learner (an actor working with the research team) when the learner failed to respond correctly to questions testing information he or she had just been taught by the teacher. Initially the research was intended to test "when and how people would defy authority in the face a clear moral imperative."[61] Milgram found that as physical proximity between the teacher and the learner decreased, the incidences of obedience to authority (providing a shock to the learner) also decreased. Moreover, when the teacher had actual physical contact with the learner before the testing period of the experiment commenced, subject obedience dropped from 62.5% to 30%.

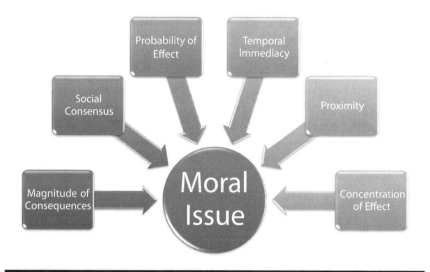

Figure 4.3   Moral intensity: Issue characteristics that affect ethical decision making.

The last feature of moral intensity is *concentration of effect*, and is an inverse function of the number of people affected by an act of a given magnitude. In other words, making a decision that will substantially harm a small number of people has a more concentrated effect than does a decision that might minimally hurt a larger group of people. For example, a change in a warranty policy denying coverage to 10 people with claims of $10,000 has a more concentrated effect than a change denying coverage to 10,000 people with claims of $10.00 (Figure 4.3).[62]

A Framework of Ethical Decision Making

The value of Jones's theory on moral intensity is particularly relevant in the role that moral intensity plays in the relationship between recognizing an issue as an ethical one and the decisions and subsequent actions taken with respect to that issue. Jones applies moral intensity to a framework of ethical decision making that includes four key components: (1) recognizing an ethical issue, (2) making a moral judgment about the issue, (3) establishing moral intent, and (4) engaging in ethical decision making and behavior.[63] This framework assumes that decision makers traverse through each stage when contemplating their response to ethical dilemmas. Jones proposes that moral intensity directly influences each of those stages.

The decision-making process begins by recognizing an issue as an ethical or moral one. To do so, the decision maker must understand that his or her decisions will affect others and that he or she has free choice in the decision that is made. Moral intensity affects the recognition of a moral issue in that it impacts the decision maker's ability to see the consequences of the decision. High-intensity moral issues will facilitate the recognition of consequences more so than low-intensity moral issues because, for example, high-intensity issues are generally more extreme (e.g., crisis issues that have greater magnitude of consequences than noncrisis issues). Likewise, decision makers are more inclined to perceive an issue as high intensity when it affects people with whom they have proximity.

Once a decision maker has recognized an ethical issue, he or she must make a moral judgment about the issue.[64] According to many scholars, moral judgments are made in accordance with Kohlberg's stage of moral development. Recall that Kohlberg has argued that the vast majority of adults are in the conventional level of moral development, in which their reasoning and judgment are facilitated by their desire to meet the expectations of others (significant others or a universal standard of what is acceptable and appropriate). Research has also found, however, that moral development may not be a stable characteristic, but that people operate within a range of moral development stages. This range can be influenced by context in such a way that moral reasoning is lower or worse in the context of real-life dilemmas than in other (i.e., hypothetical) situations. Similarly, as Jones has articulated, moral development is issue dependent. For example, decision makers may economize on the effort associated with ethical decision making when the ethical stakes are perceived to be low.[65] Moral intensity influences moral judgment when the magnitude of the consequences of the ethical issue affects the amount of effort a person will bring to bear on his or her thinking and reasoning about the issue. Here too is where cognitive biases come into play, as decision makers may be more inclined to seek confirming information for issues perceived to be of high moral intensity. In these situations, decision makers care deeply about the stakeholders (proximity effect) and want to believe that because of their close relationship to them, they know what is best and will entertain only that information that is consistent with what they already believe. When the stakes are low, however, decision makers may be more open to external information.

The third stage of the ethical decision-making framework addresses moral intent, or what the decision maker intends to do in light of the ethical judgment made in the prior stage. It is here that conflict between moral considerations and other factors (e.g., self-interest concerns) may emerge.[66] Deciding whether to blow the whistle on organizational wrongdoing is a prime example of the dilemma of moral intent. To expose one's organization for falsifying accounting information may be the ethically correct thing to do, but doing so will likely have severe, negative, and long-term consequences on the potential whistle-blower. Moral intensity can affect moral intent through social consensus. People generally want to avoid being associated with bad or evil. When social consensus (a feature of moral intensity) is that a particular decision or action is bad or unethical, people will attempt to dissociate from the decision by acting appropriately or in a morally correct way.

Finally, decision makers must take action on their moral intentions. Rest stated, "Executing and implementing a plan of action . . . involves . . . working around impediments and unexpected difficulties, overcoming fatigue and frustration, resisting distractions and allurements, and keeping sight of the original goal."[67] Although not referring specifically to crisis handling, his words are as germane to decision making in times of crisis as they are to decision making regarding moral or ethical dilemmas (and we repeat that often the two situations are highly correlated). The characteristics of moral intensity also apply to ethical behavior. Decision makers are ultimately more inclined to act ethically when the magnitude of the consequences is high, when social consensus about the issue would negatively affect one's perception by others if he or she did not act ethically, and when one is socially, psychologically, or geographically proximate to those potentially affected by the action.

Earlier in this chapter we presented cognitive biases that influence decision making. Decision makers are susceptible to cognitive biases when decisions also involve ethical dilemmas. The inability to accurately judge or perceive of future events offers one example. Bias in risk perception contributes to difficulty in judging ethical (and crisis) situations where the outcome of the decision has not yet occurred. In this case, people may underestimate the risk in future situations because they are unimaginable.[68] Many crisis events are nothing if not unimaginable. To the extent that we are biased against events that we cannot anticipate or imagine, our ability to respond ethically to them is limited. The failure to detect the relationship between simultaneously occurring stimuli poses another cognitive bias. In Chapter 3 we highlighted sense making as a critical crisis leadership competency. Yet, part of sense making is the ability to understand and interpret new or foreign stimuli. When such data are presented in isolation we have a somewhat better chance of taking notice and making sense of them than when there are multiple new stimuli that occur. The challenge of sense making becomes even more complicated when new information comes from different parts of the organization and we don't immediately see the relationship among them (Figure 4.4).

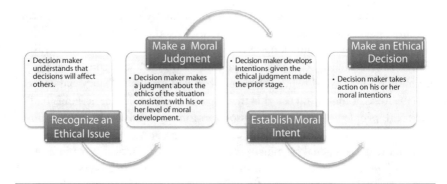

- Decision maker understands that decisions will affect others.

Recognize an Ethical Issue

Make a Moral Judgment

- Decision maker makes a judgment about the ethics of the situation consistent with his or her level of moral development.

- Decision maker develops intentions given the ethical judgment made the prior stage.

Establish Moral Intent

Make an Ethical Decision

- Decision maker takes action on his or her moral intentions

Figure 4.4   A framework of ethical decision making.

Summary

This chapter is largely devoted to the challenges, constraints, and problems in decision making. To that end, we have merely scratched the surface when it comes to presenting a comprehensive review of the decision-making literature. That said, we hope that we have drawn readers' attention to the way the mind works when it is under pressure, and how the functioning of our brain, and our framing, interpretation of stimuli, and moral reasoning can dramatically influence the decision-making process. As the manager dilemmas we presented at the outset of this chapter illustrate, managers spend the vast majority of their time making decisions, and a lot of managers feel unprepared and ill-equipped to make many of the decisions that they do make. While we do not necessarily offer a recipe for how to make decisions, we have provided food for thought for what to be mindful of when making decisions in high-pressure and ethically relevant situations such as crisis. Moreover, we hope we have whetted readers' appetite for wanting to learn more or to investigate for themselves decision-making strategies during a crisis. Our own conclusion is that part of what differentiates crisis leaders from others is that once armed with the information in this chapter, they can recognize the various cognitive biases when they experience them or create them in others, and they stay attuned to the way in which they are framing the stimuli in their environment such that they see both the threats and the opportunities of crisis situations (Figures 4.5 and 4.6).

I'm sure that my subordinates know the rational decision making model, so why don't they seem to use it?	What differentiates a crisis leader from other leaders when making decisions?
The rational decision-making model presents an ideal that assumes a number of unrealistic factors, which actually act as barriers to decision making. In addition, people are prone to use cognitive shortcuts or heuristics, which can sometimes lead to severe errors in judgment and decision making.	A crisis leader recognizes the limitations and biases of human decision making and they stay attuned to they way in which they are framing stimuli in their environment such that they see both the threats and the opportunities in crisis situations.

Figure 4.5   Leader's hot seat.

Figure 4.6   Leadership Links 4.1

- Leadership and Decision Making
  http://www.bpmforum.org/DecisionROI/PDF/Leadership_DQ.pdf
- Ethical Decision Making Simulation
  https://store.darden.virginia.edu/business-casestudy/priority-inc-player-instructions-179
- Crisis Decision Making
  http://www.au.af.mil/au/awc/awcgate/fema/247/index.htm

Endnotes

1. Mintzberg, *The nature of managerial work.*
2. Hammond, Keeney, & Raiffa, Even swaps, 137–150.
3. See, for example, the prolific writings of Max Bazerman.
4. Bazerman, *Judgment in managerial decision making.*
5. Ibid.

6. MacCrimmon, An overview of multiple objective decision making.

7. For more information on cognitive limitations see, for example, March & Simon, *Organizations*; Simon, Theories of decision-making in economics and behavioral science, 253–283.

8. James & Wooten, Diversity crises, 1103–1118.

9. Simon, *Administrative behavior*, 2nd ed.; March & Simon, *Organizations*.

10. Simon, *Administrative behavior*, 3rd ed., 72.

11. Arthur, Inductive reasoning and bounded rationality, 406–411.

12. See the work of Max Bazerman, including Bazerman & Chugh, Decisions without blinders, 84; Chugh & Bazerman, Bounded awareness, 20–25.

13. Chugh & Bazerman, Bounded awareness, 20–25.

14. Carr, *Dynamic interpretations of strategic issues*.

15. Simons & Chabris, Gorillas in our midst, 1059–1074.

16. March & Simon, *Organizations*.

17. Bazerman, *Judgment in managerial decision making*, 4th ed.

18. Kahneman & Tversky, Prospect theory, 263–291; Tversky & Kahneman, Advances in prospect theory, 297–323.

19. See, for example, Tversky & Kahneman, Judgment under uncertainty, 453–463.

20. Bazerman, *Judgment in managerial decision making*, 4th ed., 5.

21. For an extensive presentation on decision-making traps see Hammond, Keeney, & Raiffa, The hidden traps in decision making.

22. Bazerman, *Judgment in managerial decision making*.

23. Ibid., 8.

24. To view a copy of the Carter Racing case, contact Delta Leadership, Inc., P.O. Box 3024, Chapel Hill, NC 27515; carter@deltaleadership.com.

25. Hammond, Keeney, & Raiffa, The hidden traps in decision making.

26. Ibid.

27. Ibid.

28. Chattapadhyay, Glick, & Huber, Organizational actions in response to threats and opportunities, 937–955.

29. Ibid.

30. See, for example, Jackson and Dutton, Discerning threats and opportunities, 370–387; Staw, Sandelands, & Dutton, Threat-rigidity effects in organizational behavior, 501–524; Dutton & Jackson, Categorizing strategic issues, 76–90.

31. Daft and Weick, Toward a model of organizations as interpretation systems, 284–295; Cowan, Developing a process model of problem recognition, 763–776.

32. Dutton & Jackson, Categorizing strategic issues, 76–90.

33. See work by Brockner & James, Toward an understanding of when executives see crisis as opportunity, for a brief review of the literature on how events are interpreted.

34. Ocasio, The enactment of economic diversity, 287–331.

35. Thomas, Clark, & Gioia, Strategic sensemaking and organizational performance, 239–270.

36. Sitkin & Pablo, Reconceptualizing the determinants of risk behavior, 9–38.

37. Cohen, Kodak's image is picture perfect.

38. Interview on Boston NPR, April 9, 2009.

39. See, for example, the work of Cyert & March, A behavioral theory of the firm; Meyer, Adapting to environmental jolts, 515–537.

40. Brockner & James, Towards an understanding of when executives see crisis as opportunity.

41. For purposes of simplicity, *ethics/ethical* and *morals/morality* are synonymous and will be used interchangeably throughout this section.

42. Velasquez & Rostankowski, *Ethics*.

43. Jones, Ethical decision making by individuals in organizations, 366–395. Jones admits that these definitions of ethical and unethical decisions are underdeveloped. See also Cavanagh, Moberg, & Velasquez, The ethics of organizational politics, 363–374; Beauchamp & Bowie, *Ethical theory and business*, for further discussion regarding the difficulty of establishing substantive definitions for ethical behavior and decision making.

44. See, for example, Brenner & Molander, Is the ethics of business changing? 57–71; Crittenden, The age of "me-first" management, 1; Lincoln, Pressley, & Little, Ethical beliefs and personal values of top level executives, 475–487; Trevino, Ethical decision making in organizations, 601–617; Jones, Ethical decision making by individuals in organizations, 366–395; Loe, Ferrell, & Mansfield, A review of empirical studies assessing ethical decision making in business, 185–204.

45. Trevino, Ethical decision making in organizations, 601–617.

46. Ibid., 601.

47. Ferrell & Gresham, A contingency framework for understanding ethical decision making in marketing, 87–96.

48. Kohlberg, Moral stages and moralization, 34–35; Kohlberg & Turiel, *Moralization research*.

49. Kohlberg, Moral stages and moralization, 34–35.

50. Trevino, Ethical decision making in organizations, 608.

51. Blasi, Bridging moral cognition and moral action, 1–45, for example, found only weak support for the hypothesis that people at the higher stages of moral development are less likely to succumb to social pressures to conform to moral action.

52. Ferrell & Gresham, A contingency framework for understanding ethical decision making in marketing, 87–96.

53. Ibid.

54. Smith & Carroll, Organizational ethics, 95–100.

55. Brommer et al., A behavioral model of ethical and unethical decisionmaking, 265–280.

56. Ferrell & Gresham, A contingency framework for understanding ethical decision making in marketing, 87–96.

57. Vardi & Wiener, Misbehavior in organizations, 151–165.

58. Weber, Managers' moral reasoning, 687–702.

59. Jones, Ethical decision making by individuals in organizations, 366–395.

60. Milgram, *Obedience to authority*.

61. Ibid., 4.

62. Jones, Ethical decision making by individuals in organizations, 366–395.

63. Rest, *Moral development*.

64. Ibid.

65. Fiske & Taylor, *Social cognitions.*
66. Rest, *Moral development.*
67. Ibid., 15.
68. See the work of Ross & Anderson, Shortcomings in the attribution process, 129–152; Slovic, Fischoff, & Lichtenstein, Facts and fears, 67–93.

Chapter 5

Leading a Crisis Team

Teams have become a dominant mode of structuring work for most organizations. The increased use of teams can be attributed to their advantages, such as an ability to generate more information, stimulate creativity, and expedite the decision-making process. With the increasing popularity of teams, researchers and practitioners have developed models to explain their effectiveness. Yet the majority of these models of high-performance teams assume stable environments and do not consider the attributes of extraordinary teams in crisis situations. In this chapter, we will explore this topic by examining team capabilities in crisis situations. We begin by briefly discussing the research on effective teams and then discuss the skill set needed to lead teams in a crisis situation. In our discussion, we consider the role of formal crisis management teams and those teams that have to improvise during a crisis situation. In addition, we explore the significance of creating a high-reliability team culture and the importance of crisis teams working with external stakeholders.

Characteristics of Effective Teams

Effective teams are defined as a small number of people working together with complementary skills who are committed to a common purpose, performance goal, and approach in which they hold each other mutually accountable.[1] By focusing on a particular task, with a common aim, and through interpersonal relationships, teams achieve their goals.[2] As you may have noticed, not only is the size of a team important, but also that members have the right mix of skills to accomplish team goals. In essence, the complementary skills should fit together like a puzzle, where each member adds value to the skill set of the team, and this produces a synergistic effort. These complementary skills can include technical competencies, functional expertise, problem-solving capabilities, decision-making skills, and interpersonal skills. In addition to complementary skills, the adoption of a common purpose linked to performance goals is an essential determinant of team effectiveness. This is because the team's common purpose defines the parameters for their work and serves as a guide for how the team will measure its success.[3]

Beyond the skills of members, team effectiveness is determined by leadership actions that enable the team to transform its resources into a collective work product desired by its stakeholders.[4] This transformation process requires cognitive, verbal, and behavioral interdependent interactions among team members and with their task environment.[5] Hence, leading a team is a twofold process that entails (1) managing the team's boundaries by scanning its environment, monitoring the demands of external constituencies, and coordinating interdependent relationships; and (2) managing the team itself by considering design factors, such as setting the team's agenda, the type of team structure, and the team's work environment.[6]

Integral to managing the team processes is leadership's ability to explicitly link the team's purpose with mutual accountability and specific performance outcomes.[7] Mutual accountability helps the team focus on results with a mindset that the team as a whole is responsible for producing results. Specific performance outcomes focus the team on attaining goals and provide the team with a result orientation. However, when focusing on performance outcomes, effective teams not only take into account if the team's output has met the standard of the end user, but also two other very important performance metrics. One of those metrics is whether the team experience contributed to the personal well-being and development of its members, and another is whether the team experience created learning so that members have an enhanced capability to work together in the future.[8]

Composing a Crisis Management Team

In the previous section, we discussed the characteristics of effective teams. Research concludes that when teams are effective, they will outperform individuals when the task is complex, ambiguous, or demands creativity.[9] The performance advantage of teams results from efficient usage of resources, learning between team members, and cross-functional cooperation. However, how do leaders leverage and adapt the attributes of effective teams in crisis situations since they differ from routine and conventional teamwork? The rules of the game for teams change in a crisis situation because teams confront a sense of urgency and the potential of negative outcomes that will affect the organization or its stakeholders. This can create a chaotic work environment for crisis management teams that is characterized by unplanned tasks, unpredictable events, and the disruption of the organization's status quo for operations.[10] Therefore, the work of teams can differ in a crisis situation and create an additional set of leadership tasks.

In general, once a leader acknowledges the need for a crisis management team, the work begins with composing the team. Leaders composing a crisis management team should take into account all of the attributes of a high-performing team that were described earlier, but also consider the previous knowledge and heterogeneity of the team.[11] For crisis management teams, previous task knowledge held by group members influences decision-making effectiveness by encouraging productive discussions and the efficient recall of relevant information to resolve the crisis situation. Moreover, the prior knowledge of crisis management team members influences its problem-solving capabilities. Research suggests that when teams do not have prior knowledge of the task, their approach to problem solving is unsystematic in how they interpret, comprehend, and process information,[12] whereas the exposure to prior knowledge makes it easier for the team to recall accurate information and apply its use to the crisis situation. Consequently, the prior knowledge results in a crisis management team with a greater understanding of the task and a more structured and goal-oriented approach to problem solving.[13]

Similarly, heterogeneously composed crisis management teams generate better ideas.[14] This is because the differences of thought, experiences, personality, identity, and values found in heterogeneous teams can create a work environment where diverse opinions can be shared and interconnected, like puzzle pieces, to develop solutions. Moreover, team members are more likely to bring attention to blind spots in decision making by questioning each other if leadership sets a standard of inclusiveness. Therefore, when composing the crisis management team, members should possess unique skills that are complementary and actively used to resolve a crisis situation.[15]

Some organizations have composed formal crisis management teams where members are brought together to prevent, prepare, and be on call to handle crisis situations.[16] In other words, the responsibility of formal crisis management teams encompasses avoiding emergencies, planning for unavoidable crises, dealing with the crises when they happen, and mitigating the consequences of crises.[17] Since these tasks require extensive expertise from different areas of the organization, the crisis management teams usually have a cross-functional representation of members. A typical crisis management team may consist of individuals from the organization's senior leadership, technical operations, public relations, customer service, and investor relations.

In other organizations, the crisis management team may be divided into three prongs, representing the policy team, the management team, and the liaison team.[18] The policy team is normally an ad hoc team chaired by the CEO with the purpose of providing guidelines for how the organization should handle a crisis. The core work of identifying issues and implementing plans to contain a crisis is done by the management team, whereas the liaison team consists of members from different departments or areas whose roles are to lend expertise to the crisis management team and keep their respective department informed of the crisis resolution strategy.

Cisco, the global manufacturer of computer networks, is an example of organizations with several types of crisis management teams. Cisco's crisis management teams are organized by hierarchical levels, functional roles, and geographical locations.[19] Setting the crisis management policy is the Corporate Crisis Management Team. This team focuses on the big picture of crisis management and associated impact of a crisis on Cisco's shareholder value. The Corporate Crisis Management Team takes charge when a crisis situation calls for mobilizing actions across different functions, or the crisis expands to more than one geographical boundary. Working on a tactical scale, Cisco's Safety and Security Team is responsible for the daily monitoring of events that may adversely affect the well-being of customers, and other stakeholders. The Theater Crisis Management Team responds geographically to crises that pose a threat to employees, property, customers, or critical business functions, such as severe weather or power outages. The Manufacturing Crisis Management Team was activated at Cisco in response to a fear of disruptions in their supply chain because of the global recession. The goal of this team is to keep operations moving with a contingency plan for managing collapses in the trucking and air freight industries. As observed, the composition and structure of Cisco's Manufacturing Crisis Management Team provides the organization with a systematic mechanism for responding to a supply chain crisis and allows the company to continue operations as the crisis is being managed.[20] Thus, at Cisco the crisis management teams serve as "anchorage points" prepared to mobilize a diverse group of organizational members, knowledge, and resources in crisis situations.[21]

Discount retailer Wal-Mart is another organization known for its crisis management teams. In an interview, Jason Jackson, director of the company's emergency management department, describes his crisis management team as a "big operation with a lot of moving parts."[22] Wal-Mart's crisis management team consists of 38 people organized into four subteams: preparedness, alarm operations, response and recovery operations, and business continuity. Each of the subteams at Wal-Mart is organized around competencies associated with the five overlapping phases of crisis management—signal detection, preparation and prevention, damage control and containment, business recovery, and reflection and learning.[23]

For example, the alarm operations subteam is in charge of signal detection through monitoring security systems, fire alarms, and the corporate emergency hotline. The preparedness subteam is charged with the implementation, validation, testing of plans, and training. This training enables learning both before and after crisis situations. The response and recovery subteam manages the damage control and containment of crisis situations through its emergency operations center. To put Wal-Mart back on the path of recovery after a crisis, the business continuity subteam develops systems for the continuity of operations and disaster recovery.

Jackson believes that the four subteams are effective because they are diverse in skill set, but very carefully integrated and have "a good understanding of each other's businesses." In addition, each team contributes their previous knowledge acquired to manage the crisis situation. The effectiveness of team composition and integration of Wal-Mart crisis management subteams was evident during Hurricane Katrina. In contrast to government agencies that did not react until days after Hurricane Katrina, Wal-Mart's crisis management team integrated with other functional areas and quickly brought people together to make decisions and set priorities for tasks. Six days before Hurricane Katrina hit the Gulf Coast of the United States, Wal-Mart began to monitor and prepare for the storm by activating a highly organized emergency preparation with the focus on employee life safety, continuity of operations, and community support.[24] As the predictions for Hurricane Katrina worsened, the crisis management team began diffusing information to store managers to prepare inventory and employees. Wal-Mart stores were closed during the storm, but after the storm the crisis management team immediately mobilized to assess damage, reopen stores, and help the local communities that had been impacted by Hurricane Katrina.

An advantage of preestablished crisis management teams is that they have the opportunity to prepare, identify, evaluate, and respond to ambiguous threats that may lead to a crisis. Teams that excel during this "window of recovery" have developed a set of routines where they practice their detection and response capabilities for potential crises.[25] It is during these times that crisis management teams learn to prevent problems, improve operations, and develop creative solutions. Also, while working to develop solutions for a potential crisis, the team learns how to work together. Thus, when the team is confronted with a real crisis, its stress levels are reduced because of it previous experiences. Two examples of teams highlighted in research that developed routines for preparing for high-pressured work situations include Morgan Stanley's information technology group and the employees of Boston's Logan International Airport.

Morgan Stanley's information technology group practices responding to crises, such as sophisticated hackers or natural disasters, and Logan airport employees participate in scheduled practice drills for responding to terrorist attacks.[26]

Crisis Management Teams as Improvisers

In some instances organizations do not have the chance to compose a formal crisis management team, or the crisis management team has to adapt their original plans because of the complexity of the crisis or unexpected changes. These types of situations demand that the team has a skill set to improvise. Team improvising may be needed because of uncertainty, ambiguity, or time pressures.[27] Improvising in a crisis situation involves teams responding to real-time experiences that inform their actions and prepare teams for the next set of actions that must be undertaken.[28] Improvising involves simultaneously creating and executing plans, resulting in a temporal convergence of these two activities.[29] Therefore, when improvising, there is little time for following a pathway of conventional sequencing for planning, formulating, or implementing a crisis management strategy. Instead, the team constantly adapts to the situation by rapidly processing information and drawing on the intuition and mental frames of each team member as events unfold. This evolves into a task of collectively figuring out what the group knows, but more important, how to go beyond its current mindset to create order out of the available resources.

Emerging from this process is an ad hoc team structure that is built upon existing resources, but the team structure is flexible, open to change, and able to reconfigure its actions depending on the needs of the response situation. This demands that members adapt their roles by adjusting who performs tasks and how tasks are performed.[30] There may be shortcuts for managing traditional bureaucratic processes so that time is not wasted. Likewise, when crisis management teams are improvising, one's status or official job responsibilities may become irrelevant. Instead, team members may take on new activities or issue orders to others, something they may not have the authority to do in a normal state. Consequently, the team is able to cope with environmental problems, uncertainty, or resource constraints by developing novel solutions or a skill set to realign their actions to be internally or externally coherent in response to the crisis situation.[31]

Wang and Xi in their research characterize this improvisation as a fine-tuning mindset of reacting, readjusting, and restructuring.[32] Through a case study based on archival sources, they use the example of China's severe acute respiratory syndrome (SARS) crisis management teams as an illustration of fine-tuning to improvise. Between late 2002 and mid-2003 more than 8,000 people became infected with SARS, resulting in almost 800 deaths, or nearly 10% of those infected. Within weeks SARS spread across various provinces in China and ultimately to 37 countries around the world. The outbreak was labeled a near pandemic by the World Health Organization (WHO). The Chinese government reacted by making leadership and structural changes. The health minister and mayor of Beijing resigned for mishandling the SARS epidemic. The traditional hierarchy for managing epidemics was swiftly augmented with the creation of a crisis management team. The mission of this ad hoc team was to control the spread of SARS through a coordinated national effort. Communication was an integral aspect of how the team improvised to combat SARS. The crisis management team regularly met to share their experiences, develop solutions for current problems, and plan for future scenarios.

When not meeting, the SARS crisis management team was readjusting its response by reallocating resources, building temporary infrastructures, such as SARS treatment hospitals, and educating the public to improve awareness of SARS. By June 2003, SARS was under control, but some local health departments were not as vigilant and cases began to fluctuate. In response, the crisis management team urgently organized the deployment of 15 inspection teams to supervise and reinforce the building of a national SARS prevention system. As observed from this case, the act of fine-tuning is an interaction of improvising to fit the team's work with the environment and adapting to situations and over time.

Another example of a team improvising in a crisis situation is the staff of Baltimore & Ohio Museum. In February 2003 the roof collapsed during a blizzard, damaging not only the structure of the museum, but also its collection of 22 locomotives, railroad cars, and small artifacts.[33] This event forced the museum to close for 21 months, and it resulted in an additional loss of approximately $1 million invested in preparation for the Fair of the Iron Horse event to celebrate the 175th anniversary of American railroading. The improvising for this crisis team began with staff members tearing up their job descriptions and reorganizing into three core departments: Administrative and Development, Facilities and Security, and Operations.[34]

Dropping formal titles allowed team members to see things differently and experiment with new behaviors for the purposes of adaptation and flexibility. New skills emerged from team members; for example, the museum's director of Development and Sponsorship Programs used the skills acquired from working in her father's CPA firm to manage insurance claims.[35] Similarly, companies working for Baltimore & Ohio Museum in rebuilding the museum became flexible and expanded their job roles. This was the case when the Operations Team was not allowed around the museum area while steel workers were cleaning the debris. Yet, there was a need for decision making on what rubble could be discarded and which needed to be saved for restoration. As a solution to the problem, curators trained steel workers on how to identify important museum artifacts. In addition, the improvising forced staff members to interact with different functional areas. For instance, before the collapse of the roof, curatorial staff and administrative staff had a tense relationship with defined organizational boundaries, but after the crisis the departments communicated freely with each other.

In sum, by improvising, the crisis situation pushed the different teams at Baltimore & Ohio Museum to really learn what the organization can do. Instead of focusing on just restoring the museum, the teams were able to reenvision its identity and value proposition.[36] With the support of the museum's board of directors, team members began to see the crisis as an opportunity to take the museum into a new direction. A tangible outcome of this process was a rebuilt museum with 6 new buildings and 72,475 additional square feet. This transformed Baltimore & Ohio Museum into a museum that could attract a bigger audience, and host large-scale events and more exhibits. Intangibly, the opportunity presented by the collapse of a roof and the need for improvising generated new or enhanced organizational skills, such as in-house train restoration, fundraising, and marketing.

Leading the Team in Crisis Situations

As discussed in the previous sections, crisis management teams can be formalized into the organizational structure or created through an improvisation process. No matter how the team is formed, there is a need for leadership to manage the team process. Grouping people together to work on resolving a crisis does not automatically make them a high-performing team. To achieve high performance, leaders create a team culture that is designed to produce output that is more than the sum of what individual team members would contribute.[37] This type of work environment demands both individual and mutual accountability, and through a balance of contributions, team members work together to prevent or respond to a crisis. Purposeful goals co-created by the team and its leadership guide the team process; these goals help to define performance metrics.

Goal-Oriented Charismatic Leadership

Most leaders of crisis management teams focus on how to resolve the crisis and bring the organization back to a normal state. The crisis management team's performance goals are integral to its purpose and define its mission. Thus, the thought of a potential crisis or an actual crisis creates compelling performance goals because of the sense of drama, urgency, or fear of failure associated with a crisis.[38] Often a charismatic leader will emerge during a crisis event and crystallize the team's performance goals.[39] Effective charismatic leadership not only involves the nuts and bolts of crisis management, but also includes communicating the parameters for action.[40] Through their visionary communication style, charismatic leaders are masterful at influencing and inspiring teams. Charismatic leaders motivate by utilizing persuasive and positive language to convey an expectation that the team will achieve its goals, with an emphasis on high productivity.[41] Through the articulation of ideological purpose and the impression of competence, charismatic leaders engage in actions that motivate team members to accomplish desired goals. Charismatic leaders excel at managing their team when they can not only communicate rationally and clearly, but also coordinate the team's activities to focus on solvable problems.[42]

The behavior of Bobby Jindal, Louisiana's governor, while preparing his state for Hurricane Gustav exemplified goal-focused, charismatic leadership of a crisis management team. A day before landfall of Hurricane Gustav, Governor Jindal called a meeting of Louisiana's high-level emergency command team.[43] He knew that he had less than a day to mobilize and did not want bureaucracy to prevent his team from developing solutions. To achieve this goal, Governor Jindal communicated a rhetoric that directed the emergency command to be solution focused and to support their proposed solutions with data. Often in his dialogue on the emergency command team's strategy, he used military terms and sporting analogies, such as "helo assets," which is a military phrase for helicopters, and described the evacuation of residents from different Louisiana parishes as the pregame.[44]

The strategic mindset infused with symbols permeated the emergency command team to focus on the issues and corresponding solutions. Also, Governor Jindal's leadership style succeeded in minimizing the impact of Hurricane Gustav because of his ability to align his symbolic rhetoric with a plan for mobilizing team members' actions. Consequently, the crisis team was able to prioritize problems. This type of leadership style was valued by the team, because in the uncertainty of a crisis situation, members tend to be more receptive to direction.

Creating the Team's Work Environment

In addition to inspiring and providing direction for the crisis management team, leadership should create a work environment of trust among members. When trust is the foundation of a crisis management team, members believe in the competence of each other and are open with their communication. Therefore, building a work environment of trust entails balancing the paradox of members supporting each other with their ability to confront each other when necessary.[45] Team members are willing to support each other when they believe leadership and the influence of others are grounded in expertise, information, or experience that is relevant to the crisis situation.

Furthermore, the crisis management team will value trust and constructive feedback when leadership fosters inclusiveness by inviting and appreciating the contribution of team members. Inclusive leadership behaviors facilitate team processes by enabling members to both share diverse viewpoints and value listening to others.[46] Leaders exert energy into inviting and appreciating the contributions of others, and especially focus on including the voices and perspective of team members that sometimes are unheard because of status or power differences. Leadership inclusiveness of team members is associated with psychologically safe work environments where team members feel free to take interpersonal risk, speak openly, and discuss failures.[47] In particular, the practice of speaking up encourages open dialogue and for the team to try new actions and reflect upon these actions.[48] This in turn builds a repertoire of shared experiences so that the team knows what works and what does not work. Leadership encourages this behavior by being accessible and personally involved.[49] When leadership is accessible, it increases the likelihood that team members will share questions, problems, suggestions, or observations. Also, leadership's personal involvement entails managing power within the team by empowering lower-status positions and minimizing the domineering influences of high-power individuals.

In some crisis incidents, inclusive leadership emerges more in a collective form in contrast to a command-and-control individual leadership style. This was the case when in 1972 a Uruguayan flight crashed in the Andes. Survivor Pedro Algorta describes the story of how he and 15 others held out for more than two months on a snowy mountain without food, water, or medical supplies as one of inclusive collective leadership:

> We were a group of peers figuring out how to get out from the mountains, and everyone contributed according to his capabilities at that time. In some cases, one of us would "step in to the void" and make significant contributions; sometimes it was participating in a discussion and offering a new point of view, or giving an inspiring insight, or doing some generous or heroic act, or making an insuperable funny remark or improving the way we did things in order to save energies or provide relief to the injured and ill.[50]

The experience of the survivors of the Andean air crash demonstrates the significance of a teamwork environment built upon trust and psychologically safe conditions. Survival became the team's work, and everyone felt equally comfortable contributing his or her talents and using the expertise of others.

Yet, teams that are too supportive can be problematic if members perceive preserving relationships as more important than being constructively critical. This can result in groupthink or blind spots, and the team may begin to make decisions that are based more on conforming than resolving the crisis situation. To prevent distorted decision making, leaders can create a team climate that is not too dependent on hierarchy and subordination.[51] This may result in a "fuzzy" approach to decision making, but during a crisis the team environment should allow for members to cope with ambiguous information flows.[52] Thus, the team's experts can be used to deal with the demands of the crisis event. However, the use of these experts is not for reinforcing flawed beliefs held by members relating to invulnerabilities of the organization's systems, strategies, and structure. Instead, the knowledge of experts should be pooled together with information from other team members to create an interconnected mental frame for resolving the crisis.[53] It is therefore acceptable behavior for team members to monitor each other's decisions and for members to offer suggestions for coordination of work efforts and strategies for improving the team's performance.

Leaders should reward team members for adopting an inquiry approach to reflections, the decision-making process, and actions related to the crisis situation. President John F. Kennedy's behavior during the Cuban Missile Crisis is an illustration of leadership facilitating an inquiry approach to managing his cabinet team.[54] After the problems with the Bay of Pigs invasion, Kennedy revised the foreign policy decision-making process for his cabinet to include inquiry. During discussion relating to the Cuban Missile Crisis, cabinet members were encouraged to think objectively and critically so that their thoughts were not biased by a specific area of expertise or rank. Also, specific team members were responsible for acting as fact-finding probes.[55]

Their task included asking questions, weighing the pros and cons of each option, finding points of contention, and uncovering vulnerabilities. The information from fact finding was used as the basis for subteams to analyze different scenarios and formulate a strategy for each. The Kennedy cabinet's inquiry approach resulted in a methodically crafted response for blockade and a peaceful end to the Cuban Missile Crisis.

Leading the Team Culture

Similar to the work environment of trust and inclusion, a crisis management team's culture shapes its behavior. In the context of crisis management teams, culture is the shared basic assumption that teams learn as they solve problems by working together and adapting to external pressures.[56] Through their interactions, a crisis management team's culture creates norms for how it gets work done, such as through distribution of power, communication patterns, orientation to stakeholders, and working styles. In crisis situations, these cultural norms help the team make sense and respond to its environment by providing a shared approach for collective action.

Team cultures are created and transformed when leaders put into practice social processes to achieve their vision by influencing the team's shared ideologies of beliefs, norms, and values.[57] During a crisis, this entails leaders crafting a set of ideas that reduce uncertainties, can be comprehended, and convince team members to act upon them. Leadership's administrative actions create the team culture by symbolically communicating, celebrating, and embodying the vision with the goal of winning followers to share in the vision. However, cultural leadership in a crisis situation is more than just persuading team members; it is also the ability to influence how the team collectively thinks and acts. Thus, an essential skill of leading the team culture during the crisis is the ability to create a radical vision that the team can rally around and use as a springboard for action.

Flight director and leader of space shuttle Apollo 13, Eugene Krantz, is an example of cultural leadership enacting a radical vision in a crisis situation. When Apollo 13's service module exploded, Krantz and his "Tiger Team," despite negative odds, safely led the team back to Earth. Krantz built a team culture around the norms of optimism, and failure was not an option. Instead, he encouraged the team members to focus on keeping their cool and solving the problem by focusing on what was working.[58] Trust based on expertise and preparation supported the cultural norms that Krantz infused throughout the Tiger Team. The team consisted of 20 different types of specialists and experienced engineers. Yet, team members had a strong sense of camaraderie and a focus on collective actions. To reinforce the importance of team competence and cohesiveness during each phase of the crisis situation, Krantz institutionalized routines into the culture. Krantz put the team through flight simulations so that they could make correct decisions under time pressures. To facilitate communication, team members were co-located by functional expertise and not by hierarchical levels or employment status. In addition, Krantz organized the flight teams into sports leagues so they could learn to compete as a team. Krantz's actions focused on building a collaborative culture that centered upon an ideology of a positive frame of mind to work through problems and develop solutions in a time-pressured, emergency environment. Supporting Apollo 13's cultural ideology were values such as "not surrendering to failure," through a sense of hope that required the team to reframe the problems in terms of potential solution, and enabling resourcefulness by encouraging the creative use of talents, supplies, and equipment.[59]

As observed from Krantz's leadership of the flight team that safely directed space shuttle Apollo 13 back to Earth, leading the team process in crisis situations also can entail creating a culture of high reliability. A high-reliability culture emphasizes the safety of stakeholders and reliability in the decision-making process as the dominant output value by fostering mindfulness.[60] This type of team culture is appropriate when management of the unexpected is needed to prevent accidents or minimize the consequences of accidents under difficult situations. Typically, high-reliability teams function in hazardous, fast-paced, technologically complex work environments that are error-free for long periods of time, but are designed to manage unexpected events in places such as nuclear power plants, fire-fighting units, and emergency medical units of hospitals. However, crisis management teams share similarities to teams working in high-reliability organizations and can learn from how their cultural norms of mindfulness guide behavior in challenging situations. The core cultural norm of teams operating in high-reliability organizations is a mindfulness of five principles: (1) preoccupation with failure, (2) reluctance to simplify interpretations, (3) sensitivity to operations, (4) resilience capabilities, and (5) deference to expertise.[61] The mindfulness of these five principles provides teams with a compass for perceiving, thinking, and feeling in relation to problems, which transforms into the team's practices and actions. In addition, mindfulness induces awareness, and the crisis management team will make fewer assumptions and instead scan the environment to make sense of the crisis.[62]

Integrating these five principles into the culture of a crisis management team leads to members knowing that errors are unacceptable. Thus, the team discusses the potential for errors and looks for problematic signals. Often these practices demand that the team is in a constant state of unease by anticipating worst-case scenarios and being prepared to deal with these situations. A team culture fixated with failures is supported by an infrastructure that has systems for reporting when people make a mistake, but is also a just culture that does not assign blame when a problem occurs.[63] Team members exert their energies into adapting to the challenges brought to their attention by the problem and converting the lessons learned into reconfiguring their routines as a response strategy.

Likewise, the cultural norms of high-reliability teams place value on members' ability to understand the complexity of crisis situations. Leadership encourages the team to create a complex and detailed picture of the crisis situation for analysis and pays close attention to the action on the front line, because this is usually the starting point for a crisis. Team members do not simplify the problems they confront. They confront the problems by looking for a range of explanations that may explain a crisis and how to resolve it. This can involve a diversity of tasks, such as reverse engineering solutions, cause-effect analysis, or system mapping to purposely introduce complexity. An attention to system complexity also encompasses the team's ability to comprehend the relationship between everyday operations and how actions on the front line affect the crisis situation.

Somewhat similar to the inclusive leadership of crisis teams discussed earlier in this chapter, a high-reliability culture cultivates a work environment that defers to expertise of the person with the most knowledge relevant to the issue they are confronting.[64] By deference to expertise, the team acknowledges that the information critical to handling the crisis may not always come from the most experienced or highest-ranking person. Team members accept the notion that solutions for managing a crisis can come when leadership is shifted to people who currently have a solution to the problem at hand. So members at all levels of the team search for cues to manage the crisis and are comfortable sharing what they discern with others. When unexpected events transpire, information freely migrates from and to different people on the team. Team flexibility and deference to expertise complement each other through a flattened hierarchal structure and a variety of perspectives contributed by members. This is so that the information needed can be available to individuals responsible for decision making.[65]

A hallmark of a high-reliability team's culture is a norm for resilience—the ability to bounce back from the crisis by continuing operations under extreme circumstances and despite setbacks. For a crisis team to embody a norm of resilience, it possesses a mindset that the team will positively adjust to adversity and maintain focus on its operational goal and in the midst of strain.[66] Associated with the mindset of resilience is the team's dynamic capacity to adequately retain, deploy, multiply, and reconfigure its resources for adapting to the crisis.[67] A core pillar supporting resilient teams is their relationships. Relationships not only contribute to the team's resourcefulness, but also provide social, emotional, and moral support. Thus, through leveraging resources and relationships, the team's culture reinforces a cyclical process of relying upon past learning and fostering future learning to strengthen its capacity for crisis recovery (Figure 5.1).[68]

The 2009 landing of US Airways flight 1549 illustrates the power of embracing the principles of high-reliability teams. Shortly after takeoff, flight 1549 left New York's LaGuardia Airport headed for Charlotte, North Carolina. Within minutes the plane, under the direction of Captain Chesley "Sully" Sullenberger, struck a flock of birds, debilitating the plane's two engines. Immediately, Captain Sullenberger had to make a series of potentially life or death decisions. He opted to land the plane on the Hudson River rather than attempt to make it back to the airport. With the words "brace for impact because we're going down," Captain Sullenberger safely landed the jet in the Hudson River, where the plane stayed afloat long enough for all 155 passengers to be rescued from the water. The pilot's ability to make quick decisions under pressure and execute his plan resulted from both his leadership and a supporting crew that had trained for potential crashes.

Over the life of his 40-year career, Captain Sullenberger spent hours preparing for flight landings, such as the one on the Hudson River. Captain Sullenberger's career experience included commercial and military piloting. During his career, he had worked as a flight instructor, accident investigator, and safety chairman of the Air Line Pilot Association, and he wrote a paper

Figure 5.1   Characteristics of high-reliability teams.

on error-inducing contexts in information. Captain Sullenberger's career experiences suggest expertise in his trade and a preoccupation with preventing or developing solutions for system failures.

Captain Sullenbeger was not alone when he safely landed the plane and saved all of its passengers. He had a supporting flight crew that was trained to handle emergency landings. To prepare for crisis situations, air crew training entails the sophisticated use of complex simulations and exposure to research into past accidents, which revealed mistakes that cost lives or strategies that save lives.[69] Also, in some training sessions both pilots and flight attendants work together on emergency scenarios so that the entire crew has the experience of learning how to coordinate their efforts, develop sensitivity to each other's operations, and communicate in crisis situations.

However, the successful mobilization of the flight crew was not only a function of training, but also Captain Sullenberger's ability to create a climate of hope and calmness during the landing.[70] So that Captain Sullenberger could concentrate on the crisis, he relied upon other experts, such as the ferry workers, crew, passengers, and ground control staff. Each of these individuals contributed his or her skills to the safe landing of US Airways flight 1549. Moreover, as a team, the flight crew exemplified a norm of resilience by swiftly formulating a plan that channeled their previously acquired knowledge to address the problem at hand and bring and adjust its operational goals for an emergency landing.

Transcending Outside the Team

For the crew of US Airways flight 1549, the teamwork to safely land the airplane necessitated balancing internal processes with the capability to collaborate with people who are external to the team. Most crises are not isolated incidents, and the path to recovery may involve coordinating the team's work with external partners. Also, there is a need for the crisis team to consider the impact of their actions on external stakeholders, such as internal clients, customers, suppliers, competitors, and innocent bystanders. Crisis management teams that become too insular in their thoughts and actions run the risk of losing sight of the big picture and narrowly focusing on what members perceive as the essentials to prevent or resolve the crisis. This shuts out the perspectives, resources, and needs of other stakeholders that may be pertinent to the crisis management process.

For instance, Paul Levy, former executive director of the Massachusetts Water Resource Authority, attributes the 1976 Nut Island disaster to a team that did not integrate its processes with external stakeholders.[71] Levy describes the team responsible for managing the wastewater treatment plant at Nut Island as an extraordinary, hardworking team that was highly dedicated to their job. Team membership was homogeneous because of hiring practices and low levels of turnover. Over time the team evolved into a tight-knit group whose closeness was enhanced by management's neglect. So the team developed an us-against-the-world mentality. It felt no need to look outwardly for perspectives and practices. To avoid outsiders and especially management, the team formed its own operating rules and a distorted picture of reality. Because of limited contact with external stakeholders, the team lacked current knowledge of scientific practices for water treatment, felt free to engage in unorthodox approaches to plant operations, and avoided replacing new plant equipment because of the need for management's approval. The Nut Island team's parochial practices were a factor in a series of plant failures that culminated in a massive four-day discharge of untreated sewage into the Boston Harbor.

As outlined in the case study of the Nut Island team, preventing and managing a crisis calls for the team members to recognize and act upon the complex interactions of both its internal processes and external dynamics by scanning and monitoring environmental activities. Complementary to environmental scanning is the crisis management team's ability to extend their outreach to stakeholders both inside and outside the organization by taking into account the identities and interests as they chart a course for preparing for or resolving a crisis. By doing this, team members think about the implications of their actions as they relate to key external stakeholders. Each external stakeholder group may have a unique set of issues, and it is the responsibility of the team to create a coherent, interrelated strategy for addressing the crisis that takes into account external stakeholders. By building and nurturing these relationships across boundaries, externally oriented teams form a dense web of networks with contacts inside and outside the team to reach political, informational, and task-specific structures.[72]

CEO Robert Eckert's leadership of Mattel's upper management team during the recall of toys containing lead that were manufactured in China highlights the importance of integrating the internal team processes while working with external stakeholders. Mattel had a crisis prevention system before the toy recall crisis, and in preparation for a crisis, organizational members engaged in scenario planning. Eckert believes the planning was a valuable asset for the team and gave the company a head start. During the crisis, everyone on the team had a crisis communications notebook that outlined responsibilities for crisis situations, and the team met daily to plan and implement a strategy for responding to the crisis. Yet, a large proportion of the team's work involved communicating and working with external stakeholders. For instance, the team had to develop a protocol for retailers for removing toys from the shelves and accepting returns. Constant communication with consumers was necessary through Mattel's Web site, telephone lines, and the media. In addition, the team had to work with regulators, such as the Consumer Product Safety Commission, and suppliers to determine the source of the lead in the toys. Mattel even enlisted an endorsement from an industry expert, which validated its handling of the crisis situation.

Much of the research on externally oriented teams is in the context of product development teams, but the findings can be applicable to crisis management teams because both types of teams operate in a high-paced, complex environment with a need for information to flow across boundaries.[73] Similar to other types of teams, crisis management teams are interdependent with their environment and need to receive input from and provide output to the environment.[74] Through this loop of interacting with the environment, teams can justify their behaviors to the external environment and seek feedback on how they should adapt their actions in response to external demands.

The team's leadership serves as a facilitator for balancing the efforts of the team's internal and external activities. Formally or informally, leadership may engage in different roles or delegate a role to team members for interacting with the external environment to manage a crisis.[75] For example, the team's ambassador may be responsible for buffering information the team shares and representing it to external stakeholders. This person also may be responsible for controlling the communication flow between the team and outsiders, including informing external stakeholders of the team's intentional strategy, whereas the team's scout may take on the task of scanning the environment for information and resources. Another role that leadership may emphasize is that of prober, by requiring team members to interact with outsiders to diagnose the root cause of a crisis or experiment with solutions.

Similar to the process of a product development team developing a new innovation, through these different roles, the crisis management team can make sense of its external environment by executing a process of explore, exploit, and export.[76] During exploring, the scouts in the team make sense of their environment through the acquisition of knowledge. Exploiting involves the team figuring out how to interpret the information obtained from environmental cues and external relationships for its advantage. During exportation of this external information, knowledge is diffused throughout the team for use. The team's interactions with the external environment allow for the detection and correction of error.[77] Simultaneously, the team is learning by building, supplementing, and incorporating the newly acquired knowledge into its crisis management process.

In summary, successfully leading in crisis situations calls for actions that can courageously make sense out of chaos to develop extraordinary teams. This results when leaders are intentional about team membership and create a team environment where members are empowered to improvise if the crisis situation requires agility, adaptation, or flexibility. Moreover, leading a crisis team entails formulating a shared goal on which a team can concentrate its efforts. This common goal helps the team focus its actions despite the chaos and confusion that may be a by-product of the crisis.

However, leading a team in a crisis situation involves more than creating and communicating goals. It is important for leadership to create a work environment for the team that is psychologically safe, exhibits a climate of trust, and is inclusive of diverse viewpoints. Furthermore, research suggests leadership's actions should not only embody and instill in the team a system of norms for valuing the principles of high-reliability organizing, but also facilitate a mechanism for the team to build alliances with external stakeholders and look outward for resources and information. Finally, a dominant theme throughout this chapter is the significance that leadership places on team learning throughout the management of the crisis. By emphasizing a team learning orientation, the leadership fosters both reactive and reflective behavior for resolving a crisis (Figure 5.2).

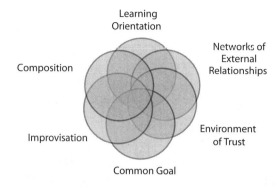

Figure 5.2   Resources for managing crisis teams.

From Theory to Practice

High-performance teams in a crisis situation are a function of leadership's ability to bring together individuals for synergistic collective action, but leadership should also acknowledge that in some cases, because of the urgent nature of a crisis and potential for negative outcomes, teams may be ad hoc and will need to improvise. No matter if you are leading a formalized crisis management team or an ad hoc team, leadership entails creating a work climate where team members concentrate on internal processes, but seek feedback and respond to their external environment. Furthermore, leadership of a crisis management team involves enabling the team to balance the contradictory demands to have a systematic approach to preparing or resolving a crisis with the mindset to be adaptable. The following points summarize ways in which leadership can create the right setting for creating a competent crisis management team (Figures 5.3 to 5.6).

■ Think strategically about the composition of the crisis management team. Team members with prior knowledge bring their familiarity to the problem-solving process, whereas diverse teams have the potential to generate better ideas because of their different backgrounds. A diversity of membership helps the team to identify blind spots and make connections for managing a crisis that may not have been realized if team members shared similar expertise or experiences. However, the advantages of a diverse team can only be realized if the leadership fosters inclusiveness by listening and valuing the contributions of each member. Team members should feel safe when they share ideas and willingly accept constructive feedback.

In a crisis, why shouldn't we just take the first people who volunteer to help?	When the crisis team is formed, what is the most important first step?
Think strategically about the composition of the crisis management team. Team members with prior knowledge bring their familiarity to the problem-solving process. Whereas, diverse teams have the potential to generate better ideas because of their different backgrounds. A diversity of membership helps the team to identify blind spots and make connections for managing a crisis that may not have been realized if team members shared similar expertise or experiences. However, the advantages of a divers team can only be realized if the leadership fosters inclusiveness by listening and valuing the contributions of each member. Team members should feel safe when they share ideas and willingly accept constructive feedback.	From the onset of bringing the team together, identify and communicate its purpose. This will guide the team actions and help with the establishment of explicit goals and performance metrics. Coupled with the team purpose, members should be mutually accountable to each other. The notion of mutual accontability reinforces to members that team as a whole is responsible for producing results.

Figure 5.3   Leader's hot seat.

- From the onset of bringing the team together, identify and communicate its purpose. This will guide the team's actions and help with the establishment of explicit goals and performance metrics. Coupled with the team purpose, members should be mutually accountable to each other. The notion of mutual accountability reinforces to members that the team as a whole is responsible for producing results.

- Empower the team with the resources needed to improvise and develop an infrastructure that minimizes the red tape associated with bureaucracies. Improvisation calls for flexibility so that team members can react to the crisis situation, and when needed readjust their roles and restructure processes. The team's ability to improvise can generate innovative solutions and serve as a springboard of new knowledge for managing crisis situations.

- Create a team culture that adopts the principles of high-reliability organizing. That is, even before a crisis, the team becomes mindful of organizational vulnerabilities and members are supported for reporting errors and crisis signals. Team members fixate their attention on the organization's operations and how it can be resilient in the midst of a crisis. Likewise, it should be a norm for team members to be reluctant to simplify the cause or effects associated with a crisis. Instead, team members ask the appropriate questions,

Why is the ability to improvise important for a crisis management team?	What sort of culture is most conducive to effective crisis management?
A team's ability to improvise can generate innovative solutions and serve as a springboard of new knowledge for managing crisis situations. Improvisation calls for flexibility so that team members can react to the crisis situation and when needed readjust their roles and restructure processes. Yet, in order to improvise, teams must be able to work within a structure that minimizes the red tape associated with bureaucracies.	Create a team culture that adopts the principles of high-reliability organizing. That is, even before crisis, the team becomes mindful of organizational vulnerabilities and members are supported for repoting errors and crisis signals. Team members fixate their attention on the organization's operations, and how it can be resilient in the midst of a crisis. Likewise, it should be a norm for team members to be reluctant to simplify the cause or effects associated with a crisis. Instead, team members ask the appropriate questions, seek out the necessary information or experts, and brainstorm scenarios for managing the crisis.

Figure 5.4   Leader's hot seat.

seek out the necessary information or experts, and brainstorm scenarios for managing the crisis.

■ Do not allow the team to become insular or embrace a parochial perspective for managing the crisis. Build networks of external relationships that can be a source of information and relationships. Encourage team members to scan the external environment for ideas and to seek feedback from external stakeholders on its performance. Consider assigning different roles, such as the ambassador to externally represent the team, or the exploiter to obtain outside information and transform it to use for the team.

■ Play a critical role in instilling a learning orientation in the team throughout the crisis management process. Team members should be encouraged to share their skills with the team and seek out new knowledge. However, a team's learning orientation goes beyond acquiring knowledge. It must be diffused throughout the team and evaluated for usefulness, and then the relevant aspects of the obtained knowledge should be applied to managing the crisis. Also, sometimes in a crisis situation, learning can entail unlearning bad habits or abandoning old ideas so that the team is in the position to discover its inadequacies.[78] Whether learning or unlearning, ultimately the team develops a memory of its learnings to prevent or use in subsequent crises.

Can team members become too cohesive?

Do not allow the team to become insular or embrace a parochial perspective for managing the crisis. Build networks of information and relationships. Encourage team members to scan the external environment for ideas and to seek feedback from external stakeholders on its performance. Consider assigning different roles such as the ambassador to externally represent the team, or the exploiter to obtain outside information and transform it to use for the team.

How do we foster reflective behavior in solving a crisis?

Leaders should play a critical role in instilling a learning orientation in the team throughout the crisis management process. Team members should be encouraged to share their skills with the team and seek out new knowledge. However, a team's learning orientation goes beyond acquiring knowledge. It must be diffused throughout the team and evaluated for usefulness, then the relevant aspects of the obtained knowledge should be applied to managing the crisis. Also, in some crises learning can entail unlearning bad habits or abandoning old ideas so that the team is in the position to discover their inadequacies. Whether learning unlearning, ultimately the teams develop a memory of its learning to prevent or use in subsequent crises.

Figure 5.5   Leader's hot seat.

Figure 5.6   Leadership Links 5.1

- Developing Teams That Thrive in Tough Times
  http://www.fvbizsolutions.com/images/High_Performance_Teams.pdf
- Teams in High Reliability Organizations
  http://www.high-reliability.org/
- Crisis Management Team Resources
  http://resources.bnet.com/topic/crisis+management+team.html
- Center for Creative Leadership, Leading Effectively Podcast on Improvisation During a Crisis
  http://www.ccl.org/leadership/podcast/transcriptWhenPlansFail nsFail.aspx

Endnotes

1. Katzenbach & Smith, *The wisdom of teams.*
2. Castka et al., Factors affecting successful implementation of high performance teams, 123–134.
3. Adair, *Effective team building.*

4. Katzenbach & Smith, The discipline of teams, 111–120.

5. Marks, Mathieu, & Zaccaro, A temporarily based framework and taxonomy of team processes, 356–376.

6. Hill, *Managing your team*.

7. Katzenbach & Smith, *The wisdom of teams*.

8. Hill, *Managing your team*.

9. Scholtes, Joiner, & Steibel, *The team handbook*.

10. Braden et al., Crisis—A leadership opportunity.

11. King, Crisis management and team effectiveness, 235–249.

12. Hmelo, Nagarajan, & Day, Effects of high and low prior knowledge on construction of a joint problem space, 36–56.

13. Larson, Foster-Fishman, & Keys, Information sharing in decision-making groups, 446–461.

14. King, Crisis management and team effectiveness, 235–249.

15. Mohammed & Brad, Team mental models in a team knowledge framework, 89–106.

16. Coombs, *Ongoing crisis communication*.

17. Littlejohn, *Crisis management*.

18. Ibid.

19. Cisco, Health & safety crisis management.

20. Darling, Seriston, & Gabrielson, Anatomy of crisis management, 343–360.

21. Gand, Acquier, & Szpirglas, Understanding organizational crisis management processes.

22. Wal-Mart.

23. Pearson & Clair, Reframing crisis management, 59–76.

24. Suburban Emergency Management Project. Wal-Mart way in disaster preparedness/response.

25. Roberto, Bohmer, & Edmondson, Facing ambiguous threats, 106–113, 157.

26. Ibid.

27. Roux, Dufort, & Vidaillet, The difficulties of improvising in a crisis situation, 86–115.

28. Miner, Bassoff, & Moorman, Organizational improvisation and learning, 304–337.

29. Chelariu, Jonhston, & Young, Learning to improvise, improvising to learn, 141–147.

30. Webb, Role improvising during crisis situations, 47–61.

31. Weick, The collapse of sensemaking in organizations, 628–652.

32. Wang & Xi, Preparing for future uncertainty, 81–96.

33. Baltimore & Ohio Museum.

34. William Davidson Institute.

35. Marlys et al., Learning through rare events.

36. Ibid.

37. Katzenbach & Smith, The discipline of teams, 111–120.

38. Katzenbach & Smith, Why teams matter, 3–27.

39. King, Crisis management and team effectiveness, 235–249.

40. Darling, Seristo, & Gabrielson, Anatomy of crisis management, 343–360.

41. Hackman & Johnson, *Leadership*.

42. Devitt & Borodzicz, Interwoven leadership, 208–216.

43. Scott, Jindal takes full command in crisis.
44. Whoriskey, Jindal presents a face of calm during the storm, A6.
45. Hill, *Managing your team.*
46. Nembhard & Edmonson, Making it safe, 941–966.
47. Edmonson, Psychological safety and learning behavior in work teams, 350–383.
48. Edmonson, Speaking up in the operating room, 1420–1452.
49. Edmonson, Managing the risk of learning.
50. Algorta, Notes from a survivor of the Andean air crash.
51. Darling, Seristo, & Gabrielson, Anatomy of crisis management, 343–360.
52. Smith, Crisis management teams, 61–78.
53. Mohammed & Dumville, Team mental models in a team knowledge framework, 89–106.
54. Garvin & Roberto, What you don't know about making decisions, 108–116.
55. Berry, How did they do it? 407–417.
56. Hill, *Managing your team.*
57. Trice & Beyer, *The culture of work organizations.*
58. Useem, The leadership moment.
59. Glynn & Dutton, The generative dynamics of positive organizing.
60. Weick & Sutcliffe, *Managing the unexpected.*
61. Ibid.
62. Naevestad, Mapping research on culture and safety in high risk organizations, 127–136.
63. Reason, Achieving a safe culture, 293–306.
64. The Lewin Group, Becoming a high reliability organization.
65. Roberts, Stout, & Halpern, Decision dynamics in two high reliability military organizations, 614–624.
66. Bunderson & Sutcliffe, Comparing alternative conceptualizations of functional diversity in management teams, 875–893.
67. Gittell et al., Relationships, layoffs, and organizational resilience, 300–329.
68. Sutcliffe & Vogus, Organizing for resilience, 94–110.
69. McCartney, Crash courses for the crew, D1, D8.
70. Rego, Crisis leadership lessons from the "Miracle on the Hudson."
71. Levy, The Nut Island effect, 5–12.
72. Ancona, Backman, & Bresman, X-teams.
73. Mylle, Team effectiveness and boundary management, 592–598.
74. Choi, External activities and team effectiveness, 181–208.
75. Mylle Team effectiveness and boundary management, 592–598; Ancona, Outward bound, 334–365.
76. Ancona, Backman, & Bresman, X-teams.
77. Wang, Developing organizational learning capacity in crisis management, 425–445.
78. Ibid.

ORGANIZATIONAL CAPABILITIES

Chapter 6

Organizational Trust Amid Crisis

By this point in the book it should be abundantly clear that a central part of what we consider to be crisis leadership is the ability to perceive and manifest the opportunity in crisis situations (we discuss the details of how that happens in Chapter 9). After all, crises can lead to either positive or negative organizational outcomes, and we believe that it is in part the actions of the leader that can tip the scale one way or the other.[1] In previous chapters we discussed, for example, the individual leadership capabilities, including critical competencies (Chapter 3), approach to decision making (Chapter 4), and responsibilities in leading a team (Chapter 5) during crisis situations. In this chapter we turn to an important organizational capability that allows leadership to flourish during times of crisis: trust. More specifically, we refer to an organization's capability to create and sustain trusting relationships with key stakeholders. We maintain that the firms that do this well are better able to address crises when they occur.

Perhaps no other crisis conjures up the centrality of trust more than the now infamous case of the Johnson & Johnson (J&J) Tylenol crisis. The pharmaceutical giant has built a reputation of being one of the most trusted brands in the world. Some of their products (e.g., medical devices and prescription medications) have the potential to save lives, while others (e.g., baby care products) touch the most sacred members of our society. What has continuously set J&J apart from competitors is its commitment first to the people who use its products, then to the company's employees, to the communities in which the firm operates, and finally to their stockholders. The firm's credo was developed by

131

its chairman and member of the company's founding family, Robert Wood Johnson, while J&J was still a privately owned entity in 1943:

JOHNSON & JOHNSON CREDO

We believe our first responsibility is to the doctors, nurses, and patients,
to mothers and fathers and all others who use our products and services.
In meeting their needs, everything we do must be of high quality.
We must constantly strive to reduce our costs
in order to maintain reasonable prices.
Customers' orders must be serviced promptly and accurately.
Our suppliers and distributors must have an opportunity
to make a fair profit.
We are responsible to our employees,
the men and women who work with us throughout the world.
Everyone must be considered as an individual.
We must respect their dignity and recognize their merit.
They must have a sense of security in their jobs.
Compensation must be fair and adequate,
and working conditions clean, orderly and safe.
We must be mindful of ways to help our employees fulfill
their family responsibilities.
Employees must feel free to make suggestions and complaints.
There must be equal opportunity for employment, development
and advancement for those qualified.
We must provide competent management,
and their actions must be just and ethical.
We are responsible to the communities in which we live and work
and to the world community as well.
We must be good citizens—support good works and charities
and bear our fair share of taxes.
We must encourage civic improvements and better health and education.
We must maintain in good order
the property we are privileged to use,
protecting the environment and natural resources.
Our final responsibility is to our stockholders.
Business must make a sound profit.
We must experiment with new ideas.
Research must be carried on, innovative programs developed
and mistakes paid for.

New equipment must be purchased, new facilities provided
and new products launched.
Reserves must be created to provide for adverse times.
When we operate according to these principles,
the stockholders should realize a fair return.

Although the credo does not specifically mention trust, the sense that trust is at the very core of J&J's operating philosophy is evident by the way it refers to the company's responsibilities to people, and commitment to such ideals as fairness, dignity, openness, and citizenship. We will highlight the way that trust pervades this credo in more detail as we proceed with the chapter.

In the early 1980s J&J was manufacturing and selling one of the most successful over-the-counter pain relievers ever, Tylenol. Although J&J had a bevy of products, Tylenol alone was responsible for 19% of corporate profits during the first three quarters of 1982, accounted for 33% of J&J's year-to-year profit growth, and held a remarkable 37% market share.[2] In 1982, the successful Tylenol run almost came to a screeching halt, and along with it J&J's long-standing reputation of trustworthiness. Someone had tampered with bottles of Tylenol extra-strength capsules and replaced the original Tylenol capsules with cyanide-laced capsules. The packages were resealed and distributed to stores and pharmacies in the Chicago area. When the tampered products were purchased and used, seven consumers died from the poisoning and J&J was immediately thrown into crisis management mode. At the time, the story of the product tampering received more media coverage than any other news event with the exception of the assassination of President John F. Kennedy.[3]

There were a number of possible avenues for handling the crisis, but guided at least in part by the culture and values of the firm, J&J's then chairman James Burke responded in such a way that consumer trust in the firm and in the product was ultimately reestablished. Burke formed a crisis response strategy team and instructed that their handling of the crisis should consider the protection of people first, and saving the product second. As a first order of business J&J used the media to order a national withdrawal of every Tylenol package and to instruct consumers all over the country to immediately stop using the Tylenol product, despite the considerable revenue loss that would come with such a mandate.[4] In addition, the company established multiple communication channels to provide information and answer questions about the crisis. Beyond the effective crisis communications, however, J&J developed a first-of-its-kind triple-seal, tamper-resistant packaging that would prevent similar incidences from occurring in the future. In the end, J&J pulled off an incredible feat: It restored public trust in its brand despite a set of circumstances that would have severely strained another firm. The J&J Tylenol crisis continues to be touted as the exemplar case in crisis handling and communications. But more important for our purposes, the case highlights the strong connection between crisis and trust.

What Is Trust?

On the surface, the notion of trust seems a simple construct. It is one of the first lessons in childhood and it factors into every stage and phase of life. We either trust a person or we do not. We are either trustworthy or we are not. Simple! At its most basic level, trust represents our ability or willingness to depend on someone else. When we trust others, we feel confident and secure in another's actions to the extent that those actions relate to or affect us. People talk casually but confidently about trust being the foundation of any meaningful relationship—personal or professional. They judge people and their effectiveness in work and in life on how trustworthy they are. And the assumptions they hold about trust are relatively universal. For example, it is not uncommon to hear people say the following: "Trust takes a long time to develop, but can be broken in an instant" or "trust has to be earned."

In reality, the feelings, emotions, and experiences of trust suggest that it is a complex phenomenon, as anyone who has experienced a betrayal can probably attest. As a construct, trust has been the study of sociologists, psychologists, organizational theorists, economists, theologians, sociobiologists, historians, and more.[5] For many years, the Russell Sage Foundation, an organization devoted to research in the social sciences, committed considerable funds for research on the topic of trust. The foundation's Series on Trust produced a host of books on the topic in an effort to examine the conceptual and empirical claims that trust and trustworthiness are central concepts in establishing and maintaining cooperative behavior.[6] One product from the series is an ethnographic book by Gambetta and Hamill, who studied taxi drivers in Belfast and New York City in an effort to identify the strategies drivers employ to establish a potential customer's trustworthiness. The selection of taxi drivers for studying trust in a work context may be a surprising one, but one that is relevant nonetheless, as taxi drivers are faced with split-second decisions regarding whether a passenger is safe to pick up. Although the book did not explicitly address the connection between trust and crisis, it became clear to the authors that crisis events in one's environment (e.g., the terrorist attacks on 9/11) can have tremendous influence on how workers (in this case taxi drivers) experience and go about their jobs.

As one can imagine, defining trust in a way that resonates similarly with everyone's unique perspective of trust is a challenge. Moreover, distinguishing *trust* from related terms, such as *dependability, cooperation, familiarity,* or *confidence,* has been difficult.[7] Yet, there are several features of trust that appear to be consistent across unique definitions of the term. In his review of the literature, and in his own research, Mishra uncovered four distinct dimensions or components of trust: competence, openness, concern, and reliability.[8]

Competence is an essential component of trust and particularly so in the context of work or organizational life. As Gabarro argues, at the base of any work relationship is a degree of trust in one's competence.[9] In the modern organization, work is a highly interdependent function, and each one of us depends to some extent on others to fulfill our role in meeting the objectives of the organization. The ability to do that requires that people are competent at what they do and that others have confidence in their competence. Competence-based trust involves respecting the knowledge, skills, abilities, and judgments of others.[10] The behavioral display of that respect, however, is what truly demonstrates a willingness or capacity to trust in the capabilities of others. In fact, people's sense of value is often closely tied to their sense of competence in their work or job. The best leaders recognize this and create opportunities to enhance a sense of competence in their employees, thereby creating an overall organizational environment characterized by *competence trust*. These organizations are then empowered with people who value learning, feel empowered to take risks, and are inclined to think creatively with respect to problem solving. Recall that these are some of the same critical competencies associated with crisis leadership, as we described in Chapter 3.

The significance of competence-based trust is particularly relevant during times of crisis. Under circumstances of uncertainty, time pressure, novelty, and severe consequences, it is imperative that employees trust their leaders to make competent decisions in an effort to resolve the crisis. Likewise, consumers and stockholders expect that firm leaders will competently resolve crises so that they are either not affected or minimally affected in the process. People are vulnerable and afraid during a crisis, and these feelings are unlikely to inspire high-quality work, much less contribute to crisis resolution. But when employees feel they can trust in the competence of their leaders, and that their organization's culture inspires competence trust, then the likelihood of their being able to work with senior leaders to resolve a crisis increases. In short, competence trust at the interpersonal level (e.g., between a boss and subordinate) and the organizational level (e.g., a culture of competence trust) can facilitate not only effective handling of crises, but also, ultimately, a crisis leadership mindset across the organization whereby crises are resolved in such a way that the firm and its stakeholders will be resilient following a crisis.

Openness, and to use a related term, honesty, is another key element of trusting relationships. To create effective workplaces employees must trust their leaders to be open with them about strategic plans for the organization as well as with mundane information and decisions. When leaders are open with employees they are better positioned to attract and retain followers and to promote organizational change and innovation.[11] In addition, openness can lead to trust by helping organizations characterized by silos, or heavily matrixed organizations, become more coordinated.[12] As we will describe in more detail in Chapter 9, organizational change and innovation is a positive consequence of perceiving and manifesting opportunity in crisis situations. In addition, Chapter 3 highlighted organizational agility, or a leader's ability to work across functions, as a critical crisis leadership competency. What we can infer from the work of Mishra and others is that being open creates an environment that allows leaders to be effective in organizational agility and promotes creativity and innovation in problem solving.[13] Taken together, organizations that are experienced by employees as open and honest can facilitate crisis leadership. Employees are often the first to recognize the warning signs of a pending crisis. When employees feel comfortable communicating these concerns to senior leaders, rather than fear rejection of their ideas or punishment for bringing negative news to their attention, then there is a greater likelihood that further investigation into the problem will commence. This may be all that is necessary to ward off a potential crisis. In less open environments, however, leaders may be more reticent to hear or heed the warning signs.

Trust is as much a function of *concern* as it is openness and competence. Some scholars have described concern as one party's belief that he or she will not be exploited by another.[14] Stated in the affirmative, concern represents an interest in someone other than oneself and engaging with others in such a way as to demonstrate care for their well-being.[15] To be clear, the concern dimension of trust involves a balance of concern for self and a concern for other. If one is perceived as being overly or exclusively concerned for others, his or her sincerity may be called into question and consequently trustworthiness is ultimately undermined. Mishra identified a number of studies that found concern to be a meaningful part of organizational life. Similarly, Kanter found, for example, that care and concern are extremely relevant in boss-subordinate relationships. In her book *Men and Women of the Corporation*, the data suggest that middle managers show they can be trusted by "caring about the company more than anything else."[16] In other research she found that employees are more likely to trust top managers when they believe that managers will care about employees' job security.[17] Finally, during times of significant organizational change, employees evaluate management on the extent to which it can be trusted to be concerned with employees' welfare and interests.[18] Beyond concern at the interpersonal level, other research suggests that concern operates at the organizational and even institutional level as well.[19] For example, in the political environment people are elected to office by constituents in part based on their perception of the degree of concern the candidate has for the interests of the community in which he or she intends to represent.[20]

Concern plays a tremendous role in crisis. Crises are traumatic events and stakeholders seek guidance, reassurance, and a sense of concern from their leaders. If they do not trust that crisis handlers have their best interest at heart, then effective functioning and participation will dissipate quickly. To highlight this point, consider the handling of Hurricane Katrina that hit the Gulf Coast region of the United States in 2005. Nearly every aspect of the crisis was mishandled, and residents all along the coastal region and in New Orleans, in particular, experienced tremendous pain and suffering as a result. There was very little indication that the crisis handlers were competent at dealing with the safety of the residents, managing the potential and actual levy breach, communicating and coordinating among federal and state officials, evacuating the community, adequately anticipating and managing the subsequent crime, and so on. The mishandling of this crisis resulted in outrage across the country and accusations that the crisis handlers, including then president George W. Bush and others at the levels of local state and city government, were not adequately concerned for the victims. Whether a lack of concern led to the poor handling of the crisis, or whether the poor handling led to a perception of lack of concern is more or less irrelevant. In this case, perceptions of limited concern from their leaders clearly had a negative impact on the victims and other stakeholders of Hurricane Katrina.

The last dimension that characterizes trust is *reliability*. The confidence that can be gained from knowing what to expect from another person, whether the expectations are positive or negative, is generally perceived to be reassuring. We are comforted by consistency. We can plan around reliability. Reliability is akin to credibility and dependability, all generally considered to be positive virtues. Several scholarly definitions of trust are explicit in the importance of reliability and consistency,[21] and others note that during a crisis, a leader's reliability is especially important for assessments of trustworthiness by stakeholders.[22] As with the previous dimensions of trust, reliability is important not only for hierarchical or interpersonal relationships but also for the broader organization. Customers, suppliers, and in some cases competitors may all rely on a firm's perceived reliability to gauge the level or type of engagement they will have with the firm.

To these four dimensions of trust (competence, openness, concern, reliability), we add a fifth dimension, one that may be so fundamental to trust that we become blind to its importance. That dimension is *vulnerability*. When conducting workshops on trust with executive audiences, James will often share the following two definitions of trust: (1) *Trust* is a relationship of mutual confidence in agreed upon performance, honest communication, expected competence, and a capacity of unguarded interaction[23]; and (2) *Trust* is a state involving confident positive expectations about another's motives with respect to oneself in situations entailing risk.[24] When asked what aspects of these definitions resonate with participants, the executives consistently point to the notion of "unguarded interaction" in the first definition and "situations entailing risk" in the second. Each of those phrases connotes a sense of vulnerability. Mishra acknowledges that his own definition of trust (which we provide below)[25] is grounded in the notion of vulnerability, or a willingness to take action where the potential for loss is perceived to be greater than the potential for gain.[26] In other words, trust is a demonstration of behavior in which one risks harm by the person in whom trust has been placed. Managers show trust in subordinates by allowing them to perform work and make decisions using their best judgment, rather than demanding that subordinates follow a strict set of rules or even expectations about how work should be achieved. To the extent that the subordinates' performance reflects on or has implications for the manager, then the manager has behaviorally demonstrated trust by being vulnerable to the actions and work output of his or her subordinates. The manager has taken a risk or displayed unguarded interaction. As one group of authors put it, "Without vulnerability, trust is unnecessary because outcomes are inconsequential for the trustor."[27]

Incorporating all five of these dimensions into a definition of trust, Mishra offers the following: "Trust is one party's willingness to be vulnerable to another party based on the belief that the latter party is 1) competent, 2) open, 3) concerned, and 4) reliable."[28] By definition then, trust is a multidimensional construct.[29] In addition, the various dimensions are activated for different types of relationships (e.g., personal, professional, political) and across various levels of analysis (e.g., individual, group, organizational).[30] The logic of trust then is as follows: The more dimensions in which one is trusted, the more he or she will be characterized as trustworthy. The same holds true for the perceived trustworthiness of organizations. Organizations that demonstrate reliable performance, that are perceived to have concern for the welfare of their customers, that have a culture of openness and honesty, and that are competent in their work are more trustworthy than those organizations that may be perceived positively on only one or two of those dimensions. Organizations are vulnerable in that they have to trust that information that is shared with employees will not be abused, that employees will perform to the best of their abilities to produce high-quality work that will enable the firm to be competitive, and so on. In sum, as we consider trust in organizations, an interesting opportunity for further study is whether particular dimensions of trust are more or less important in determining overall trustworthiness. Likewise, researchers might consider the conditions under which some dimensions of trust are more or less relevant (Figure 6.1).

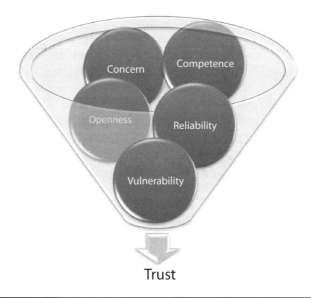

Figure 6.1   Components of trust.

Forms and Evolution of Trust in the Workplace

Trust in professional relationships develops gradually, and it evolves from one stage or form to another. In an effort to differentiate trust in a work context from trust in personal or romantic relationships, Lewicki and Bunker identified three forms of workplace trust.[31] The first they call *calculus-based trust*, and it is based on the element of consistency of behavior (similar to the dimension of reliability as described by Mishra). With calculus-based trust a person assesses another's trustworthiness by whether or not she does what she says she will do. This form of trust is sustained both by a fear of negative consequences (not getting a bonus as a result of lackluster job performance) and by the rewards that can be gained from preserving it. In this way, trust is a market-driven, economic calculus derived by weighing the potential outcomes of creating trust relative to the cost of destroying it.[32] At work, one's professional reputation is built largely upon this calculus. When a person falls short on calculus-based trust and is deemed untrustworthy, his or her reputation suffers, along with his or her potential for advancing up the organizational hierarchy. As Lewicki and Bunker state, "So even if there are opportunities to be untrustworthy, short-term gains from untrustworthy acts must be balanced (in a calculus-based way) against the longer-run gains of maintaining a good reputation."[33]

Not only must individuals be concerned with calculus-based trust, but so too must organizations. Employees and potential employees, customers, suppliers, and all other stakeholders calculate the overall consistency with which a firm produces its products or services its clientele. When these groups are short-changed by firm behavior that is considered to be inconsistent or unreliable, then the organization becomes less trusted, and ultimately less reputable. Under these circumstances, the demand for the firm's products and services will decline as will profitability and competitiveness.

Knowledge-based trust is built on the notion of predictability, or the ability to anticipate another person's actions.[34] The foundation of knowledge-based trust is information, and this form of trust is developed over an extended period of time during which information about one's behavior is conveyed. As a result, one with a history of interaction can learn to predict the other's behavior, and the more accurately one can predict another's behavior, the more trustworthy he or she is deemed to be. Managers and leaders rely on predictability in their organizations. They use knowledge-based trust to make decisions and communicate expectations to stakeholders. This is in part why crisis situations are so off-putting. By their very nature crises are not predictable events, and the unpredictability of crisis-related circumstances continues as the crisis event unfolds over time. Thus, the ability to function during a crisis when knowledge-based trust has declined is yet another mark of a true crisis leader. We will discuss more on how to deal with this later in the chapter.

Identification-based trust is a result of identifying with the wants and intentions of others.[35] This form of trust is characterized by a mutual understanding that is so well developed that each party can effectively act on the other's behalf. Clearly strong marriages or other significant personal relationships are marked by identification-based trust, but such trust is relevant in the workplace as well. Direct reports are often needed to fill in for their boss at meetings or when engaging with a key client. During times of crisis, when one is simultaneously pulled in multiple directions, there is a tremendous need to be able to rely on others to perform and make decisions in ways in which they may be unprepared. Yet it is imperative that one feels as if his or her interests are protected and his or her wishes carried out. The opportunity for "checking up" on others simply does not exist during a crisis. This is also why a highly competent crisis leadership team (as discussed in Chapter 5) is so relevant. Together, the team members can fill in the "gaps of incompetence" that might exist for any one individual.

In professional relationships, Lewicki and Bunker describe the development of trust as an evolutionary process, moving from one form of trust to another.[36] There are several assumptions that must be accepted for this assertion to be realized. First is that as relationships evolve, so do the stages of development through which the relationships traverse. They argue that the evolution of trust moves from calculus based, to knowledge based, to identification based, as a result of the display of relationship-enhancing activities. Second, only after the parties involved in the trust-building relationship confirm that trust has been established at one level is it possible for the next level of trust to be attained. Third, the development of trust may stall before achieving identification-based trust. This may occur, for example, if the nature of the relationship requires only calculus-based or knowledge-based trust. Circumstances under which a relationship may not move beyond calculus-based trust, for example, include relationships that are intended to be temporary or that only require transactional exchange, and cases in which one or more violations of trust have already occurred. A crisis, if nothing else, can be perceived as a violation of trust, as we discuss in the next section.

The Flip Side of Trust: Betrayal

No discussion of trust would be complete without at least a brief mention of betrayal, and depending on its source and nature, a crisis might be perceived as the ultimate betrayal. We argue that a betrayal is simply the perception that one party's actions are sufficiently negative as to violate the other party's trust. The consequences of a betrayal for the violated party are experienced both cognitively and emotionally. Cognitively, the violated party thinks about the significance of the violation, its ramifications on others, where the fault for the violation lies, and so on. Emotionally, the violated may experience feelings of sadness, despair, hurt, anger, or revenge. In both cases, the consequences of a violation can be so severe as to be debilitating, which poses a problem in the workplace that requires fully functioning employees.

We believe that acts of betrayal can be intentional or unintentional, and they can be minor or major in their perceived scope. We illustrate the possible forms that a betrayal can take and offer some examples in Figure 6.2. Yet regardless of how a betrayal is labeled, the pain associated with any betrayal can prove problematic, precisely because it hits us at the core of what we consider important, namely, our set of values, assumptions, beliefs, and expectations about how the world should operate, and how people should behave in the world. Let us be clearer. Any given action only has meaning or is judged positively or negatively because we give it meaning and choose to judge it in a particular way. When we judge a person's behavior positively, we want to reinforce it and reward the person who performed it. But we do not usually consider how the action, or our interpretation of the action, is fundamentally tied to our core set of values and beliefs. Yet, behavior that we judge to be bad can be hurtful precisely because

Figure 6.2 Forms of betrayal in organizations.

it violates what we believe to be true about the world. It violates our core set of values, assumptions, beliefs, or expectations. Behavior that has no effect on our values, for example, generally has no effect on us—we simply do not care enough about it to be aroused one way or the other. Yet when we do perceive that a core value or belief system has been violated, we tend to draw a set of negative conclusions about the person or group of people who performed the betrayal. Those negative conclusions subsequently lead to negative feelings, which ultimately manifest in negative behavior.[37] When the negative behavior is directed back to the person that caused the initial betrayal, we refer to that as revenge. But what is worse is when the person who was initially violated takes his or her negative emotions out on someone else, and in so doing violates a core set of values or beliefs of a new target. Now this person will likely experience a betrayal, and the cycle starts anew.

Imagine an employee who values hard work and believes that he has been performing at a high level, only to learn from his supervisor during a performance evaluation that his performance is substandard. The employee will interpret that message negatively because it is inconsistent with his beliefs about his own performance. He experiences the message and the message bearer (the boss) as a violation (or the boss as a traitor), and because of the negative conclusions and subsequent emotions that will likely be elicited, the employee's performance declines. The dip in performance serves to further violate the boss's core assumptions of how employees should behave at work, and now both parties feel betrayed.

For many people, a crisis is a form of betrayal. Acts of malice, including sabotage, workplace violence, or rumors, can certainly be perceived as a violation of someone's trust, and the J&J Tylenol tampering crisis is a perfect example. In this case, one of the world's leading pharmaceutical companies and product brands might have been devastated by the malicious acts of one or more people. At stake for J&J was not only the financial loss associated with pulling the firm's top-selling product off of the shelves but, even more important, the company's reputation as a trusted manufacturer of medical products and equipment. In the end, reputational loss as a result of a crisis can be far more difficult to overcome than financial or other losses. Adopting crisis leadership behaviors, including communicating effectively through the use of appropriate rhetoric, choosing the most effective communication strategy for the type of crisis, and taking appropriate risk (see Chapter 3 for more on these crisis leadership competencies), is of paramount importance in order to preserve and rebuild trust during and after a crisis.

In the J&J crisis, the potential to feel betrayed could manifest in many ways. Because it was unclear who had tampered with the bottles of Tylenol and how the tampering had been achieved, the possibility that the guilty party had come from within J&J had to be considered. Under this scenario employees, victims, and individual and institutional consumers (e.g., hospitals) could perceive that the firm had not lived up to its promises as outlined in the company credo. Moreover, they might easily presume that the firm could not be counted on to reliably deliver safe products or that the firm was not particularly competent at ensuring the quality of its products, both of which impede a sense of trust. For stakeholders affected by the crisis, the sense of betrayal materializes because of a strong set of values, beliefs, and expectations consumers and employees have about how J&J operates and what it should deliver. The cyanide-laced capsules were inconsistent with the J&J image and with the core beliefs and expectations that the firm espoused.

In the absence of having an identifiable culprit to blame, J&J could easily have been the target of consumer and employee backlash. And yet it was not. The reason is that J&J leadership took considerable risk by swiftly and decisively taking action to remove all Tylenol products from store shelves worldwide (which might be considered an extreme measure given that the evidence of product tampering was localized to one city), and they communicated openly with stakeholders. This behavior is in contrast to the more defensive stances that we often see firms in crisis take.[38] Rather than assume a posture that would distance the firm from the incident, J&J was proactive in setting and executing an agenda with respect to how the crisis would be handled, and a significant part of that agenda involved frequent open and honest communication with stakeholders. It was this combination of value-driven action and frequent communication that preserved a sense of trust within J&J and among its constituents.

The Role of Trust in the Relationship Between Crisis Leaders and Followers

In Chapter 5, we discussed the importance of leading crisis teams. The crisis team perhaps best represents the significant role of trust during a crisis. By its very nature a crisis team is essentially a temporary group that has come together for a very specific and likely short-lived purpose—to resolve the crisis. Based largely on the work of Goodman,[39] temporary groups generally have the following characteristics:[40]

- Participants with diverse skills are brought together for the purpose of their unique expertise.
- Participants have limited history with one another.
- Participants have limited prospect for working together again or in a more permanent capacity.
- Tasks are complex and involve interdependent work.
- Tasks involve a deadline or time pressure.
- Tasks are nonroutine and not well understood.
- Tasks have severe consequences.
- Continuous interrelating is required to produce an outcome.

By now it should be easy to recognize the similarity in the description of temporary groups and the core elements of a crisis. As Meyerson and colleagues wrote,[41]

> Temporary groups often work on tasks with a high degree of complexity, yet they lack the formal structures that facilitate coordination and control. They depend on an elaborate body of collective knowledge and diverse skills, yet individuals have little time to sort out who knows precisely what. They often entail high-risk and high-stake outcomes, yet they seem to lack the normative structures and institutional safeguards that minimize the likelihood of things going wrong. Moreover, there isn't time to engage in the usual forms of confidence-building activities that contribute to the development and maintenance of trust in more traditional enduring forms of organization.

By their very nature, as a temporary group the work of a crisis team requires trust to be effective, yet the opportunities for building trust in the traditional way (e.g., over time, through repeated interactions, by demonstrations of fulfilled commitments, and so on) are precluded. Thus, the trust that develops for more permanent forms, such as the trust in a boss-subordinate relationship, or the trust between an organization and its customers, is qualitatively different than what we should expect for the more ephemeral crisis team. Meyerson and colleagues have referred to this new form as *swift trust*.[42] Stated simply, swift trust is a form of trust that develops quickly and without the benefit of history or repeated interaction to assess the competence, openness, concern, and reliability of the parties involved. Moreover, swift trust is more likely to develop under unusual circumstances, such as a crisis situation. Although their theorizing about swift trust was not predicated on crises or crisis teams, the notion that swift trust is required for effective crisis handling is clear in three ways.

First, crises invoke vulnerability for all involved. Crisis handling teams are vulnerable in that the consequences of their decisions and actions have the power to affect, positively or negatively, the circumstances of many stakeholders. Depending on the outcome of their actions, the jobs or reputations of crisis team members may be at stake. Victims or potential victims are vulnerable in that they may find themselves lacking control over their own circumstances, and the actions of another party can determine their fate. Trust, as we have already defined, is rooted in the notion of vulnerability. Thus, when a crisis occurs, crisis leaders and the crisis team are faced with an awesome responsibility to carefully manage the vulnerability that is shared across all parties. Yet, there are reasons to expect that the crisis team will rise to the occasion and work in the best interest of as many stakeholders as possible. Consider, for example, the outpouring of support and resources, including volunteer labor, money, and supplies, that are offered to communities or families following a natural disaster. In this circumstance an entire organization or community is threatened and crisis handling ultimately requires benevolent effort from everyone, including strangers. In short, crises can evoke altruistic behavior from the most unlikely people, and the willingness to trust relative strangers (swift trust) increases.

Second, as we have stated many times, crises involve uncertainty and ambiguity. A great deal of energy and resources can be depleted in trying to predict how the crisis will unfold, the ultimate scope of the crisis, the extent of the damages that will be incurred, who will be adversely affected, and more. Energy directed toward resolving or limiting the uncertainty of the crisis can distract from crisis handling. To add to that uncertainty by questioning or doubting (distrusting) the capability of the crisis handlers would likely be completely debilitating. So even if we are unfamiliar with those formally tasked with managing the crisis (i.e., those with whom we have no history upon which to base a sense of trust), people may be more inclined to simply trust them to have their best interests at heart as a means of reducing the uncertainty associated with the crisis itself and getting on with the task of crisis resolution.[43] In other words, in times of crisis, there is a willingness to suspend doubt. As one salient example, consider a house fire. When the homeowner calls 911 for help and the firefighters arrive on the scene, it is unlikely that the owners will stop to interview the rescuers to ensure proper training and experience before they let them proceed with the business of putting out the fire.

Webb offers a related interpretation of the role of uncertainty in the relationship between crisis and trust.[44] He suggests that crises increase the likelihood of cognitive biases, faulty decision making (see Chapter 4 for more on biases in decision making), and organizational errors—clearly circumstances that can erode competence-based trust in those charged with handling the crisis. In addition, because one's dependency on others is greater during times of crisis, there is a premium for determining the trustworthiness of those dealing with the crisis. To the extent that crisis handlers can reduce the uncertainty of the situation, by performing competently, for example, the more likely they are to be able to garner the support and resources that are necessary to resolve it, and the more likely people will fall in line to follow the directives of the crisis team.

Third, the relationship between trust and crisis handling plays out to the extent that both crises and trust are fundamentally associated with risk. Without risking one's vulnerability, there is no real demonstration of trust. Likewise, regardless of whether the source of the crisis is man or nature, whether the crisis has been brewing for some time before eruption or occurred suddenly, or whether the crisis was an accident or intentional, it will ultimately entail risk. In the midst of crisis, victims and other stakeholders must be willing to risk the crisis handling to an individual, but more likely a team of individuals (a temporary group) that came together quickly and specifically for the purpose of addressing the crisis. As Luhmann observed, temporary groups "require trust as an input condition in order to stimulate supportive activities in situations of uncertainty or risk."[45] Failure to offer swift trust under these circumstances can impede the group's ability or perhaps willingness to engage in effective crisis handling. What victims and others must also consider is that without the actions of the crisis response team the crisis will likely get worse.

Although there are many reasons why we would expect the development of trust in a crisis, we do not want to discount the challenges associated with swift trust in times of crisis either. To demonstrate trust under these circumstances means victims and other stakeholders cannot dwell on the fact that the crisis handling team is likely a newly formed, fleeting, or untested team—all characteristics that are unlikely to inspire trust. Yet, to give these characteristics undue weight would limit the trust placed in those charged with managing the crisis and potentially undermine their ability to resolve it. Moreover, as Meyerson and colleagues point out, temporary does not mean trivial.[46]

The Role of Trust in Crisis Response

Clearly, being perceived as trustworthy is an important leadership and organizational characteristic. As we have described up to this point, crisis situations can heighten the need people have to feel confident in the trustworthiness of their leaders and of the organizations. When trust pervades the organization, employees are more likely to act in the best interest of the firm and to follow the edict of their leaders certainly in times of relative calm, but also in times of uncertainty. But when trust is not present during times of crisis, employees may be more inclined to behave in ways that preserve their own self-interest rather than the interest of the firm. So how, specifically, does organizational trust translate into how a firm will respond during a crisis?

In Chapter 3, we discussed a highly theorized firm response to crisis, rigidity.[47] Briefly, the threat-rigidity hypothesis assumes that crises and other threatening events will evoke a set of behaviors in which the firm and its decision makers will employ well-learned responses to deal with the threat, restrict information processing, and centralize decision making. These activities are considered to be rigid responses to crisis. The consequences of such rigid responses to a crisis situation are that it may prevent the firm and its crisis handlers from realizing and pursuing creative and innovative ways for addressing the crisis, and more important, may prevent them from manifesting opportunities from the crisis.[48] We argue that a more decentralized approach to decision making may facilitate these outcomes, and trust is one mechanism by which decentralized decision making can occur.

Stated simply, centralization and decentralization are the extent to which decision making is distributed to people throughout the organization (decentralized decision making) or limited to those individuals at the higher levels of a firm's hierarchy (centralized decision making). Considerable research shows that decision making in response to a crisis becomes more rather than less centralized, in part because top managers may want to demonstrate control and legitimacy to key stakeholders in light of the uncertainty that a crisis can pose.[49] Alternatively, others have suggested that decision making becomes more centralized during a crisis because those at lower organizational levels want to distance themselves from the situation to avoid making mistakes that might be punished.[50] Regardless of the reason, trust plays a central role in the tendency to centralize decision making when experiencing a crisis, and here is why. For top managers to delegate decision making to potentially less experienced and lower-status others at a time when the organization is experiencing threat is a risk. To do so requires that that firm leaders yield authority to others, which in turn ultimately increases their dependency on this untested group. What the newly empowered group chooses to do with this authority is unknown to the leaders who ceded control, and therein lies the risk as the group may act opportunistically[51] or incompetently[52] in response to the crisis.

This is the fear that we expect would characterize the average manager. After all, it is virtually human nature to assume a defense posture (literally and metaphorically) in light of a threat. The crisis leader, however, will recognize this circumstance as an opportunity for trust building within the organization. Rather than assume the worst in others and try to defend against it, a crisis leader will recognize that times of immense pressure can often bring out the best in people, and that when called upon to serve, such pressure can act as a positive force. Moreover, for those organizations whose culture is already defined as trusting, a demonstration of trust through decentralized decision making will likely motivate the entrusted to rise to the occasion and perform at an enhanced level. In times of crisis this might take the form of creative problem solving and innovation. One example comes from a prestigious academic institution that over a period of months has had their financial stability and endowment plummet as a result of the economic crisis that began in earnest in 2008. In response, there was a mandate that the university reduce its expenses by 10%. Although the administration dictated a number of ways in which faculty, staff, and others were to change their behavior (e.g., no business or first-class travel for trips overseas, closing of some dining facilities), the administrators also encouraged employees from all levels within the university to identify and implement ways in which the university might deal with the economic challenge. In an update e-mail to the university community several months later the administration reported the following:

> We have looked carefully at more than 300 creative suggestions for savings that came in from the community . . . and the ideas have led us to a number of cost-saving measures, primarily operational in nature. . . . Some of these changes have required us to alter our daily routines or to do things differently. Fortunately, the impact of some measures we've already implemented seems to have been largely unnoticed. Indeed, during a recent Board of Visitors meeting where menus were scaled back and materials were more modestly produced, participants reported being impressed with the changes. And an added benefit is that many of these measures are good for the environment.

From this example, we see creative engagement by employees when called upon to participate in the decision making during a financial threat. Moreover, by opening the decision making up to a broader group beyond top managers, the organization received an array of ideas from people with different experiences with and perspectives about university operations. Consequently, there would likely have been many cost-saving avenues that would have been missed had decision making been centralized at the upper echelon of the university.

The last benefit of decentralized decision making during a crisis is that by involving employees in the decision-making process, they become part of the solution and they begin to feel ownership for the organization and for their ideas for helping the organization succeed amidst the crisis. The demonstration of trust that decentralization conveys in employees is likely to be reciprocated with other trust-inducing behavior by employees. In other words, it is unlikely that employees that have been entrusted with decision making and problem solving at a time when the organization is most vulnerable will respond in a way that would undermine that trust. To the contrary, we expect them to work with senior leaders to collaborate on brainstorming and crisis resolution. So the leap of faith for the leader willing to push decision making down the hierarchy during a crisis may very well be rewarded with enhanced employee performance and a better understanding about the capabilities of his or her employees. Furthermore, by demonstrating a willingness to trust, leaders will in turn gain the respect and trust of employees. To reinforce the display of trust by top managers, employees will likely continue to function at a high level and continue to engage in trust-worthy ways. As they do, managers will reward employees' efforts with greater decision-making autonomy. Earlier we described the cycle of betrayal; here we have described the cycle of trust (Figure 6.3).

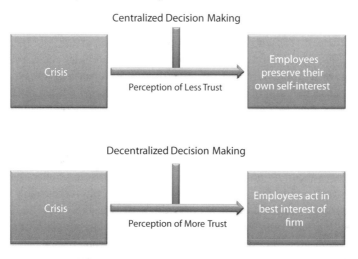

Figure 6.3   Perceptions of trust in centralized and decentralized decision-making crisis environments.

From Theory to Practice

Building trust in an organization is not easy, but it is a key ingredient in becoming a high-performing organization in general, and one that is able to effectively prevent, respond to, and learn from crises. Below are a few ideas for generating trust:

- *Communicate, communicate, communicate.* Attempting candor and open and honest communication for the first time in the midst of a crisis is likely to be met with some resistance. Therefore, we cannot emphasize enough how important it is for leaders to establish a norm of open and honest communication. By this we are not suggesting that leaders share confidential information, or information that if leaked prematurely might do more harm than good, but rather we encourage them to be appropriately candid about all aspects of the business, in good times as well as bad. Doing so can go a long way toward building a culture of trust. Moreover, information flow to various stakeholders will occur more easily when there is a norm or expectation of communication and an infrastructure that supports communication efforts across organizational levels, departments, and other boundaries. A culture of communication is created in at least two ways. First is from the interactions that occur at the boss-subordinate dyadic level. In this case, individual managers make it a point to communicate openly with their subordinates and to encourage and reinforce subordinate communication upward. Part of promoting communication at this level is the use of dialogue. By dialogue we mean conversation that seeks to uncover the underlying values and assumptions that motivate people's behavior. The foundation of the conversation is largely anchored around inquiry, or asking questions and listening carefully to the responses. Through inquiry and patient listening we are more likely to suspend judgment or stereotypes we tend to form about people, and in that suspension we reduce fear and build commitment to one another and to the broader organization. A second way to build a culture of communication is from the top. In this case, senior leaders create a norm of communication by sharing information not only about business strategy but also about the values and expectations of behavior. Only once a culture of communication exists can we expect trust to proliferate throughout the organization, and when there is trust we can more readily and collaboratively respond to threats and other crisis situations.
- *Tell the truth and face the facts.* In Jim Collins' acclaimed business book *Good to Great* he identified the ability to confront the brutal facts as a distinguishing factor between those companies that were merely good and those that were great.[53] When confronted with challenges leaders cannot afford to ignore warning signals, yellow (and in some cases red) flags, or

those moments when the hairs on the back of one's neck stand up. These are all an indication that a potential problem or crisis is likely imminent. But in an effort to protect themselves or other important stakeholders, the urge to withhold information or manipulate it in such a way that distorts the severity of the problem becomes extremely strong. It takes a brave leader (regardless of hierarchical level) to tell the truth and face the facts, but in the long term doing so will far outweigh the short-term benefits of denial.

■ *Align behavior with values.* We started this chapter describing the J&J Tylenol tampering crisis, and we hold the way J&J dealt with the crisis as the gold standard for crisis handling. In what could have been a tremendous loss for the firm financially and reputationally (as one of the world's most trusted brands), J&J is instead lauded for its crisis handling. It achieved this distinction because the firm's response to the crisis was aligned with its espoused values. In other words, it acted in a way that was consistent with what the firm believes about what (or in this case who) is important and how people should be treated. Its messaging and actions were consistent with its values. Consequently, people trusted the firm to do the right thing. Aligning behavior with values goes a long way toward building and sustaining trust (Figures 6.4 to 6.6).

How do we facilitate the flow of information to stakeholders?

Establish a norm of open and honest communications. Be appropriately candid about all aspects of business, in good times as well as bad. Doing so can go a long way toward building a culture of trust and facilitating information flow across organizational boundaries.

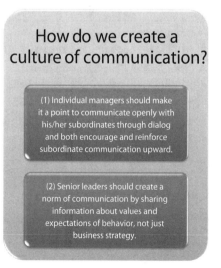

How do we create a culture of communication?

(1) Individual managers should make it a point to communicate openly with his/her subordinates through dialog and both encourage and reinforce subordinate communication upward.

(2) Senior leaders should create a norm of communication by sharing information about values and expectations of behavior, not just business strategy.

Figure 6.4   Leader's hot seat.

> **What's wrong with witholding information until a problem is sever enough to merit more attention?**
>
> When confronted with challenges, leaders cannot afford to ignore warning signals, yellow (and in some cases red) flags, or those moments when the hairs on the back of one's neck stand up. These are all an indication that a potential problem or crisis is likely imminent. It takes a brave leader to tell the truth and face the facts, but the potentially long-term advers consequences of doing so far outweigh the short-term benefits of denial.

> **How do we become a company that people trust to do the right thing?**
>
> Aligning behavior and values goes a long way toward building and sustaining trust. Espousing moral values then treating people (employees, customers, suppliers, and even competitors) in a way that is consistent with those values will say a lot about the trustworthiness of your organization.

Figure 6.5   Leader's hot seat.

Figure 6.6   Leadership Links 6.1

- Trust Matters Blog
  http://trustedadvisor.com/trustmatters
- Articles and Trust Blogs on Trust
  http://totaltrust.wordpress.com/things-weve-written-on-trust/
- Trust Assessment Tool
  https://store.darden.virginia.edu/businesscase-study/trust-assessment-wheel-1316

Endnotes

1. Marcus & Goodman, Victims and shareholders, 281–305.
2. Historical information regarding Johnson & Johnson came from a case study written by the department of defense about the Tylenol crisis. To access the case, go to http://www.ou.edu/deptcomm/dodjcc/groups/02C2/Johnson%20&%20Johnson.htm.
3. Ibid.

4. Broome, Center, & Cutlip, *Effective public relations.*
5. See, for example, Gambetta, *Trust: Making and breaking cooperative relations*; Lewicki & Bunker, Trust in relationships, 133–173.
6. See the Russell Sage Foundation Web site for more information and a complete listing of the work they have produced on trust: https://www.russellsage.org/publications/books/subjects/TRUST.
7. See, for example, the work of Barber, *The logic and limits of trust*; Luhman, Familiarity, confidence, trust, 94–107.
8. Mishra, Organizational responses to crisis, 261–287.
9. Gabarro, *The dynamics of taking charge.*
10. Reina & Reina, *Trust and betrayal in the workplace.*
11. Kirkpatrick & Lock, Leadership, 48–60.
12. Davis & Lawrence, *Matrix.*
13. Mishra, Organizational responses to crisis, 261–287.
14. McGregor, *The professional manager.*
15. Ouchi, *Theory Z.*
16. Kanter, *Men and women of the corporation*, 65.
17. Kanter, *Change masters.*
18. Kotter & Schlesinger, Choosing strategies for change, 106–114.
19. Mishra, Organizational responses to crisis, 261–287.
20. March & Olsen, *Rediscovering institutions.*
21. Ouchi, *Theory Z.* Also, Gabarra defined trust in boss-subordinate relationships as consistency of behavior. See Gabarro, *The dynamics of taking charge.*
22. Kirkpatrick & Lock, Leadership, 48–60.
23. Reina & Reina, *Trust and betrayal in the workplace.*
24. Boone & Holmes, The dynamics of interpersonal trust, 190–211.
25. Mishra, Organizational responses to crisis, 261–287.
26. Deutch, Cooperation and trust, 275–319.
27. Moorman, Zaltman, & Deshpande, Factors affecting trust in market research relationships, 81–101 (quote from p. 82).
28. Mishra, Organizational responses to crisis, p. 267.
29. Bromiley & Cummings, *Organization with trust.*
30. Mishra, Organizational responses to crisis, 261–287.
31. Lewicki & Bunker, Developing and maintaining trust in work relationships, 114–139.
32. Ibid.
33. Ibid., 120.
34. Lewicki & Bunker, Developing and maintaining trust in work relationships, 114–139.
35. Ibid.
36. Ibid.
37. The language and general ideas associated with values, assumptions, beliefs, and expectations (a.k.a. VABES) come in large part from colleagues in the organizational behavior area at the Darden Business School. For many years, the Darden School of Business first-year teaching team used a case study intended to draw out

the importance of VABES within the context of personal leadership, and in the course of that teaching they would make the connection among VABES, cognition (conclusions), feelings, and ultimately behavior.

38. In an extensive qualitative study of firms experiencing crisis situations, James and Wooten found that more than 90% of firms' initial verbal rhetoric following the crisis was defensive. James & Wooten, Diversity crisis, 1103–1118.

39. See, for example, Goodman, *Temporary systems*; Goodman & Goodman, Some management issues in temporary systems, 494–501.

40. Meyerson, Weick, & Kramer, Swift trust and temporary groups, 167.

41. Ibid.

42. Ibid.

43. Ibid.

44. Webb, Trust in crisis, 288–301.

45. Luhmann, Familiarity, confidence, 103.

46. Meyerson, Weick, & Kramer, Swift trust and temporary groups, 167.

47. Staw, Sandelands, & Dutton, Threat rigidity effects on organizational behavior, 501–524.

48. Brockner & James, Towards an understanding of when executives see crisis as opportunity, 94–115.

49. See, for example, D'Aveni, The aftermath of organization decline, 577–605; Herman, Some consequences of crisis which limit the viability of organizations, 61–88.

50. Mishra, Organizational responses to crisis, 261–287.

51. Arrow, The economics of agency, 37–51.

52. Donaldson, A rational basis for criticism of organizational economics, 394–401.

53. Collins, *Good to great*.

Chapter 7

Organizational Learning Amid Crisis*

On April 22, 1999, four former and current employees filed a class action lawsuit against Coca-Cola, alleging that the firm discriminated against its African American workers. Specifically, the lawsuit claimed that the firm's corporate hierarchy created conditions in which black employees were clustered at the bottom of the pay scale, averaging $26,000 a year less than their white counterparts. In 1995, Coke's leadership became aware of internal criticism and dissatisfaction with the treatment of black employees when a group of black executives lamented a dearth of African Americans in senior management positions and described an environment in which they felt humiliated and ignored.[1] Two years later, a Labor Department review found that Coke had violated federal antidiscrimination laws and demanded that the company redress its diversity challenges. Although many Coke executives agreed that it was best to settle the lawsuit quickly rather than participate in a public and protracted legal battle that would likely further damage the firm's reputation, Coca-Cola's then CEO, Douglas Ivester, denied the allegations both in an e-mail sent to employees and publicly in statements made to the media.[2] In addition to the denial, the firm commented that the employees' complaints were without merit and that the allegations had "significant errors of fact."[3] As the case progressed, Coca-Cola was perceived

* Originally published in a slightly different form in Wooten, L. P., & James, E. H. (2004). When firms fail to learn: The perpetuation of discrimination in the workplace. *Journal of Management Inquiry, 13*(1), 23–33.

by many as having mishandled the lawsuit. Public relations experts, customers, and sociopolitical interest groups accused Coca-Cola of acting defensively and being slow to respond to the charges. The firm's image was tarnished, both by the allegations and by the firm's handling of them.

A little more than a year later, another Atlanta-based firm, Georgia Power, was presented with a class action racial discrimination lawsuit of its own, representing approximately 2,000 black employees. Like Coca-Cola, several Georgia Power workers accused the firm of discrimination against blacks with respect to salary and promotion treatment. In addition, however, the lawsuit claimed that over a period of years black employees had felt threatened by the display of hangman's nooses throughout the workplace and by other forms of physical harassment from white colleagues. An internal investigation following the allegations indeed found that a total of 13 ropes tied in the form of a noose had appeared in eight different Georgia Power facilities, one of which had been placed around the neck of a black figurine and laid on the desk of an African American employee. Initially Georgia Power executives seemed surprised that a noose continued to symbolize racism for black Americans, but soon after the lawsuit was filed the firm's president and CEO, David Ratcliffe, commented that he now understands how offensive anything that looks like a noose would be and that they have no place in the work environment.

Georgia Power took a substantially different approach to managing the lawsuit than Coca-Cola. First, Ratcliffe vowed swift and effective action against any employee involved in harassing others, and he quickly expressed a sense of concern for the targets of the alleged discrimination and harassment. Second, rather than outright deny the charges, he accepted the possibility that some of the allegations of discrimination *may* be accurate, and publicly acknowledged that the company's record on racial issues was imperfect. Third, Ratcliffe declared diversity as a major interest for the firm and proceeded to launch a series of employee focus groups and surveys investigating the company's diversity practices. Moreover, the day that the lawsuit was filed, Ratcliffe announced a 12-member diversity advisory council that he would co-lead along with an African American member of the firm's board of directors. Fourth, a few weeks later he created a new position of vice president of diversity action and, upon review of more than 50 individual employee complaints about compensation, made salary adjustments in some cases. Within a year's time, the diversity efforts had yielded more than 30 initiatives to improve the firm's diversity practices, and Ratcliffe outlined these initiatives on a closed-circuit television address to employees. Finally, Ratcliffe personally sought out African American employees to talk to in order to facilitate his understanding of their experiences as African American employees at Georgia Power. At the conclusion of these meetings Ratcliffe said, "Now that I understand it, I have a sensitivity that I must have."[4]

Georgia Power's response to its discrimination lawsuit, and its quick action to manage it, was the antithesis to the actions of neighboring Coca-Cola. Coke's rhetoric and behavioral responses about the lawsuit can be characterized as defensive,[5] and as a result, the firm was hit with fairly extensive criticism for its handling of the discrimination crisis. One could argue that the allegations against Georgia Power were more severe and certainly more sensational (e.g., psychological harm because of the display of nooses) than those against Coca-Cola, in which case we might expect Georgia Power to have received the lion's share of negative publicity. Yet, Georgia Power executives learned from their careful observations of Coca-Cola's incident and applied that learning to the handling of their own situation. The fact that one company learned from another following a crisis was apparently so unusual that it made headlines with the following story that appeared in the *Atlanta Journal Constitution* newspaper, "Georgia Power Learns From Coca-Cola Bias Suit: Utility's Response Shows Lessons Gleaned From Soft Drink Giant's Actions."[6]

In this chapter we build on one of our previously published articles to highlight the important role that organizational learning plays in crisis leadership.[7] The Georgia Power story provides one example of how learning can facilitate crisis handling and, as we will argue later in the chapter, how learning can also influence a firm's susceptibility to future crises. We use the discrimination lawsuits as a specific type of crisis on which to build our arguments with respect to learning, primarily because of the continuing significance of diversity in organizational theory and the practical implications of diversity for managers and the organizations they lead.

Why Discrimination Lawsuits Are a Noteworthy Crisis

Throughout the 1990s and early into the 2000s, allegations of wide-scale and egregious acts of employment discrimination and harassment proliferated the news media. One of the more notorious cases involved the Texaco Corporation; the firm was accused of unfairly compensating and promoting white employees to the detriment of black workers. In addition, however, private meetings of senior executives talking disparagingly about black employees and plotting to destroy incriminating evidence had been secretly recorded and leaked to the media, and thereby turned the lawsuit into a public relations crisis for Texaco. Around the same time that the Texaco crisis was unfolding there were a growing number of reports and lawsuits claiming rampant sexual harassment and discrimination against women and minorities in some of the country's most prestigious Wall Street firms. In an earlier paper we argued that discrimination-related class action lawsuits are a crisis for organizations, and that they are particularly challenging to address because of the sensitivity Americans tend to have regarding matters of diversity, especially as it relates to race.[8] Throughout the remainder of this chapter we illustrate why organizational learning is so important to the crisis handling of such lawsuits and why organizational learning with respect to diversity issues can be so difficult.

Workplace discrimination occurs when a firm engages in deliberate or unintentional bias against a group of employees that are protected by civil rights legislation. Generally, the categories that are included in legislation include race, gender, religion, national origin, and disabled or veteran status. The Civil Rights Act of 1991 protected employees by giving them an increasing opportunity to file discrimination claims against employers. Class action lawsuits are of particular concern to organizations because they represent a grievance brought by one or more individuals against a company whose actions have harmed a group or class of people in a similar way. When such cases are recovered successfully, all members of the class receive a portion of the amount paid by the offending organization. Class action lawsuits are costly in the same way as other forms of crises. In some cases, settlement fees alone can reach hundreds of millions of dollars. On top of that, firms have other expenses to contend with, including potential back pay settlements to plaintiffs, punitive damages, public relations fees, and the costs associated with organizational policy and structure changes,[9] not to mention the opportunity costs of having management time and attention spent on the lawsuit rather than the operations of the business. Financial consequences are even more evident when one considers the total cost to shareholders. Although Texaco paid out upward of $176 million to the plaintiffs in its case, one study found that the total cost to shareholders exceeded $500 million.[10] Another researcher found that the value of firms involved in class action discrimination lawsuits fell more than 15%, and that the average loss to shareholders typically exceeded the amount firms were required to pay in legal and out-of-court settlements. Finally, in addition to the financial considerations, class action lawsuits create reputation concerns for an organization. Negative media attention can portray an unflattering picture of the firm and adversely affect key stakeholders, including employees, customers, and potential job applicants.

There are many reasons why firm leaders should be adept at handling discrimination lawsuits. First, within the past couple of decades there has been widespread focus on diversity issues and management from both the scholarly and practitioner communities.[11] With this increased attention, we might expect today's leaders to have a better understanding of how to prevent discrimination and effectively manage discrimination lawsuits. Second, the frequency with which U.S. firms experience discrimination lawsuits and the notoriety associated with many of them represent opportunities for firm leaders to learn from the experiences of others. However, it seems as if many firms continue to struggle with diversity management, and with preventing and resolving discrimination lawsuits. An unfortunate consequence has been burgeoning settlement fees paid by firms and an inability to fully capitalize on employee talent. In essence, poor diversity management can result in a crisis for the organization.

In this chapter, we advance a view that failures in managing discrimination, and discrimination lawsuits in particular, reflect failures in learning by firms. Crises offer tremendous learning opportunities, and yet, all too often, firm leaders fail to take advantage of the learning that crises can provide. Bazerman and Watkins have argued that there are four ways in which organizations fail to learn from prior failures, their own or others' (Figure 7.1).[12]

We define discrimination management fairly narrowly as the prevention of systematic inequity in the workplace that has the potential to lead to discrimination lawsuits. Discrimination is an extraordinarily complex issue, and there have been numerous theoretical attempts to explain why a diverse workforce poses a challenge for organizational leaders and employees alike. For example, discrimination has been examined at the individual level of analysis, focusing on such factors as stereotypes[13] and prejudice,[14] the interpersonal level,[15] the group level,[16] and the organizational level, including structural considerations.[17] This body of

Figure 7.1   Why organizations fail to heed prior failures.

research has focused on somewhat immutable characteristics such as attitudes, as well as individual and organizational demographic profiles. Focusing on these issues clearly has and will continue to help scholars make strides in developing theory around matters of diversity. Because prejudicial attitudes and structural limitations of organizations are difficult to change, however, these same aspects of diversity may be less productive in terms of helping managers and diversity professionals eradicate discrimination. So rather than tackle the broader issue of diversity, we have elected to concentrate on an issue that we consider to be a subset of, and perhaps a more focused aspect of, diversity—discrimination and the lawsuits it generates.

We chose this aspect of diversity for three reasons. First, when managed poorly, lawsuits can become an organizational crisis and, like all other crises, will require immediate organizational attention not only to bring the issue to resolution but to prevent future crises. In fact, at one point discrimination lawsuits ranked among the leading type of crises faced by business leaders in the United States, with the number of class action discrimination lawsuits rising more than 100% in 2003.[18] Second, valid lawsuits generally represent the consequence of egregious diversity mismanagement practices by a firm, and they reflect in a concrete way the consequences of mistreating an important stakeholder group, whether they be employees, customers, or suppliers. In this regard, they epitomize the type of crisis for which the organization is often deemed responsible. Because the nature of the problem is often behavioral, we believe that there is a greater likelihood of successfully changing behaviors than there is of changing relatively immutable or inherent individual factors (i.e., attitudes). Third, discrimination lawsuits are one of the more serious and challenging aspects of managing workforce diversity and demand a different skill set than managing routine diversity issues such as personnel staffing or promotion decisions. Moreover, because discrimination lawsuits represent extreme cases, using them to illustrate how organizations learn, or fail to learn, can help researchers and practitioners better understand organizational behavior that is "transparently observable."[19] For these reasons, we believe that applying concepts associated with organizational learning to the crisis of discrimination lawsuits can serve as an effective and generalizable example for understanding the role of organizational learning as it relates to any type of crisis.

Below, we describe some of the most widely reported perspectives of organizational learning. Based on the primary tenets from these perspectives, we identify key organizational barriers that we believe prevent firms from learning how to manage workplace discrimination and successfully resolving discrimination lawsuits. We close with examples of learning in practice as they relate to the barriers we identified.

Perspectives of and Barriers to Organizational Learning

The concept of organizational learning is rooted, in part, in individual-level learning theories,[20] such as the one advanced by Skinner advocating learning as a function of the consequences and reinforcements that follow a behavior.[21] Behavior followed by favorable consequences tends to be repeated; behavior followed by unfavorable consequences tends not to be repeated. According to Skinner, when desirable consequences consistently follow a behavioral response, permanent behavioral change, or learning, has occurred. Thus, at its core, learning generally involves the process of acquiring new information and implementing a change in behavior as a result. The relationship between learning and behavior change is a powerful one and is central to not only individual-level learning theories in psychology,[22] but also what some organizational scholars have referred to as adaptive learning.[23] Adaptive learning is believed to shape an organization's knowledge base by incorporating the firm's previous experiences into organizational routines (e.g., policies and procedures) that then serve to guide firm behavior.[24] Thus, the concept of organizational learning captures the sense that firms continuously adapt to a changing business environment by drawing on organizational knowledge—a repertoire of skills and routines—that come to bear on a particular circumstance.[25]

Adaptive Organizational Learning Perspective

The adaptive organizational learning perspective assumes that learning is a function of changing behavior in response to experience.[26] In keeping with this idea, researchers refer to organizational learning as a change in routines (e.g., rules, procedures, strategies, codes) and beliefs as a result of failure.[27] This assertion is based on three central tenets: (1) firm behavior is based on routines, (2) behavior in an organization is history dependent and therefore focused on activities and interpretations of the past rather than expectations of the future, and (3) firms are target oriented and measure their success according to the achievement of some goal. Organizational learning is also thought to be largely experiential[28] and, following Bandura's beliefs about individual learning,[29] suggests that changes in routine firm behavior are a function of trial-and-error experimentation. Specifically, dysfunctional routines will cease when they are associated with failure (e.g., inability to meet targets) and functional ones will continue or increase when they are associated with success.[30]

Each of the three tenets of adaptive learning gives rise to potential barriers that may explain firms' failure to effectively manage and prevent crises such as lawsuits. In addition, the trial-and-error experimentation that should facilitate organizational learning may not fully apply when the learning is associated with nonroutine events such as a crisis.

Barrier 1: Dysfunctional Routines

Discriminatory Routines

Central to the adaptive learning approach is the notion of organizational routine behavior. This idea contributes to a firm's failure to learn how to manage discrimination lawsuits, or other crises, in that there are generally no organizational routines in place to deal with such challenges. Moreover, where routines do exist, they generally relate to negative, albeit unconscious, firm behavior that perpetuates rather than eliminates discrimination. In other words, although most organizations do not intentionally or even knowingly discriminate against their employees, there may be unconscious but systemic routines in place that can lead to discriminatory behavior and outcomes. One study, for example, discovered an institutionalized practice that adversely affected racial minority employees.[31] In this firm, decision makers assigned new minority hires to minority supervisors believing that doing so would help the new hire during the socialization process. However, these supervisors were, on average, in less powerful positions in the organization and therefore less able to help their workers succeed and advance within the firm. Over time, a trend developed: Minority employees had a significantly lower rate of advancement than that of their white counterparts. Once tacit norms such as this become routinized in the organization, a dangerous pattern emerges—one leaving the firm vulnerable to allegations of discrimination.

Reliance on Reactive Learning Routines

Another dysfunctional organizational routine is one grounded in single-loop or reactive learning.[32] Reactive learning occurs when an organization detects a problem and uses existing policies or procedures to correct it. This strategy often precludes firms from paying attention to why the problem occurred initially. Thus, if organizational problem solving simply involves corrective action without questioning the firm's fundamental assumptions, or organizational norms, then only reactive learning has occurred.[33] When an organizational problem leads the firm to question whether its culture or normative procedures may have caused the problem, the learning is double-loop or reflective.[34] Reflective learning essentially demands a rethinking of the organization's norms and operating rules and indicates the organization's capacity to change its "view of the world" by replacing obsolete perspectives and systems with approaches that are more effective.

According to Argyris, one type of learning is not necessarily better or worse than another type.[35] In fact, both reactive and reflective learning are necessary aspects of organizational life. Reactive organizational learning is appropriate for routine or repetitive issues, whereas reflective learning is appropriate for complex, nonroutine occurrences such as crises.

We believe that despite the relative frequency with which discrimination claims are made, they are not necessarily routine problems, but rather are complex and idiosyncratic. For example, our research reveals that depending on the cause or source of discrimination (e.g., an individual's action, structural constraints, or system-wide policies and procedures), some response strategies (both behavioral responses and rhetorical responses) may be more or less appropriate. Likewise, we found that management strategies for handling discrimination vary by the target group being discriminated against, with discrimination against women, for example, typically being handled differently than discrimination against African Americans.[36] Last, our prior research indicates that not all discrimination strategies are perceived as equally effective. In some cases, stakeholders respond more favorably to those strategies in which a firm acknowledges responsibility and adopts corrective action than to those that diffuse responsibility or pursue damage control activities. In other cases, defensive posturing is perceived as not only an acceptable response, but also an effective one.[37]

Given the findings above, we argue that discrimination cases vary based on a number of contextual factors. As such, they represent situations that are complex and difficult to manage, and therefore call for reflective learning strategies. What we found, however, is that firms tend to adopt reactive learning strategies for managing discrimination allegations. In so doing, they fail to learn what factors within the firm are the underlying causes of the problem of discrimination and ultimately fail to resolve those specific issues. The firm then risks being vulnerable to repeated claims of discrimination. We argue that the same is true for any other form of crisis, especially when the source of the crisis is the organization (e.g., organizational policies or values) or management (e.g., managerial decision making). Failure to consider the fundamental ways in which the organization's norms and procedures contribute to the set of circumstances that allowed for the crisis to materialize will likely ensure that the same or a similar crisis will recur. In other words, firms become vulnerable to *predictable surprises*,[38] or smoldering crisis events, as we described in Chapter 2. Recall that such incidences occur when firm leaders fail to heed evidence that a potentially devastating problem is imminent. Prior to wide-scale allegations of discrimination, there are almost always subtle and even not-so-subtle warning signals that if recognized, might not materialize into a lawsuit.

To illustrate our point about reactive learning routines we use the case of Home Depot's 1997 sex discrimination lawsuit. In this case, Home Depot vehemently denied the allegations and chose to resolve the dilemma by complying with court-ordered mediation that required the firm to settle financially with the targets of the discrimination.[39] In addition to the financial settlement, the Equal Employment Opportunity Commission (EEOC) required Home Depot to make changes to its existing human resources (HR) programs. However, there was no thorough investigation to determine what specific aspects of the firm's HR policies were problematic. Moreover, because the changes were imposed externally, rather than suggested and implemented by the firm's own decision makers following a thorough audit of firm practices and culture, the resolution may have failed to address the relevant issues. By not questioning *why* the firm was accused of discriminatory behavior, Home Depot did not benefit from the deeper-level understanding that results from reflective (double-loop) learning. Failure to adopt reflective learning may lead to a higher likelihood that perceived discriminatory behavior would continue to exist in the organization. In fact, in less than a five-year time period Home Depot has faced two large-scale discrimination lawsuits. In both cases, the firm chose to adopt a reactive strategy for handling the lawsuits.

Organizational Defensive Routines

Organizational defensive routines may also prevent learning as it relates to the prevention and management of discrimination. Similar to an individual's ego defense mechanism, organizational defensive routines are actions, policies, and norms of behavior that prevent organizations from experiencing embarrassment or threat.[40] These organizational defenses hinder employees from taking responsibility for their decisions. Instead, organizational members may defend themselves against ineffectiveness by blaming others.[41] Argyris characterized organizational defensive routines as antilearning, and suggested that when a firm is confronted with threatening or embarrassing information as a result of its own behavior, defense routines will bypass or cover up the information.[42] The firm subsequently offers excuses that maintain the cover-up. This tendency to conceal negative information may result in missed opportunities for learning and the continuation of the behavior that caused the initial problem.

Common organizational defensive routines during a threatening event include (1) denying the problem—stating, for example, that the incident did not occur or that the firm was not responsible—and (2) justifying firm behavior.[43] By employing these types of defensive routines, firms hope to preserve a favorable image and dissociate themselves from the negative event.[44] The organization is then rewarded for its masking or distancing from the problem and continues to deny that discrimination is something with which the firm has a problem. In 1995, a lawsuit charging Publix, a grocery store chain, with hiring and retaining women in dead-end, low-wage jobs and blocking them from management track positions provides an illustration of a defensive routine. A spokeswoman said on behalf of the firm, "Publix denies that it discriminates. Most female employees choose not to take career-track jobs because of the long hours."[45] In this case, there is not only a clear denial of untoward behavior by the firm, but rhetoric that offers an ostensibly plausible explanation for why the alleged victims of the discrimination may find themselves in jobs that limit their advancement and salary potential. The organization has offered what can be perceived as an effective and appropriate response. As a result, it avoids the taint of discrimination. However, the denial rhetoric may also prevent the firm from fundamentally rethinking, and perhaps improving, the way jobs are designed and how to take full advantage of its workforce. In this regard, an opportunity was lost.

Other examples of organizational defensive routines include making reference to institutional policies to defend and excuse firm behavior.[46] Interestingly, the existence of formalized antidiscrimination policies (e.g., EEOC statements) often allows organizations to view discrimination incidents as anomalies or infrequent occurrences. Over time these antidiscrimination policies become legitimized through their rule-like status and create the appearance that discrimination cannot exist in the organization. Gingiss Formalwear, which operates a chain of tuxedo shops, is an example of a firm that responded to allegations of racial discrimination by referencing its institutionalized policies. During its 1998 racial discrimination lawsuit, Gingiss's president stated that:

> An investigation into claims of racial discrimination found evidence of the illegal behavior in several of our shops. . . . I would like to unequivocally state that Gingiss Formalwear does not discriminate against any of its employees, applicants or customers on the basis of race . . . that would be a violation of our policies.[47]

By referencing institutional procedures during an image-threatening event, firms attempt to decouple the organization from the situation,[48] but by doing so the organization fails to look inward and critically reflect on the work environment that inadvertently contributed to the discrimination problem. Thus, when defensive routines are enacted, the opportunity for learning how to behave differently regarding the management of diversity may diminish, leaving the firm susceptible to additional allegations of discrimination.

Limited Learning-Based Routines

Dysfunctional organizational routines are not the only routine-based barrier to learning how to manage and prevent discrimination lawsuits effectively. In many cases, firms fail to prepare adequate routines for managing and preventing a discrimination lawsuit. This lack of preparation is surprising given the attention that firms generally give to other employee-related issues, such as workplace safety. In such cases, firms will often have documented procedures or routines for preventing and dealing with safety concerns. Unfortunately, such documentation is rare when it comes to managing and preventing a discrimination lawsuit. There are typically no policy manuals that describe in detail the procedures to follow when and if allegations of discrimination arise in the workplace. Rarely are there drills, review sessions, or forums where issues of discrimination and, more important, how to prevent or manage them are openly discussed. Rather, any discussion that does occur is likely to be in a closed-door meeting with key personnel, including a human resources representative or an attorney. Moreover, such discussions generally occur only after a problem has surfaced.

In sum, based on the various situations described above, we infer that the negative organizational routines that can promote discrimination, coupled with a firm's failure to institutionalize procedures to prepare for the consequences of discrimination, suggest a breakdown in the learning process. Thus, taking the barriers together, it seems to us that the presence of some negative routines and the absence of positive ones will increase the likelihood that discrimination will continue to exist and that discrimination lawsuits will follow.

Barrier 2: History-Dependent Learning

Limited History of Discrimination Lawsuits

A second assumption of the adaptive learning approach is that organizational behavior is history dependent and therefore focused on activities of the past rather than expectations for the future. Further, behavioral change or learning is adopted incrementally as a response to feedback.[49] Stated simply, organizational learning occurs when there are opportunities to learn and gain feedback from one's previous experience. Despite the sensational and newsworthy element of some discrimination lawsuits (e.g., Texaco), the frequency of large-scale discrimination lawsuits, just like with other forms of crises, tend to occur across firms rather than within the same organization. In other words, any one firm may have a very limited history with discrimination lawsuits. Consequently, there are few opportunities for obtaining feedback and adopting new and better strategies for managing them. As we found in a sample of nearly 50 organizations that had experienced a discrimination lawsuit within a 10-year time frame, fewer than one-third of those firms had experienced a previous large-scale lawsuit upon which to draw learning opportunities.[50] Furthermore, less than 10% of the firms in that subset had experienced more than one prior lawsuit. Although many firms can face small-scale discrimination lawsuits—those generally brought by an individual—such cases tend not to garner widespread media attention. Rather, such cases are generally quietly resolved without most of the world taking notice.

Certainly a history free of lawsuits is a desirable record. Yet it can also serve as a barrier to learning how to manage a lawsuit when or if one should arise because there is little opportunity for obtaining feedback regarding firm performance in that domain. Moreover, a limited history with a particular type of challenge or organizational vulnerability (i.e., diversity) may lead firms to become complacent in that area. Ironically, without this history and the feedback associated with it, firms may be prevented from learning better strategies for managing domain-specific crisis situations.

Lapses in Organizational Memory

Organizational memory is an aspect of an organization's history in which firm knowledge and behavior are captured and stored in such a way that they become accessible in the future. Stated differently, organizational memory is viewed as the means by which knowledge from the past is brought to bear on present activities, which may require applying the knowledge in a new manner or a different combination.[51] Organizational memory consists of both the knowledge and experiences of firm stakeholders as they relate to a firm's culture, management, communications, and decision-making styles.[52] Mechanisms such as documented policies, strategies, and paradigms serve as repositories in an organization's memory, as do the individual memories of firm employees.

Managing and preventing discriminatory firm behavior requires that an organization acquire and store relevant knowledge in its memory, and possess the capability to retrieve and transfer this knowledge. Organizations may fail to acquire knowledge for handling discrimination because the information may rest with only a subset of organizational members and is never diffused throughout the organization. Alternatively, the knowledge may be imperfectly shared among its members.[53] If, for example, a firm's HR department is the only unit responsible for managing diversity and the challenges that arise from it, then there is little opportunity for HR to transfer its knowledge for resolving diversity dilemmas to individual managers. Managers, in turn, fail to learn for themselves how to handle future discrimination challenges. Ironically, managers might be important assets to the firm and its crisis handling if they were able to resolve a discrimination claim, or other problems, before it reached the point at which HR and other stakeholders must become involved. Through discussion and the employment of effective conflict resolution techniques the manager may be just the person who can calm the waters enough to bring the matter from a boil to a slow simmer. Yet in the absence of sharing or transferring information, the people who can be most helpful in crisis resolution may be among the least involved in the process. We believe that it is imperative to transfer organizational knowledge across units and to err on the side of including more people in the problem-solving process.

Even if a firm obtains relevant knowledge regarding the management of discrimination, and that knowledge is diffused throughout the organization, there is not always a clear link between what is learned and actual behavior change. The ability of a firm to utilize knowledge effectively can be constrained by human biases and errors (see Chapter 4 for more detailed discussion on biases in decision making), by the way the organization currently interprets information, and by its frame of reference. For example, in 1995 employees at Coca-Cola recommended to senior management a number of initiatives to enhance workforce diversity and prevent the "glass ceiling" for African American employees. Senior management failed to pay adequate attention to the message or recognize its importance to employees. There was an error in judgment with respect to how to deal with the information. In choosing not to heed their recommendations, senior managers essentially discounted the opinions and suggestions of an important stakeholder. Shortly thereafter, Coca-Cola was faced with the first of two racial discrimination lawsuits.[54]

In some organizations, the knowledge for managing discrimination may not exist internally, but is held by people and entities external to the firm, including competitors, consultants, and regulatory agencies. In these circumstances, attaining the necessary knowledge requires vicarious learning or the ability to acquire information from those external to the firm. When organizations intentionally seek to learn the best practices from others, particularly those that are deemed to be an industry standard, we call that benchmarking, the goal of which is to make improvements in their own process or strategy. Benchmarking diversity best practices can go a long way toward improving a firm's own diversity efforts, or toward eliminating systems or processes that contribute to discrimination. Yet benchmarking is not foolproof. Oftentimes, firms will adopt one particular practice or initiative by another firm and expect similar results. What they fail to recognize, however, is that what makes something a best practice in one organization is not necessarily the practice itself, but the entire infrastructure that supports it and is aligned with it. This infrastructure includes a leadership philosophy, numerous organizational and job design features, and a culture, without which any one particular practice will become less effective. So in considering best practice strategies for responding to a diversity crisis, leaders should bear in mind that it is not merely a firm's behavioral or verbal response to the crisis that made it effective, but a response that is in the context of a supporting cast of aligned organizational characteristics.

Barrier 3: Target Orientation

Focusing on the Wrong Target

In addition to organizational learning being a function of firm routines and interpretations of past behavior, Levitt and March suggest that organizations learn by associating behavior with a specific target.[55] In other words, changes in firm behavior occur based on whether outcomes of firm behavior meet expectations. According to this view, when outcomes fall short of anticipated targets, firms will likely adopt new behaviors. This pattern may be repeated until firms have satisfactorily met their objective. Simply stated, evaluations of success or failure are important for determining future action.

The target-focused aspect of organizational learning is particularly important for understanding the perpetuation of discrimination and the lawsuits that often accompany it. Of paramount importance is identifying what the appropriate target objective should be with respect to a firm's handling of discrimination issues. Unfortunately, this may be a difficult task as targets may change over time, conflict with other organizational goals, be ambiguous, or lack support from key firm decision makers. In determining the objective to be achieved following a discrimination lawsuit, decision makers must consider, among other things, the various constituencies that are affected by the lawsuit, firm image, available resources, and consequences of firm action.

In an effort to identify what firm decision makers claim to be their goal or target for resolving discrimination lawsuits, we examined multiple data sources, including newspaper accounts, radio and television transcriptions, and internal firm documents that depict communication regarding discrimination lawsuits. We examined accounts from 49 firms that were targets of discrimination lawsuits during a 10-year span (1990–2000). Our search resulted in 71 data sources and, combined, yielded 551 separate accounts of discrimination lawsuits.[56]

We used these data to code the accounts, or statements, provided by firm spokespersons (e.g., CEOs, firm attorneys, and communications representatives) and found that the desired goals in resolving discrimination lawsuits varied across organizations and were generally firm specific. Consequently, there may be limited opportunity for other firms to learn from an organization's handling of a discrimination lawsuit. For example, a spokesperson for Fleet Bank, a firm accused of racial discrimination, stated that Fleet would provide a financial settlement to the alleged victims primarily because it wanted to end the lawsuit and put the case behind them. These and other statements led us to believe that the target objective of Fleet's discrimination management strategy was to bring the lawsuit to an immediate close and to return to "business as usual." From our reading of the accounts associated with the Fleet lawsuit, there was little to no emphasis on understanding what caused the discrimination or how to prevent it in the future. In other words, there seemed to be little interest in reflective learning.

As another example, the Hooters restaurant chain indicated that it would fight its allegations of sex discrimination and harassment in court because doing so would help preserve the firm's reputation with its customers. This and other evidence leads us to believe that the firm's objective in this case was impression management. Again, there seemed to be little to no focus on uncovering the root cause of the discrimination, or even whether or not the discrimination actually took place. Ironically, Hooters, a firm some believe promotes a sexually charged environment, actively tried to promote a favorable image of its firm in light of a sex discrimination lawsuit.

The cases of Fleet Bank and Hooters represent merely two of the various end goals that firms try to achieve in their efforts to resolve a discrimination lawsuit. Overall, our review of scores of discrimination accounts led us to the following conclusion: A firm's target objective following a lawsuit is one generally concerned with lawsuit resolution rather than discrimination prevention. By focusing on the immediacy of the lawsuit and how to bring it to closure, firms may fail to think long term and consider how they might prevent future lawsuits from occurring. In this case, the learning that has taken place is how to resolve a crisis, not necessarily how to prevent one. A crisis leader will consider both.

Failure to Identify Diversity Challenges as Important Managerial Targets

In addition to targets being important at the organizational level, they are also important for individual-level learning within organizations. Yet when discrimination management and prevention are not identified as important individual learning objectives, the likelihood that leaders will respond poorly to allegations of discrimination increases. In fact, the same might be said for any number of areas in which a crisis situation arises. As the saying goes, what gets measured gets done. In the absence of having concrete or even implicit expectations and performance measures around learning how to effectively manage diversity, the chances are that diversity challenges will be responded to ineffectively. In other words, because senior leaders set the tone of an organization, employees interpret messages from them about what is important and how they should focus their time and energy. Issues that are low on the organization's priority list are unlikely to have a prepared repertoire of responses for how to address the challenges that accompany them. As a result, when confronted with a crisis in a low-priority domain, management responses will reflect trial by fire rather than

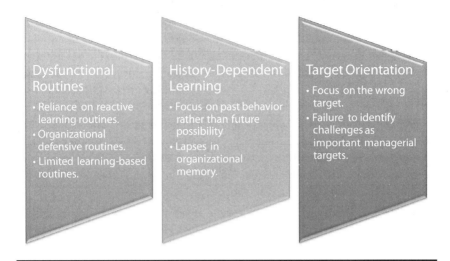

Figure 7.2 Barriers to organizational learning.

a well-planned strategy. Under these circumstances, the likelihood of a quick and smooth resolution becomes less probable.

As we close this section on barriers to learning, we revisit a central tenet from individual-level learning theory; namely, the potential for reward and the desire to avoid punishment tend to motivate learning. This particular premise may speak to why some firms may fail to learn how to manage discrimination. Essentially, without consequences, positive or negative, the likelihood that managers will learn how to effectively respond to discrimination challenges effectively is likely to diminish. At Mitsubishi, for example, a firm accused of widespread discrimination and harassment of female employees, management's strategy for handling the issue was to "blame the victims" rather than the individuals accused of discrimination.[57] In fact, of the 89 separate cases of discrimination uncovered at one Mitsubishi plant location, only 11% resulted in disciplinary action (i.e., dismissal) against those responsible for the discriminatory behavior.[58] Little or only symbolic punitive consequences following discriminatory acts are unlikely to motivate behavioral change. Likewise, if successful diversity management strategies go unacknowledged, such desirable behavior may not be repeated in the future (Figure 7.2).

Learning From Failure

A crisis can be interpreted as the ultimate business failure, yet the organization has only failed if it fails to learn from the crisis. In his seminal article on learning from failure, Sitkin argues that failure is an essential prerequisite for effective organizational learning and adaptation.[59] Consistent with the perspective we have been advocating throughout this book, a fundamental aspect of crisis leadership is the ability to promote organizational learning and to guide the organization through the learning process before, during, and after a crisis. Doing so should position the postcrisis organization for resilience and, as we argue more forcefully in Chapter 9, for the capability to be better off after the crisis than it was before. Learning plays a role in this process in that it can facilitate organizational adaptation and innovation. Sitkin states, "Modest levels of failure can promote a willingness to take risks and foster resilience-enhancing experimentation."[60]

Failure is a deviation from expected and desired results, and it includes those errors that could (and generally should) have been avoided, as well as the unavoidable adverse outcomes from experimentation and risk taking.[61] Conventional wisdom suggests that success is what organizations should strive for and that failure is to be avoided. Failure represents an inadequacy in such critical areas as planning, decision making, executing, and more. Consequently, much of the organizational scholarship on learning has focused on success, or the ability to learn from that which has been proven to work well. In practice, success tends to promote the maintenance of the status quo, and as long as environmental and other factors remain constant, there is little incentive to alter the practice of repeating what is known to work.[62] Eventually, however, scholars began to examine organizational failure as an important mechanism for learning,[63] and have argued that "the process of learning from failure can be analyzed in terms of the factors that foster more or less effective learning."[64] For our purposes, an important aspect of crisis leadership is the ability to learn, including learning from mistakes and failures.

Learning from failure can take the form of the organization adopting the practice of heeding the early warning signals that foreshadow a potential crisis. In the case of discrimination allegations, there are almost always signs that there is unrest among employees. When left unattended, these simmering problems can escalate to a class action lawsuit, as was the case with Coca-Cola, Texaco, and many others. Sitkin refers to these signals as small losses and claims that their value lies in their ability to draw management attention to previously overlooked problems and inconsistencies and challenge leaders to examine current practices and procedures before a full-fledged crisis (e.g., discrimination lawsuit) emerges.[65] Small losses or failures signal unequivocally that there is a recognizable problem or a need to address a novel predicament. Moreover, because they are generally less threatening than a problem of crisis proportions, small failures may not only capture management attention but also help to avoid some of the less productive behavioral responses to threat, including hypervigilance,[66] threat-rigidity responses,[67] reliance on overlearned behaviors,[68] and escalation of commitment to prior routines.[69]

Failures, like crisis events, should challenge leaders to move beyond the status quo. A failure, especially an organizationally imposed crisis, implies that something has gone awry and that the attention, evaluation, and cognitive processing of the firm's leaders are required. In theory, failure should move leaders from complacency and satisfaction to action. Yet, organizations that systematically and effectively learn from crises and other failures are rare, and the reasons for this are many.[70] One paramount barrier to learning from failure is rooted in human nature. Organizations are composed of psychologically and emotionally complex human beings who tend to find failure (especially their own) difficult. There are strong instinctive tendencies to deny, distort, or ignore feedback that indicates that one has failed.[71] Furthermore, to the extent that people closely identify with their work process, work outcomes, and decision making, when a failure occurs in their area of responsibility, a natural first reaction is to dissociate from the failure in order to protect their self-esteem and self-image. Within an entire organizational system, this tendency is exacerbated because a collection of individuals inadvertently collude to ignore or repress failure. Stated differently, large failures in which the potential for losses is significant are more likely to engender a protective organizational response rather than an exploratory one. Thus, acknowledging one's individual mistakes or failures, as well as organizational failures, is inherently unappealing. The unfortunate consequence of not doing so, however, is that the organization is precluded from a learning opportunity.

Despite the face-saving incentive to ignore failure, Sitkin offers several motivations that might stimulate learning from failure.[72] First, failure provides a clear and decisive target, and we know from goal-setting theory that action (and in this case corrective action) is more likely to be initiated when there is a specific rationale or objective to be achieved.[73] As we alluded to earlier in this chapter, however, the challenge for the crisis leader will be identifying the appropriate target in which to commence action. Second, mistakes, failures, losses, and other threats, and the adverse consequences they can spawn, can fuel a general willingness to consider new alternatives and to reconsider institutionalized practices or traditions. New approaches to problem solving will likely manifest in opportunities that otherwise would not have been realized.

An Example of Learning in Practice

Up to this point we have articulated a number of reasons that make it difficult for firms to live up to their potential as learning organizations when it comes to managing and preventing a specific type of crisis: workplace discrimination. Despite these barriers to learning, we continue to be optimistic that leaders can and will learn how to lead organizations that are composed of a bevy of diverse members. In fact, many firms have already learned, and we believe will be stronger and less vulnerable to future diversity dilemmas as a result. Thus, ending as we began, Georgia Power is an example of a firm that did try to overcome many of the barriers we have identified and, in the process of managing a racial discrimination lawsuit, was able to learn from the mistakes of others.

Rather than adopt defensive routines that serve to cover up or dissociate the organization from the allegations of discrimination, Georgia Power adopted a crisis leadership stance that included an openness to learn about and confront the problems it faced. For example, Georgia Power's president and CEO, Ratcliffe, promised to investigate the allegations, validate alleged victims who had been affected by wrongdoing, and enact a set of consequences for those employees involved in the discriminatory or harassing behavior. After a series of follow-up investigations related to the discrimination charges, other Georgia Power managers not only acknowledged the disparities in promotion and compensation between white and black employees but took swift action to bring the affected employees to parity.[74] Ratcliffe formally stated that if discrimination is a problem at Georgia Power, "We've got to do a better job of training and teaching our folks how to deal with different kinds of people."[75]

Georgia Power also engaged in reflective learning by rethinking its organizational norms regarding diversity management. Its goal was to ensure that the firm's work environment valued differences and capitalized on employee diversity for the long-term success of the company. Reflective learning was manifested, in part, by the creation of a new department within the company to discern the systems, practices, or policies that contributed to poor diversity management. Furthermore, this reflective learning process entailed examining the corporate culture and then creating a new environment that could eventually model how to discover and use the talents of all Georgia Power's employees to their fullest.[76] This approach to learning and manifesting the opportunities that come from diversity is consistent with what Thomas and Ely refer to as a *learning and effectiveness* paradigm for managing diversity.[77] The authors argue that such a strategy is a powerful and positive means to capitalize on diversity because of an intentional focus on integration and internalizing the differences that exist among employees so that the firm can learn and grow as a result of those differences.[78]

Last, Georgia Power began the process of creating an organizational memory such that information about and responsibility for diversity management was diffused throughout the company. This included (1) designating a senior leader responsible for diversity management who would report directly to the CEO; (2) appointing managers responsible for *corporate concerns* to handle discrimination allegations and the development of supplier relationships with women and ethnic minorities; and (3) developing a Diversity Action Council that includes members external to Georgia Power, who can contribute an additional perspective to diversity management issues.

Although Georgia Power was able to overcome some learning barriers, this behavior did not resolve all discriminatory practices within Georgia Power. Shortly after Georgia Power began to tackle its discrimination problems, five hangman's nooses were displayed at company facilities.[79] This ongoing challenge to extinguish discrimination behavior and racial harassment demonstrates that an organization's routines, both positive and negative, are deeply ingrained in its culture, and organizational culture can act as a facilitator or inhibitor of organizational learning.[80] In short, culture is about shared mental models that reflect deeper and more pervasive aspects of organizational life. Attempts to change these mental models require a long-term effort because the origins of these routines are embedded in history and transmitted through socialization, education, and personal movement.[81] Thus, the challenge for companies that seek to engage in reflective learning is to understand that while some familiar organizational routines are altered in a favorable way as organizations learn, some dysfunctional routines may continue. This demands that reflective learning must continuously adapt to an organization's environment by identifying which routines to pursue and which routines to try to eliminate.

It should be noted that although reflective learning is optimal, there may be some situations in which reactive management approaches for preventing and resolving workplace discrimination are appropriate and beneficial. This is especially true when management strategies are consistently implemented over a long period of time, and are not merely a Band-Aid approach to discrimination challenges. Advantica, the parent company of Denny's restaurants, is an example of an organization that employed a reactive learning approach after being accused of mistreatment of minority customers and denial of career opportunities for minority employees.[82] Like the Coca-Cola and Texaco cases we have already discussed, the case of discrimination at Denny's became a full-fledged crisis for the organization when customers and other interest groups publicly boycotted the restaurants nationwide and started a public media campaign highlighting the firm's mistreatment. These accusations ultimately resulted in Denny's paying $54.4 million to settle two class action lawsuits. In response to the legal sanctions, Denny's complied with EEOC mandates, including agreeing to have all of its 45,000 employees undergo diversity training and to pursue new relationships with minority-owned vendors. Stakeholders of the company acknowledged that the training would likely not have occurred if Denny's had not been mandated to implement it. Yet, the mandate did serve to help Denny's learn how to begin to create a work environment that at the very least respects its diverse customer and employee base. Over time, the firm became increasingly committed to achieving a functional diverse workplace and eventually began to implement diversity initiatives on its own accord. An overarching culture that reflected the learning and effectiveness paradigm toward diversity began to emerge, and ultimately Denny's started receiving accolades for its commitment to diversity.

Based on the learning strategies of both Georgia Power and Denny's we began to ponder the following question: Is the motivation for learning and type of learning more important than the results obtained from the learning process? Georgia Power was quick to engage in reflective learning, but still struggles with discrimination problems. Conversely, Denny's long-term reactive learning resulted in fundamental changes for the corporation's diversity practices and public accolades that view Denny's as the corporate model for multicultural sensitivity.[83] Both cases illustrate that firms can learn from discrimination crises and are able to change their routines and beliefs as a result of failure. It is unfortunate, however, that too many times it takes a crisis to prompt firms to think about creating inclusive work environments. Success in other areas of the business may blind organizational leaders, narrow their perspective, or create complacency when it comes to what is often perceived to be a less tangible contribution to firm performance—the diversity of its workplace.

In closing, we argue that firms can learn from crisis situations and that the best crisis leaders embrace these failures as a learning opportunity. Facilitating this learning process requires that firms acknowledge that barriers do exist but are surmountable, and also to recognize that learning often requires changes to an organization's mental model. Learning from crises provides an excellent opportunity to challenge the organizational routines that may stand in its way of excellence. Moreover, firms that can engage in reflective and in some cases reactive learning can develop an organizational memory that helps to prevent future crises. In so doing, we believe that firms will increase their likelihood of creating a work environment where employee differences become an organizational asset instead of a litigation liability (Figure 7.3).

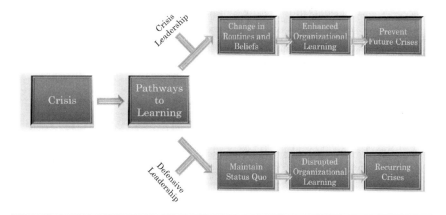

Figure 7.3   Pathways to learning during crises.

From Theory to Practice

Organizational learning, especially in response to a failure, does not happen on its own. It requires intentional leadership, fortitude, commitment, and focus. It also involves a process that includes organizational activities associated with identifying and analyzing failure.[84]

- The ability to proactively identify organizational failures is a critical first step in the process of learning from them. An important by-product of identifying failures early and often is that they can be stopped before they are compounded, infiltrate other aspects of the organization, or made irrevocable. Clearly, had the Coca-Cola executives paid attention to the warning signs that many of its African American employees were disgruntled, they could have avoided the public outcry that culminated in the class action lawsuit. By contrast, the Georgia Power leadership took initiative to learn more about the concerns that its employees communicated. Although a lawsuit was eventually filed, it was evident that the leadership was well aware of the diversity challenges and was working with employees and others to rectify past wrongdoings and avoid such challenges in the future. Again, a critical impediment to identifying failure is overcoming the psychological and emotional ramifications that threats pose to one's self-esteem and self-image. Leaders must demonstrate a willingness to let down their guard and show vulnerability when under duress because it is only during those times that the opportunity for learning will emerge.

Moreover, leaders must set the example for other employees to follow. They cannot expect employees to identify and acknowledge failures, especially of their making, if their leaders are not behaving similarly.

■ A key organizational impediment to identifying failures is not having access to data that would indicate failure. After all, bad news rarely travels up the organizational hierarchy. To counter these powerful tendencies, firm leaders can take the initiative to develop systems and procedures that allow the data necessary to identify and learn from failures to emerge. Once the psychological and organizational impediments to learning have been addressed, a culture that values small failures as learning opportunities can emerge.

■ Following the identification of failure leaders must discuss and analyze them. This requires a more extensive conversation than simply recognizing or acknowledging that a failure has occurred; it requires taking a deep dive into *why* it has occurred. Reflective learning, or engaging in analysis that will explore the root cause of the failure, is a central aspect of the analytic process. This analysis includes looking for trends or patterns and asking questions that might implicate organizational members, norms, practices, or systems. In addition, a failure analysis takes time and requires a spirit of

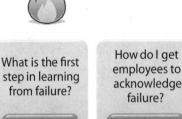

What is the first step in learning from failure?	How do I get employees to acknowledge failure?	We've identified the failure. What's next?	How do we encourage reflected learning and analysis?
Proactively identifying organizational failures is a critical first step. An important by-product of identifying failures early and often is that they can be stopped before they are compunded.	Creating a culture of safety and rewarding, rather than penalizing those who bring mistakes to top management attention, will help employees feel more comfortable with acknowledging failure.	Once a failure has been identified, the next step is to engage in experimentation. You must move away from statue quo and experiment with new ways of addressing a problem.	Leaders must fight the urge, in themselves and others, to consider a problem over simply because it has been resolved. Learning requires that leaders create a norm or standard for engaging in a reflected analysis of the situation, and include that behavior in performance measures.

Figure 7.4 Leader's hot seat.

Figure 7.5   Leadership Links 7.1

- The Fifth Discipline Fieldbook Series:
www.fieldbook.com
- Appreciative Inquiry
http://appreciativeinquiry.cwru.edu/
- Society for Organizational Learning
http://www.solonline.org/

inquiry and openness and a tolerance for ambiguity. Many organizations, however, reward people for being decisive, efficient, and action oriented, behaviors that are in many ways counter to those necessary for reflected learning and analysis. So what can leaders do? First, they can establish formal processes or mechanisms for employees to discuss, analyze, and apply the lessons of failure. Second, they can ensure that these discussions and lessons are communicated throughout the organization and not only among the subgroup of employees to whom the failure initially applied. Third, they can model a spirit of inquiry such that it becomes a cultural norm to ask the *why* question and to attempt to get below the surface of organizational challenges. This modeling will be facilitated if people are not penalized for revealing information or data that potentially implicates themselves, coworkers, or supervisors. Instead, leaders can reinforce and reward behavior that exposes dangerous activity or systems that somehow threaten the organization (Figures 7.4 and 7.5).

Endnotes

1. Winter, Coca-Cola settles racial bias case.
2. Ibid., A1.
3. Unger, Discrimination lawsuit, H1.
4. Information about the Georgia Power discrimination lawsuit was extracted largely from the writing of Douglas Blackmon. The complete article can be found at the following website: http://www.slaverybyanothername.com/2001/04/racial-bind-bl ack-utility-workers-in-georgia-see-nooses-as-sign-of-harassment/ (accessed June 2, 2009). The original article appears in the *Wall Street Journal*. Blackmon & Harris, Suit alleges pattern of bias at a Southern Co. unit; Managers "had no idea."
5. James & Wooten, Discrimination crises.
6. Quinn, Ga. Power says five nooses displayed, F1, 2000b.
7. Wooten & James, When firms fail to learn, 23–30.
8. To learn more about discrimination lawsuits and crisis handling please refer to James & Wooten, When firms fail to learn.

9. Terpstra & Kethley, Coca-cola settles racial bias case, A1.

10. Pruitt & Nethercutt, The Texaco racial discrimination case and shareholder wealth, 685–693.

11. Souza, The diversity trap, 83; Hemphill & Haines, *Discrimination, harassment, and the failure of diversity training*.

12. Bazerman & Watkins, *Predictable surprises*.

13. Essed & Stanfield, *Understanding everyday racism*, 237–271.

14. James, Brief, Dietz, & Cohen, Prejudice matters, 1120–1128.

15. Thomas, The dynamics of managing racial diversity in developmental relationships, 169–194.

16. See, for example, Ely & Thomas, Cultural diversity at work, 229–273; Ibarra, Homophily and differential returns, 422–447; Ibarra, Personal networks of women and minorities in management, 56–87; Ibarra, Race, opportunity, and diversity of social circles in managerial networks, 673–703.

17. Kanter, *Men and women of the corporation*; Lefkowitz, Race as a factor in job placement, 497–313.

18. Institute for Crisis Management, 2004.

19. Eisenhardt, Building theories from case study research, 532–550.

20. Starkey, *How organizations learn*.

21. Skinner, *Contingencies of reinforcement*.

22. For example, ibid.; Bandura, *Social learning theory*.

23. For example, Levinthal & March, A model of adaptive organizational search, 187–218. Herriott, Levinthal, & March, Learning from experience in organizations, 219–227. Glynn, Lant, & Miliken, Mapping learning processes in organizations, 43–83.

24. Nelson & Winter, *An evolutionary theory of economic change*.

25. Matthews, Organizational foundations of economic learning, 113–124.

26. Glynn, Lant, & Milliken, Mapping learning processes in organizations, 43–83.

27. Levinthal & March, A model of adaptive organizational search, 187–218.

28. Levitt and March, Organizational learning, 319–340.

29. Bandura, *Self-efficacy*, 191–215.

30. Cyert & March, *A behavioral theory of the firm*.

31. Lefkowitz, Race as a factor in job placement, 497–313.

32. Argyris, Double loop learning in organizations, 115–125.

33. Argyris & Schon, *Organizational learning*; Baker & Sinkula, The synergistic effect of market orientation and learning orientation on organizational performance, 411–427.

34. Argyris & Schon, *Organizational learning*; Senge, *The fifth discipline*.

35. Argyris, *Overcoming organizational defenses*.

36. James & Wooten, Diversity crisis: How firms manage discrimination lawsuits, 1103–1118.

37. James & Wooten, *Actions speak louder than words*.

38. Bazerman & Watkins, *Predictable surprises*.

39. Bueno, Home Depot's agreement to settle suit could cut 3rd quarter earnings by 21%, B18.

40. Argyris, *Overcoming organizational defenses*.

41. Rahim, Managing organizational learning, 5–8.
42. Argyris, *Overcoming organizational defenses.*
43. Benoit, *Accounts, excuses, and apologies.*
44. Schlenker, *Impression management*; Elsbach & Sutton, Acquiring organizational legitimacy through illegitimate actions, 532–550; Elsbach, Managing organizational legitimacy in the California cattle industry, 57–73.
45. Harris, Revolt at the deli counter, 32.
46. Meyer & Rowan, Institutionalized organizations, 340–363; Scott, The adolescence of institutional theory, 493–511.
47. Simpson, Suit accuses Gingiss of race bias, 22.
48. Oliver, Strategic responses to institutional processes, 145–179; Elsbach, Managing organizational legitimacy in the California cattle industry, 57–88.
49. Levitt & March, Organizational learning, 319–340.
50. James & Wooten, *Being in the spotlight.*
51. Walsh & Ungson, Organizational memory, 57–93; Hargadon & Sutton, Technology brokering and innovation in a product development firm, 716–749.
52. Kransdorrf, Flight organizational memory lapse, 34–40.
53. Hargadon & Sutton, Technology brokering and innovation in a product development firm, 716–749.
54. Deogun, Coke was told in '95 of need for diversity, A3.
55. Levitt & March, Organization learning, 319–340.
56. James & Wooten, *Being in the spotlight.*
57. Pomerenke, Class action sexual harassment lawsuit, 207–219.
58. Ibid.
59. Sitkin, Learning through failure, 231–266.
60. Ibid., 237.
61. Cannon & Edmonson, Confronting failure, 161–177.
62. Sitkin, Learning through failure, 231–266.
63. See the following for reviews of the literature on organizational learning: Huber, Organizational learning, 88–115; Levitt & March, Organizational learning, 319–340.
64. Sitkin, Learning through failure, 237.
65. Ibid.
66. Janis & Mann, *Decision making.*
67. Staw, Sandelands, & Dutton, Threat-rigidity effects in organizational behavior, 501–524.
68. Weick, A stress analysis of future battlefields, 32–46.
69. Staw & Ross, Behavior in escalation situations, 39–78.
70. Cannon & Edmonson, Failing to learn and learning to fail (intelligently), 299–320.
71. Edmonson & Cannon, 2005.
72. Sitkin, Learning through failure, 231–266.
73. Locke & Latham, *A theory of goals and performance.*
74. Quinn, Ga. Power learns from Coca-Cola bias suit cases similar, F1.
75. Jacobs, Georgia Power hit with bias suit, A1.
76. Poe, Making sure diversity gets a chance, H2.

77. Thomas & Ely, Making differences matter, 79–81.
78. Ibid.
79. Quinn, Ga. Power says five nooses displayed, F1.
80. Schein, Three cultures of management, 9–20.
81. Levitt & March, Organizational learning, 319–340.
82. Rice, Denny's changes its spots, 133–142.
83. Ibid.
84. The ideas presented about the process of learning from failure are adapted largely from Cannon & Edmonson, Failing to learn and learning to fail (intelligently), 299–319.

Chapter 8

Crises and the Global Environment

Often research and the practice of crisis leadership explore this topic with a focus on the United States or through a particular national or regional lens. Yet, author Marion Pinsdorf titled her 2004 book *All Crises Are Global*.[1] She argues that for centuries crises, such as plagues, have spread across domestic borders or wars that in many instances were global in planning and execution. In today's world, the globalization of organizations, more efficient and open infrastructure, and technological advancements have expedited the need for leaders to develop competencies for managing crises in a global environment. Because of these macro-environment changes, with ease, money, information, diseases, and people can move across borders. Similarly, a natural disaster or severe weather does not limit itself to a particular border or its effects.

In essence, we can surmise that the "world is flat," and all of these factors contribute to the globalization of crises, and add another layer of complexity and uncertainty to leading an organization during a crisis. The transnational and interconnected nature of crises has somewhat merged the distinction between international and domestic crises.[2] Many environmental, technological, and infrastructural factors have external effects on a global scale and result in organizational crises. Political instability in another part of the world can ensue into a crisis because of an organization's supply chain or customers. Likewise, the transnational aspects of economic and financial transactions can have consequences in a crisis situation.

Developing organizational capabilities for managing a crisis in a global context requires a mindset and integrated, supporting systems that can quickly bring together and mobilize stakeholders from different parts of the world to resolve the crisis. This calls for leaders not only to be center stage in the organization's home country, facilitating the development and use of crisis management competencies, but also to peruse its different international locations to understand the implications of a potential crisis or impact of a current crisis. However, what are the specific organizational competencies necessary to manage a global crisis, and how do these competencies differ from when the crisis is global? In this chapter, we explore these questions by reviewing the research on global organizational competencies and linking this body of knowledge to managing the global environment in crisis situations. In addition, we present illustrative cases to highlight specific competencies.

A Global Mindset in Crisis Situations

Organizations that are effective in their home environment can sometimes share attributes with an effective global organization, but a major differentiating factor of an effective global organization is the ability to both retain certain competencies and adapt or develop new skills in response to its different international operations. Leading a crisis in a global environment accentuates the need for organizations to be attentive to the focal area of a crisis (e.g., social, political, employees, or natural disaster), the institutional players, and the location of a crisis.[3] The ability to do this can be framed as a global mindset.

From an organizational perspective, a global mindset is the collective cognitions of its members to comprehend, articulate, and manage the multiple strategic and cultural realities on both global and local levels through generating, allocating, mobilizing, and integrating resources across geographical borders.[4] Cognitively a global mindset directs the organization's attention and use of information so that it can understand issues beyond a single country, culture, or context. It is an altered way of thinking that frames behavior to encompass the complex interconnections of the global environment by comprehending the world from a broader perspective. A global mindset is sustained by leadership's knowledge of the different macro-environment and cultural aspects of an interdependent world, and the skills to diffuse this knowledge throughout the organization.[5]

Strategic Framing of Global Crisis Situations

In a crisis situation, enacting a global mindset means scanning the world from a broadened perspective to identify and respond to threats. This involves processing and sense making of different perspectives to create a global community of knowledge and using this knowledge to strategize a course for leading the crisis. Often this knowledge is filtered through frames. Frames are organizational lenses that bring the world into focus during a crisis and help manage complexity, ambiguity, and dynamism in a global environment.[6,7] Frames can be built upon simple generalizations or complex theories that represent the organization's view of an event and provide a mental model for interpreting and directing actions. Similar to maps, organizations utilize frames as windows to view and analyze their thought processes and as tools for navigating their environment.[8] Research conceptualizes four types of global mindsets that can be used as organizational frames during crises.[9] Each of these mindsets develops in organizations over time and is symbolic of the organization's structure, strategies, political systems, human resource management practices, and culture.[10] Moreover, a global mindset is the by-product of an organization's history and evolves by an iterative process of change through new experiences, social processes, and shifts in the mix of organizational members.[11]

The Defender

The defender is a traditional global mindset with a strong focus on domestic operations, and events external to the organization's home county are not a strategic priority. When the organization confronts a crisis that transcends its domestic boundaries, it relies upon the government, stakeholder organizations, or nonprofit organizations to take charge. A defender mindset neglects making a connection between its organization's operations and activities in its foreign locations.

For example, in 2008, citizens of mainland China called for a boycott of Carrefour, the French retailer, because of widespread unsubstantiated rumors that one of Carrefour's major shareholders had been making donations to the Dalai Lama.[12] The suggestion of a boycott was triggered not only by rumors of the firm's connection to the Dalai Lama, but several other events. They included an incident in Paris when Tibet supporters attempted to take the Olympic torch away from a Chinese wheelchair-bound torchbearer, a growing dissatisfaction for Western retailers, and the belief that China is demonized in the West. Although many Western retailers have locations in China, Carrefour was targeted because of its large customer base in China.[13] The boycott began when a girl demonstrated at a Carrefour store by carrying pictures of the Olympic torch relay. The pictures of her boycotting activities were quickly reported online through blogs, instant messaging, websites, and e-mails. Within five days, the Chinese citizens' commitment to the boycott expanded out to at least 70 million Microsoft Messenger users, who added a red heart followed by "China" as a signature. During the early period of the boycott, Carrefour denied the allegations of its support for illegal political organizations, and stated that the rumor was fabricated. Also, Carrefour threatened to pursue legal action against individuals or organizations that spread the rumor. As the boycott progressed, Carrefour expressed as a foreign enterprise in China that it did not want to become involved in politics or sports and suggested the company was not concerned with the boycott because there was no significant impact on sales.[14] Yet, both the Chinese and French governments intervened.[15] Officials from the Chinese Communist Party urged citizens to take care of their own business and put efforts into supporting the country. The French government sent a delegation to China to express regret for the Olympic torch incident in Paris.

Carrefour's defensive mindset and lack of response for handling the boycott damaged its reputation. Even though Carrefour had warning of the pending boycott, it took a passive role by making no plans to manage the looming crisis.[16] During the crisis, Carrefour's response appeared insensitive by lacking sympathy for the feeling of the boycotters. Carrefour was content to be a bystander as both the French and Chinese governments intervened, and it missed the opportunity to leverage the Chinese government's views on the crisis. When the Chinese government encouraged the boycott to cease, Carrefour could have aligned the government's stance with its public relations strategy. Moreover, Carrefour could have utilized the boycott to emphasize its positive contribution to the Chinese economy, such as its employment of 40,000 Chinese workers.[17]

The Explorer

Similar to the defender mindset for managing global crisis, the explorer's dominant focus is its domestic environment, but it takes a more active role in the administration of foreign operations by centrally managing from the home office.[18] Initially, when organizations with an explorer mindset formulate a global strategy the goal is growth of the organization through increased sales or distribution of services. The organization takes a cautious approach to implementing a global strategy by assigning staff to explore the foreign terrain and explain the implications of nationality differences to the home office. The home office uses this information for centralized decision making and to coordinate administrative tasks. Thus, in a crisis the home office oversees management of the situation through standardization with some modifications to account for national differences.

For instance, in 1998 when the Russian economy experienced hyperinflation, and its citizens could not afford the basic necessities, McDonald's Russian locations confronted a smoldering crisis that developed over time because of economic conditions in Russia.[19] George Cohen, founder and senior chairman of McDonald's Russia, and Khamzat Khasbulatov, president of McDonald's

Russia, led this crisis by using the home office resources and practices to guide their actions. Cohen and Khasbulatov were able reduce the prices of menu items because of supply chain efficiency, but maintained the core menu that was the central component of McDonald's brand. Efficiencies in the supply chain were accomplished by employing McDonald's European network of suppliers to train Russian suppliers, and by building its own food production facility to ensure consistent quality of local meat, dairy, and baked products.[20] When McDonald's initially opened restaurants in Russia, the company imported human resource management practices from the United States through the design of recruitment policies, compensation systems, and training practices that ensured service standards were not compromised. During the economic crisis, McDonald's was able to be selective when hiring employees and designed a compensation system based on productivity.[21] Also, senior managers were sent to Hamburger Universities, which are McDonald's corporate training centers in Toronto, Canada, and Oak Brook, Illinois, and the employees trained in Russia received standardized training similar to that of McDonald's employees in other locations. The centralized management of product standardization training and customer service practices resulted in customer loyalty, which enabled McDonald's to weather Russia's economic crisis.

The Controller

The controller global mindset focuses on leading through stringent policies that are dictated by the home office of an organization. There is little adaptation to its foreign environment, and instead the controller global mindset imposes the home culture and practices on its foreign operations.[22] In many instances, a controller global mindset embraces an ethnocentric orientation that can be expressed by a view that the headquarters location and its national practices are the optimal way to conduct business because of superiority in abilities and skills.[23] Consequently, leadership from a controller global mindset can result in minimal concerns for stakeholders beyond the home country because of the superior attitude.

During a crisis, organizations with a controller global mindset will perceive it as a threat and respond rigidly and defensively.[24] This rigid response to the crisis is a coping mechanism for managing system disruptions that challenge the organization's basic assumption, subjective sense of the world, or existential core.[25] It evolves into enactment of control that integrates organizational rhetoric and behavior by depending on parochial knowledge, limited sources of information, and past experiences to resolve this crisis.[26] As the demands of leading the crisis intensify, senior management of organizations with this mindset will decrease their search for alternatives for resolving the crisis and assimilate previously acquired information into their dominant and familiar precept or seek information that confirms the choices they have already made.[27] Similarly, the control mindset may try to mask the organization's actions by manipulating the crisis situation to redefine events, displace perceptions of the crisis, or place blame on others.[28]

With limited information and confirmation biases, actions for leading the crises are guided by the values and managerial traditions of the organization's headquarters and home country.[29] For example, in 1994, when Mitsubishi Motors Manufacturing of America (MMMA), an auto manufacturer with corporate headquarters in Japan, confronted a sexual harassment crisis in its Normal, Illinois, assembly plant, its first response was to deny the allegations. As investigations into MMMA progressed, the company argued that the harassment incidents were isolated and not a normal pattern of practice for which it should be held liable.[30] However, female MMMA employees reported to the U.S. Equal Employment Opportunity Commission (EEOC) that the company was a work environment in which women were oriented toward the Japanese culture and told they should not work in factories or make eye contact with men. By 1996, not only was a sexual harassment lawsuit filed by 22 individual female employees, but also the EEOC filed its own class action suit against MMMA. At the time, this was the largest sexual harassment lawsuit ever filed in the United States, and the potential legal liability was estimated at $200 million.[31]

Within a short period of time, the crisis began to receive additional media coverage, and another class action lawsuit was filed. However, Mitsubishi, the Japanese parent company of MMMA, underestimated the negative consequences of this media coverage.[32] The miscalculation led to a threat of consumer boycotts. In response to the growing crisis, MMMA organized a support committee of its employees. With thousands of signatures, this group of employees purchased a full-page ad in the local paper stating that they were proud to be employed by MMMA and support their company.[33] During the same time, MMMA's general counsel encouraged the firm's employees to use phone banks at the plants to complain to their congressperson about the sexual harassment allegations and to organize a demonstration against the EEOC.[34] MMMA provided buses for employees to travel to Chicago so that they could march outside of the EEOC headquarters. Employees who chose not to participate were required to report to work or be docked one day of salary.

Mitsubishi's leaders in both the United States and Japanese headquarters perceived organizing employees to take a stance against the EEOC as a strategy for controlling the situation. Even though the crisis occurred in a different country than the corporate headquarters, the underlying frame of reference for leadership actions drew upon socially acceptable behaviors and legal practices in the home country of Japan.[35] In Japan, the management of business activities is strongly linked to national societal values, and consequently there is the tendency for a single set of Japanese moral principles to be applied in its international operations.[36] Moreover, a Japanese company operating in Japan has the option of ignoring sexual harassment lawsuits because there is minimal threat of costly litigation.[37] The MMMA sexual harassment crisis illustrates that facing a challenge with the controller global mindset can manifest into an enactment of organizational routines that do not adapt to changes in the operating environment.[38] Also, the MMMA case highlights what happens when organizations focus on the "taking charge" aspect of the crisis and do not consider global environmental conditions, such as the economy, demographics, or sociopolitical factors when planning response actions. The organization exposes its weaknesses to environmental threats.[39] This is particularly problematic when organizational learning is not incorporated into the leadership process, since acquiring knowledge of the operational environment of a foreign subsidiary is critical for crisis resolution.[40]

Interestingly, a few weeks after the EEOC rally, MMMA changed its strategy. Its public relations campaign backfired when the media, congresswomen, civil rights leaders, and women's organizations questioned the motivations behind its actions.[41] MMMA hired former U.S. Labor Secretary Lynn Martin to examine its human resource management practices.[42] Martin's recommendations resulted in the creation of a training program on sexual harassment, the hiring of an affirmative action administrator to respond to harassment or discriminatory complaints of employees, and managerial changes at the Illinois plant. Hence, the pressures of stakeholders shifted MMMA actions from defending and controlling to adapting organizational practices to accommodate the workplace norms of its U.S. subsidiary.

The Integrator

The integrator mindset strategically frames cross-national and multicultural perspectives to develop an awareness of geographical differences and the corresponding capabilities needed to lead when a crisis occurs beyond the organization's domestic borders.[43] Organizational members perceive global operations holistically and pay close attention to the complex patterns of relationships that exist between an organization's partners and subsidiaries. By paying close attention, the organization has the ability to bridge and leverage national differences to synergistically design and execute crisis management strategies. The foundation of an integrator mindset is a learning organization. Knowledge management is a core competency, and even in crisis situations organizational members seek to constantly learn and transfer knowledge within the organization and across boundaries for it to be absorbed, adapted, and innovated. The focus on learning enables the organization to become resourceful and resilient as it responds to a crisis by analyzing the crisis experience and using the knowledge acquired as a basis for change.[44] Since the integrative mindset is programmed for change, the process can involve the organization working with members across geographical boundaries for not only learning new concepts as a result of the crisis, but also unlearning old habits that are unproductive or detrimental to the well-being of the organization.

Although some have criticized Union Carbide for its response to the Bhopal, India, disaster, several of the company's actions illustrate an integrative mindset for handling a global crisis.[45] This crisis occurred in 1984 when a Union Carbide in Bhopal experienced a disastrous release of methyl isocyanate, a toxic gas used to manufacture pesticides. The release of this toxic gas resulted in the deaths of more than 3,800 people, and over 170,000 were injured.[46] Union Carbide's role in the Bhopal crisis was attributed to a major planning failure of senior management, which did not imagine or take seriously a worst-case scenario.[47] Thus, Union Carbide's approach to managing the crisis was largely reactive. From the onset of the crisis, leaders at Union Carbide coordinated activities between its corporate headquarters in Danbury, Connecticut, and the plant in Bhopal, India. Union Carbide's leaders went back and forth between both locations as they worked to contain and recover from the crisis. Communication systems were designed to be double-looped between operations in the United States and India and were inclusive of key constituents, such as government officials, shareholders, customers, suppliers, and employees.[48] Union Carbide's inclusion of government officials and shareholders suggests a strategy to create linkages with groups who provide authority, control, or regulation of the crisis situation,[49] whereas employees, suppliers, and customers represented key functional linkages that provided input or received output. By implementing plans for communicating with both groups of constituents, Union Carbide managed its global environment by investing time and energy in relationships.

Union Carbide efforts for managing the crisis extended beyond the corporate headquarters and the Bhopal, India, site of the disaster. The firm's West Virginia facility was quickly closed after the Bhopal incident since it also manufactured methyl isocyanate.[50] The West Virginia plant remained closed until safety measures were reexamined and Union Carbide analyzed the cause of the Bhopal tragedy. For investigating the cause of the crisis, the organization created several teams with members that represented various departments throughout the organization. These teams traveled between the United States and India analyzing how the chemical reaction occurred by working backward and experimenting with different environmental controls, constraints, and errors. Throughout Union Carbide global operations, the teams microscopically examined manufacturing processes and risks management. The Bhopal accident was a motivator for leadership to set up a corporate policy on risk assessment to understand the hazards involved in worldwide production of its products and to champion a movement to improve the industry's safe management of chemicals.[51] Also, leadership prioritized achieving the goal of becoming "second to none" in the environmental performance of Union Carbide's businesses by establishing global health, safety, and environmental standards.[52] For these standards, Union Carbide's corporate office decides upon the specific environmental goals for the firm's global business subsidiaries, but it adapts the implementation of these goals to the different macro-environments of each country.

In summary, as observed from Union Carbide, the enactment of an integrative global mindset involves leadership working within a central command structure. However, the central command structure is not a protective silo for leaders to build barriers. Instead, it is used to coordinate crisis containment and resolution efforts that extend beyond the organization's domestic boundaries.[53] Through vertical and horizontal coordination, leaders are able to expedite the decision-making process and deploy resources to appropriate locations. Concerted coordination breeds knowledge by revealing vulnerabilities throughout the organization. Similarly, because of the pressurized nature of a global crisis situation, some organizations will use the crisis as an opportunity to learn by actively acquiring and sharing information with international subsidiaries, and this creates a platform for changing behaviors that caused the crisis (Figure 8.1).

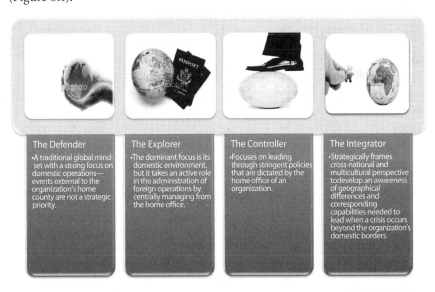

The Defender	The Explorer	The Controller	The Integrator
•A traditional global mindset with a strong focus on domestic operations—events external to the organization's home county are not a strategic priority.	•The dominant focus is its domestic environment, but it takes an active role in the administration of foreign operations by centrally managing from the home office.	•Focuses on leading through stringent policies that are dictated by the home office of an organization.	•Strategically frames cross-national and multicultural perspective to develop an awareness of geographical differences and corresponding capabilities needed to lead when a crisis occurs beyond the organization's domestic borders.

Figure 8.1   Global mindset.

Cultural Framing of Global Crisis Situations

In addition to thinking strategically, a global mindset incorporates cultural attributes of nationalities as insights for leading a crisis. The cultural perspective of a global mindset focuses on the diversity and inclusion within an organization's international locations by overcoming an ethnocentric mindset.[54] In an ideal world, organizations employ the cultural dimension of a global mindset to frame cultural awareness and as a filter for incorporating foreign values into its practices.[55] In essence, the cultural dimension of a global mindset is a cosmopolitan attitude that transcends national models of organizational culture by incorporating complex repertories to understand cultural identities.[56] This state of mind in organizations is reflected when leaders have a sense of others' cultures that is a consequence of listening, looking, intuiting, and reflecting.[57]

In some instances, the cause of a crisis or behavior during a crisis can trace its roots to an ethnocentric mindset that has a home country cultural orientation or polycentric mindset that has the host country cultural orientation.[58] Moreover, an organization's cultural orientation can be a defining attribute of the crisis and challenge the organization's prevailing norms, beliefs, and practices.[59] This can be the case when an organization has operations in different countries and cross-cultural conflicts ensue into a state of crisis. For example, when the German-based automaker Daimler-Benz merged with American-based Chrysler Corporation, a crisis arose in integrating the cultures of two companies that effected the long-term survival of the merged firm.[60] The societal values of each firm's country were reflected in the two firms' corporate cultural norms, and this was indicative in differences in communication styles, leadership practices, and work systems.

Drawing from its American heritage, Chrysler had a free-spirited open culture in contrast to the more traditional, top-down management style of Daimler-Benz.[61] Work practices and decision-making processes at Daimler-Benz were consistent with German work values and were described as conservative and efficient,[62] whereas Chrysler was known for innovation and being daring. From the onset of the merger, Chrysler's president was charged with managing the integration of the two diverse cultures. He did not believe cultural differences would be an issue and thought a culture would develop that integrated both companies' work values.[63] However, each firm held on to its national and organizational culture. Consequently, the forecasted synergies of the merged companies were not realized and the merged firm experienced financial decline. After nine years, Daimler-Benz and Chrysler separated, and the Chrysler division was sold off to Cerberus Capital Management.

As with the merger of Daimler-Benz and Chrysler, national cultural differences can influence an organization's behavior during a crisis. National culture shapes the organizational mindset by acting as the collective programming that distinguishes a group of humans from one country to another.[64] National cultural differences can be observed along five dimensions: power distance, individualism, masculinity, uncertainty avoidance, and long-term orientation.[65] Power distance is the extent to which members of a society expect power to be unequally distributed. The individualism dimension of a national culture focuses on the degree the society values individual or collective achievement and interpersonal relationships. The masculinity dimension of a national culture refers to the distribution of roles between genders, and if that society reinforces the traditional masculine roles of control, power, and achievement. Uncertainty avoidance deals with the society's tolerance level for ambiguity. Countries with high uncertainty avoidance are rule-oriented societies that create laws, regulations, and rules to reduce uncertainty. The long-term orientation dimension describes the importance a society places on the future versus the past and present.[66] Societies with a long-term orientation value attitudes and actions that affect the future, such as perseverance, thrift, or shame. In contrast, societies with a short-term orientation place emphasis on respect for tradition, fulfilling social obligations, and protecting one's reputation.

In a comparative study of both U.S. and Japanese airline crises, significant differences were revealed in leadership practices for responses to crises when examining several dimensions of national culture.[67] From the beginning of a Japanese crisis, President Takagi of the Japanese Airlines (JAL) took responsibility for the accident and was highly visible. Although the airline did not claim human error was the cause of the crash, its general assumption of responsibility minimized any uncertainty related to the crisis. President Takagi and JAL's top management team were available to answer questions from the government and interact with victims' families. JAL's president displayed strong masculinity by being assertive and decisive when developing a course of action for leading the crisis. Likewise, a masculine cultural orientation was exhibited when only middle-aged men were assigned to assist families of the crash victims, reinforcing the Japanese value that older males are more equipped than females or younger males to handle crisis situations. JAL's responses to the crash were hierarchical and centralized. This created demarcation differences between levels of power to indicate who was in charge of the crisis.

During the same time range, the American airline Delta never took responsibility for the crash of its airplane. Delta's public relations director was ambiguous in his statements about the cause of the crash, and suggested that weather was the possible cause. When questions could not be answered, Delta spokespersons were comfortable saying "I don't know," and the media was accepting of this response. This arm's length approach for responding to a crisis could be indicative of U.S. tolerance for uncertainty. Both the CEO and president of Delta Airlines kept a low profile during the crisis resolution phase and did not meet with families of survivors. Also in comparison to JAL, Delta Airlines was more decentralized in its management of the crisis. Approximately a dozen senior managers collectively led the organization through Delta's disaster plan.

Other research has described the national cultural attributes that influence a leader's global mindset during a crisis as a "software of the mind" with the capacity to unconsciously program behavior. Guiding this software of the mind are national cultural differences in people's orientation to interpersonal and environmental relationships. These national cultural differences can be segmented into a Western and Eastern approach of crisis leadership.[68] A Western approach to crisis leadership is rooted in rational practices supported by universal ideas on how organizations should resolve crises. The cultural norms and practices of a Western approach to crisis leadership assume there is a systematic process for preventing crises, and when crises occur there is a structured course of action for containing and resolving them. On the other hand, an Eastern approach to crisis leadership may be predisposed to the view that crises are destined events that cannot be prevented. For instance, a research study found that leaders of Malaysian organizations engaged in less crisis prevention planning, and when crises occurred took the orientation of "allowing things to happen."[69] This is in contrast to the Western leadership approach that embraces the orientation "making things happen" in crisis situations through critical inquiry and problem solving. An explanation for this difference is that Malaysia and other Eastern cultures may be inclined to rely on deterministic explanations for crises, and this results in leaders seeking fewer systematic explorations of causality. Consequently, these organizations did not engage in learning how to build leadership practices that can be used during a crisis.

Interestingly and somewhat similar to Malaysian firms, research indicated that crisis prevention plans and formal processes for resolving crises were not major practices of businesses in Africa.[70] Instead, for firms in Africa, the mindset for leading in crises is dictated by national cultural practices. For example, in Africa the written word is not the most important way for remembering information, but there is an emphasis on the oral transmittal of history, and this practice is a barrier to creating codified plans to manage crises. Furthermore, this research discovered that in Africa the cultural mindset that shaped leadership behavior in a crisis was influenced by the African tradition of the palabre. The palabre is an informal forum with a hierarchy where openly and freely an organization problem can be discussed among it members and constituents. The palabre combines Hofstede's cultural dimension of high power distribution with low individualism into a practice of collective actions governed by hierarchy. When the African firm Burkina Faso confronted a financial crisis, it created a council of wise individuals to listen, discuss, and analyze the crisis from different angles. In sum, the palabre served as a suggestion box and ideas were combined to form a collective resolution for the crisis.

Stakeholders and the Global Environment of Crises

The previous section integrated research on a global mindset with crisis leadership. Interwoven throughout the research on global mindset are the challenges of managing stakeholders in a global environment. Hence, to effectively lead a crisis in a global environment, it is essential to have an understanding of the nature of the relationships between an organization and its stakeholders. As you may recall from Chapter 2, stakeholders are any person, group, or organization affected by the firm's operations or who can influence the firm's attainment of its goals.[71] Strategizing about interactions with stakeholders entails leaders acknowledging that stakeholders will try to influence the decision-making process so that it is consistent with their needs. Another tenet of incorporating stakeholders into the crisis management process is that balancing the interests of various stakeholders is important since an organization cannot survive unless, in the long run, it gives key stakeholders fair treatment.[72]

When a crisis transcends geographical borders, the management of stakeholders intensifies. The need for coordination and control expands to a global scale so that the organization can efficiently monitor and influence the outcome of the crisis situation.[73] Yet, as different segments of stakeholders are further removed from the centralized point of command, organizations become more vulnerable to losing control. Also, complicating the globalization of a crisis are the conflicts of interest that may arise between different stakeholders, and relationships that are dependent on each other for resources. This is because resource-dependent relationships between organizations can be characterized by power dynamics to compete or control scarce and valuable resources needed for survival.[74]

For instance, when in 2003 the Canadian beef industry experienced a crisis because of cows infected with bovine spongiform encephalopath (BSE), more commonly known as mad cow disease, it was not prepared to manage stakeholders outside of its national borders.[75] After Canada became identified as a country with BSE-infected cows, many countries issued trade embargos and Canadian beef suppliers were unable to export their cattle livestock. Canadian consumers did not reduce their consumption of beef because of trust in their government's view that the beef was safe, but trade embargos from international trading partners resulted in long-term negative economic consequences for the industry. Within a year, some Canadian cattle producers claimed bankruptcy or went out of business. Industry representatives became frustrated and blamed different government agencies as a defense mechanism. This anger was not limited to Canadian government agencies. The Canadian cattle producers especially became incensed with the United States and contended that its trade embargo was unreasonable and ineffective because the industry is highly integrated between the two countries.

The global nature of the beef industry necessitated the Canadian beef producers to move beyond the closed-system mentality to manage the strategic complexity of the crisis. With the involvement of multiple stakeholders who had the power to impact the resolution of the crisis, the Canadian beef industry experienced an escalating loss of control until the United States lifted the trade embargo. For the Canadian beef industry, the globalization of commercial, economic, and sociopolitical forces redefined power and resource dependency relationships. This resource dependency of the Canadian beef industry on stakeholders outside of its country constrained its strategic choices and put the industry in a holding pattern until trade embargos were lifted.[76,77]

As illustrated in the Canadian beef industry incident, in a global environment, organizations have less control of stakeholders beyond geographical borders. This is because local governing policies and cultural practices can change the rules of the game, and there is less pressure to cooperate as geographical boundaries expand. Moreover, power dynamics can come into play and be influenced by the stakeholders' capacity to threaten or cooperate during the crisis. Often this is determined by both the resources the stakeholder controls and the resources it seeks from the organization in crisis.[78]

Megacommunities

The globalization of a crisis demands that organizations consider not only resource dependency and coordination of stakeholders, but also the creation and utilization of megacommunities where stakeholders work together to prevent, contain, and resolve crises of mutual interest.[79] A megacommunity is a community of organizations from the sectors of business, government, and nonprofit whose leaders and organizational members deliberately come together across national boundaries for the purpose of achieving a goal they cannot achieve alone. As discussed earlier in this chapter, often the goals of different organizations cannot be achieved alone because of the increased interdependent and global flow of human activities, knowledge, and resources around the world. The complexity, abruptness, and unpredictability of a crisis in a global environment along with limits of human capital create a challenge for organizations.

Furthermore, each of the three sectors—business, nonprofit, and government—have developed specialized skill sets for dealing with global crises but have not eliminated barriers for sharing this knowledge.

Yet, frequently and quickly crises are diffused globally and expeditiously across the three sectors. Take, for example, the impact that the very small nonprofit, activist organization Global Resistance had on Coca-Cola, which cost the companies millions of dollars in lost sales in India and legal fees. Global Resistance is based in California, and in 2004 had a grants-funded budget of $60,000 from sources such as the Unitarian Church social.[80] Global Resistance's founder, Amit Srivastava, is the only full-time employee, and the organization has a part-time webmaster. Despite its small size, Global Resistance developed a grassroots campaign against Coca-Cola manufacturing practices in India that mobilized other nonprofit organizations, college students, communities, and local Indian government units. Amit Srivastava and his supporters accused Coca-Cola India's operations of stealing water, poisoning the land, and selling soft drinks laced with toxic pesticides. Although the claims were unproven, the protests of these activists resulted in government officials of the southern state of Kerala, India, shutting down a $16 million Coke bottling plant. Likewise, in Varanasi, India, the local governmental officials accused Coca-Cola of similar behavior and blamed the firm for drought conditions.

The core of the strategy of Global Resistance's campaign against Coca-Cola centered on using the Internet to communicate its message, having its supporters fax thousands of letters to Coca-Cola's headquarters regarding their practices in India, and serving as intermediary for coordinating protest efforts. This strategy brought together all different types of people and organizations from different countries. Although Coca-Cola had more resources than Global Resistance, it ignored the energy that could be created from an informal megacommunity until it escalated into a crisis. Global Resistance created energy around this issue by serving as initiator of the protest against Coca-Cola and by connecting different transnational sectors, such as international activists and the Indian government, to form collaborative partnerships. Often, initiators such as Global Resistance build energy on an international scale to create or resolve crises through a megacommunity motivated by some combination of egoistic (voluntary or self-serving) and altruistic (mandated or problem-focused) reasons.[81]

As observed from the Coca-Cola crisis in India, organizations cannot ignore the global strength of megacommunities. If an organization is connected with an interest of the megacommunity, it is a member of it by default status.[82] In the case of Coca-Cola, its stakeholders' claims of offensive behavior earned the firm latent membership status, but for a long period of time Coca-Cola was disconnected from the megacommunity. Eventually Coca-Cola could not ignore the actions of the megacommunity created by Global Resistance. Although environmentalists and community groups still want to shut down some of Coca-Cola India's manufacturing plants, the company has been pressured to become involved in the megacommunity.[83] In response, Coca-Cola developed a corporate social responsibility plan for directing its treatment of water and the environment. This plan included policies for assessing the scarcity of water risk and the creation of efficient systems to reduce the amount of water needed to produce a liter of soft drink from 2.5 liters of water to 1.0 liter of water. Also, Coca-Cola has established the goal to be a water-neutral consumer of environmental resources by investing in water recycling and conservation efforts.[84]

The Coca-Cola water pollution example highlights a megacommunity forming across domestic borders with a combination of initiators and reactors to resolve a crisis. In other incidents, megacommunities are more purposeful and cooperate to manage global crisis situations. When a megacommunity is a concerted, planned effort, the different members representing the business, nonprofit, and government sectors come together as collective leaders to partner on an international scale.[85] These different organizations agree to work together because of overlapping vital interests around a shared issue, and this issue may sometimes have intersecting geographical implications. Equally important to overlapping interests are a convergence of commitment to mutual action and structured organizing principles that draw upon diverse networks.[86] Structure is ingrained in megacommunities by an explicit formative stage that establishes a protocol and a sense of joint mission. The structure of a megacommunity is not rigid, but adaptable because of environmental circumstances and the evolution of the megacommunity through learning by collective interactions.

A megacommunity can evolve into a strategic bridge that leverages its knowledge or resources for the benefit of subsequent crises that will demand collaboration.[87] The public health sector is one arena where we sometimes see the formation of global megacommunities as strategic bridges to resolve crises. Take the case of the 1995 outbreak of the Ebola virus in Zaire. A group of nonprofit organizations and government agencies were able to quickly halt the spread of the virus because of the work of a megacommunity formed in 1976.[88] In 1976, when there was a previous outbreak of the Ebola virus in Zaire, a diversity of organizations came together to prepare for the next outbreak by investing in research on the Ebola virus and creating an organizing system for disaster response to it. So in 1995, when the Ebola virus resurfaced in Zaire, nonprofit agencies from across the globe and the Zaire government, with the support of research by pharmaceutical companies, were able to bridge the knowledge learned in the last 19 years into a systematic approach of surveillance, education of susceptible populations, and isolation procedures that would contain the outbreak of the Ebola virus.

Rapid Reflection Forces in Global Learning Communities

The research on megacommunities emphasizes the importance of creating global learning communities to prevent and manage crises. When an organization can partner with other organizations in its sector to create a global infrastructure for crisis management, it benefits participants by bringing together diverse perspectives to reflect upon the crisis, develop solutions, and formalize a process for managing knowledge across geographical boundaries. Patrick Lagadec and his colleagues describe this type of learning community as "rapid reflection forces."[89] Comparable to the military use of "fast action forces" to implement ground strategy, rapid reflection forces are teams with leadership representation from different organizations that clarify an industry's crisis management strategy by defining possible scenarios and response plans to these scenarios. In a global environment, the value created by a rapid reflection force is that these industry leaders do not come together just to create quick fixes for a crisis, but also the group is committed to advancing their understanding of the crisis situation and creating initiatives to prevent or contain future crises. Rapid reflection forces address the complexity and interdependent aspect of global crises by bringing leaders together to collectively ask questions that help the group dissect the crisis and its implications for various systems and stakeholders. Based on the knowledge codified during the inquiry phase, rapid reflection forces formulate strategic initiatives that are support mechanisms for when the next crisis occurs.

The Paris Initiative, which brought senior postal executives to Paris from 30 countries one year after the 2001 anthrax crisis to share and learn from each other's experiences, is an insightful example of a rapid reflection force.[90] This alliance of international postal executives formed in response to a crisis that began September 18, 2001, just one week after the major terrorist attacks on the United States. Four anthrax-contaminated envelopes and thousands of hoaxed anthrax envelopes paralyzed the U.S. Postal Service, and this had rippling effects on the international postal system for a 10-week period. From the onset, this crisis highlighted the interdependence of the global postal network that connects together international, national, local, and regional public carriers (such as the U.S. Postal Service or France's La Poste), corporate carriers (such as Federal Express or DHL), third-party mail-sorting companies, and transportation mail delivery firms. A crisis in one segment of this interconnected industry has effects on the entire global system. Complicating the anthrax crisis was the unpredictability of attacks and that the attacks could not be isolated to one part of the global postal system.

The 2001 anthrax attacks exposed the vulnerabilities of the global postal system. Postal systems realized there was not a global mechanism for sharing real-time information across geographical boundaries.[91] For instance, the chairman of France's La Poste was in New York when he heard the news of two persons infected with anthrax in Germany, but he could not get in touch with his German or English counterpart.[92] Tensions among the leadership team at La Poste remained high until that evening when the news reported that Germany's anthrax case was proven false. This was a wake-up call for La Poste's leadership, and they were determined to act quickly and bring together colleagues from PostEurop—an association of 48 European public postal operators created to optimize postal operations and foster greater cooperation among its members. Although members of PostEurop were formed as an association because of the interconnectedness of the global postal system, this group had not established a coordinated effort to deal with a crisis on an international level.

Therefore, in response to the anthrax attacks, this group came together to create an infrastructure so that as an alliance, European postal services would be ready to respond to crises, and especially crises that could paralyze the European postal network.[93] In November 2002, a meeting convened in Paris, and in addition to members of PostEurop, experts in public health, crisis management, security, and the vice president of the U.S. Postal Service attended. By convening as a rapid reflection force, members had an opportunity to discuss experiences and lessons from the anthrax crisis, and to share ideas so that they could improve processes and develop operational capabilities for the collective management of global postal crises.

The outcome of the conference was the creation of a network of crisis managers and security officers within the European public postal services, and a system that connected European postal officers during the first 24 hours of the crisis.[94] The purpose of this system is to exchange information about solutions being implemented by each country and to serve as a virtual meeting place so that during a crisis, members of PostEurop can work as an interorganizational network to formulate concerted responses to crises. Two months after the Paris meeting, this rapid reflection force had its first test when PostEurop received a notice from the U.S. Postal Service about a possible anthrax contamination in the Washington, D.C., area.[95] Although this anthrax threat was a hoax, the network created at the Paris Initiative provided European postal services with reliable and timely information on the incident, and this enabled network members to assess the scope of risk.

Using Technology to Enable Crisis Resolution

To effectively and resolutely lead an organization throughout the crisis life cycle requires the coordination of people and other resources, the synthesis and interpretation of information, and communication that spans multiple stake-holders.[96] Moreover, large-scale and global crises often require that both private and public organizations work together[97]; therefore, the leaders of these groups must function collaboratively and with a shared understanding of the end goal and the means for attaining it. The challenges associated with global crises are exacerbated largely because the coordination, synthesis, and communication must take place despite barriers associated with geographical boundaries and physical access to a region, language barriers, differences in cultural norms, political and geopolitical considerations, resource constraints, and more. Thus, the process of gathering and disseminating information across these obstacles can result in undesirable and even dangerous delays in crisis handling and deci-sion making.[98] Consider, for example, the case of the 1989 Exxon Valdez oil spill on Bligh's Reef in Prince William Sound, Alaska. The vessel was located in a remote region and the oil was dispersed over a vast amount of territory. Accessing the location to commence the clean up was going to be a challenge, and the remoteness of the territory meant that traditional communication chan-nels were nonexistent. Yet, within a few hours of the spill an Exxon command center was set up in Houston, Texas, where Exxon USA and Exxon Shipping corporate headquarters were located. Cleanup supplies and equipment were assembled from around the world from Houston. In a matter of a few days, executives connected with experts on oil spill cleanups across the globe and had enlisted personnel and major contractors from the United Kingdom, Canada, Australia, Norway, Colombia, and Malaysia to gather in Valdez to respond to the spill.[99] The ability to pull together a cross-national team to respond on short notice underscores the importance of collaboration, coordination, and infor-mation dissemination. Technology, and information technology in particular, is becoming increasingly important in facilitating these activities and ensuring effective crisis handling.

Technology can be a firm-specific asset, and like all other resources and assets can be used to implement competitive strategies.[100] The more technologi-cally advanced a firm, the more potentially competitive it becomes in the indus-try. In this way, technology is a differentiator of sorts in that it has the capability of distinguishing firms and firm performance. In the book *Good to Great*, Jim Collins devotes a chapter to technology accelerators, and offers data indicating that great companies think about and use technology differently from average ones.[101] It is not that technology itself propels a company past its competition, but rather that technology aids an existing innovative business idea or solu-tion. Thus, a solid strategy coupled with pioneering technology can differentiate high-performing companies. In fact, research has demonstrated that the inter-action between technology and other nontechnology resources influences per-formance.[102] This interaction functions in one of three ways: (1) compensatory (a change in one offsets a change in the level of another), (2) enhancing (a change in one may increase the impact of the other), or (3) suppressing (the presence or a change in one resource lessens the impact of the other).[103]

So while technology can play a clear role in firm performance and sustaining a competitive advantage, we believe technology and information systems can also serve in a similar capacity in the context of crisis handling. To lead under pressure requires focused attention throughout the crisis life cycle, from signal detection to business recovery and learning. Effective leaders prepare for and develop plans for managing across each phase. A central aspect of those plans should include a clear understanding of the ways in which technology can and should facilitate crisis handling. Yet, because technology and information systems (IS) are generally considered to be a firm-specific resource, companies have relied on their technological capabilities in the spirit of competition. They focus on developing technology that is valuable, rare, and difficult to imitate, appropriate, or substitute. By protecting technology resources against imitation or substitution a firm can sustain an existing advantage.[104] In fact, researchers have attempted to examine how firms function in hypercompetitive, fast-moving, and volatile environments (all characteristics of a crisis).[105] The resulting dynamic capability model suggests that competitive advantage is achieved by creating new resources (i.e., technology) to realize congruence with the changing circumstances.[106] However, when there is a need for organizations to work together, as in the case of a global crisis, technology can and should be a powerful tool for facilitating collaboration and coordination. To this point, recent research extends the dynamic capability perspective to crisis settings that require a cooperative response rather than competitive positioning.[107] As Schneider noted, crisis situations require not just a fast response, but an immediate response, and a delay in crisis response may result in a humanitarian crisis of a larger magnitude than the damage caused by the crisis itself.[108] Consider the double tragedy of Hurricane Katrina when it hit the Gulf Coast region. The affected communities were victimized first by the hurricane and again by the slow and inefficient crisis response at all levels. This was a case of clear failure in collaboration and coordination as well as a failure to adequately utilize technology in a coordinated effort.

As we have said throughout this book, crises are chaotic and unstable events, and the coordination required to resolve them can be onerous.[109] In large part, this is because roles and responsibilities of crisis handlers (which may not have been identified prior to the onset of the crisis) are uncertain.[110] Moreover, global crises offer an additional level of complexity. Leidner and colleagues argue, however, that by understanding how technology is coordinated during a crisis, and the central role it plays both as a resource and as a coordinated mechanism, "organizations and government agencies can be better positioned to mount a swift response to future crises." Their research attempted to answer the following questions related to technology and crisis: What technology resources are needed in crisis response? How are these resources bundled with other resources? How are they effectively coordinated? To address these questions they examined the crisis response to the severe acute respiratory syndrome (SARS) outbreak in Singapore and the Asian tsunami. Below, we discuss their findings in order to highlight the important role of technology in managing large-scale and global crises.

The Role of Technology in the SARS and Asian Tsunami Crises

To use an example of crisis handling from Chapter 5, the Chinese government made good use of technology during the SARS epidemic. The SARS outbreak began in Singapore in March 2003, and, by April 2003, it had spread from a few cases to a national outbreak. In a two-month time period, Singapore deployed a massive crisis response plan that focused on the contact tracing of SARS patients. The tracing involved the identification of all of the places a patient had visited and required the participation of multiple government agencies, including the Ministries of Education, which provided contact information and promoted crisis containment awareness in schools and businesses; the Ministry of Community Development and Sports, which taught childcare centers on preventive tracking measures; the National Environment Agency, which managed the data on identifying and tracing contacts; and the Ministry of Home Affairs, which carried out quarantine orders. The Defense Science and Technology Agency (DSTA) developed an information technology system to support the large-scale contact tracing and data management activities across these various groups. In addition, technology-based diagramming and networking applications were used to document, organize, and disseminate across agencies the complex data that were being produced by the tracing. On May 30, 2003, the WHO removed Singapore from its list of SARS-affected countries.

One year later, on December 26, 2004, a tsunami devastated 13 countries' coastlines, killed nearly 300,000 people, and left millions more homeless. Almost immediately after the tsunami struck, more than 160 aid organizations and United Nations agencies commenced crisis handling and relief operations from a coordination center in Singapore. Again the DSTA served as a central player in the crisis containment effort, primarily in its work to set up an IT infrastructure and applications to store and disseminate information, which it did within hours. The IT system enabled the various agencies to exchange updated crisis-related data, such as the aid supplies delivery schedule and the ground situation report. The system was also able to track relief personnel deployment in those regions hit by the tsunami and send text alerts as well as messages to and from field personnel. While the development and implementation of these systems was ongoing, other agencies set up a contact center to manage inquiry calls from victims' families and friends. Using this technology, crisis handlers were able to identify psychologists and other mental health specialists, as well as volunteer organizations, and deploy them to appropriate places to provide counseling and other services to those areas most hard hit. In short, within the first 20 days of the tsunami, the IT system fostered a collaboration network among multiple agencies in carrying out the crisis relief activities.

Although there were problems and lessons learned in the handling of both the SARS and tsunami incidents, it is clear that technology can play an important role in facilitating effective and efficient crisis handling within and across global environments. From their research Leidner and colleagues argue that the combination of leadership, information technology infrastructure, and collaborative networks is a critical organizational asset.[111] When these assets are linked with existing capabilities (specifically the ability to build and apply IT, the ability to recognize signals, and the ability to see the big picture)[112] organizations become more adept at preventing and handling crisis situations. In fact, the authors conclude that "Singapore's existing IT infrastructure provided the foundation for the crisis management effort, and not just in terms of its technical underpinnings. The IT infrastructure resources proved to be a critical antecedent for engendering collaboration, coordination, and IT knowledge across the involved entities to quickly develop capabilities in response to the crises."[113] Similarly, although Exxon was heavily criticized for its public relations handling of the Valdez oil spill, the company was able to effectively leverage sophisticated technology and other resources from across the globe to quickly mobilize a complex set of relationships to commence a cleanup initiative of enormous proportions.

Bundling Technology and Crisis Leadership

In managing a global crisis, technology is only as good as the leadership that supports and uses it. In large-scale or global crises, multiple leaders are required and technology can serve as one of the primary means by which those leaders are able to connect and coordinate. However, because crises are generally rare and often unforeseen events, the likelihood that existing technology will be able to perform in the precise way that meets the needs of those leaders is small. Thus, leaders must have the foresight to see the possible utility of technology and then invest appropriately in developing a flexible IT infrastructure that will position their organizations to handle threatening situations even before they arise. When IT infrastructures are in place, crisis handlers are better positioned to respond and deploy needed resources. In the case of the SARS and Asian tsunami crises, had Singapore lacked the IT infrastructure and IT development capability, it would have had to bring in external IT staff. Yet, no matter how sophisticated or skilled this new group, it would have lacked the collaborative and decision-making network that facilitated the fast development of crisis information systems. In short, any organization's IT infrastructure is only as good as the extent to which the organization's leadership values it to be.[114]

In Chapter 2 we discussed signal detection and sense making as two critical crisis leadership competencies. Specifically, the ability to recognize signals and then make sense of the data presented is critical in influencing response time and response quality in a crisis. Technology is important in both signal detection and sense making in that it can facilitate the recognition of potential problems. Moreover, according to Turoff, leaders who are unable or simply refuse to recognize signals are also less likely to make adequate investments in IT and are less likely to design adequate response systems when a crisis does occur.[115] On the other hand, leaders who engage in signal detection and sense making, and then use information technology to disseminate information, mobilize resources, or engage in collaborative problem solving with others, are demonstrating a critical set of core crisis leadership behaviors.

Finally, we must emphasize the role of an IT infrastructure in coordination activity during a crisis. Coordination is the mechanism that enables an organization to transform existing resources into action. Based on Leider and colleagues' research, one of the primary coordinating mechanisms during a crisis is IT structures.[116] Although standard operating procedures and face-to-face meetings are the typical coordination mechanisms in small-scale or local crises, for global crises that involve numerous parties, broad-reaching stakeholders, and enormous financial and other resources, coordination will largely involve more organizational structural techniques.[117] Contrary to the dominant centralized and command-and-control structures that characterize most responses to emergency situations,[118] recent studies argue that loosening rather than tightening communication and decision-making structures during a crisis may be more appropriate.[119] In the case of both the SARS and tsunami crises, for example, agencies were able to respond quickly and mobilize resources (people and technology) because of a flatter and more nimble organizational structure.[120]

In summary, astute leaders acknowledge the interaction between a crisis and the global environment. In this chapter, we contend that leading a crisis in a global environment involves processing and sense making of different perspectives to create knowledge. An aspect of this knowledge building is developing a strategic mindset for interpreting and directing actions. In addition to thinking strategically about the global environment of a crisis, the mindset should incorporate cultural attributes of different nationalities to understand identities and associated behaviors. Furthermore, leaders should build and manage relationships

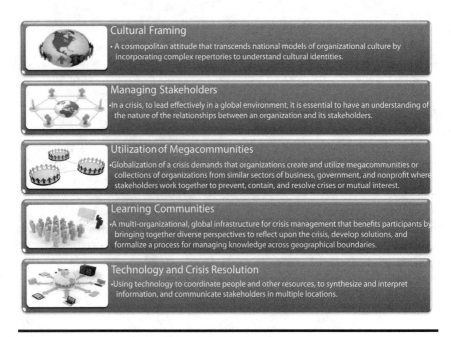

Figure 8.2   Global crisis leadership considerations.

with stakeholders in the organization's global environment. During the life cycle of a global crisis, managing stakeholders is a balancing of interests so that key stakeholders receive fair treatment. Options for collaborating with international stakeholders to prevent or resolve a crisis are the formation of megacommunities or industry-specific rapid reflection forces. Last, this chapter highlights that the global environment necessitates the importance of using technology to prevent or resolve crises. Technology facilitates double-loop communication and the coordination of stakeholders across national borders (Figure 8.2).

From Theory to Practice

The globalization of crisis adds another layer of complexity and uncertainty to leading an organization during a crisis. Leaders must broaden their mindset and actions to take into account the sociocultural, political, economic, and demographic patterns beyond their domestic borders. Also, leading crises in a global environment calls for expanding your networks of stakeholders to include members from different geographical areas and sectors. By expanding the network to collaborate with a diversity of stakeholders, you enhance the potential for organizational learning, increase resources, create effective infrastructures for mobilizing action, and expedite the crisis resolution process. The following points summarize ways in which leaders can manage the global environment of a crisis:

- Be cognizant of the organization global mindset. This is a collective approach that an organization uses to process information and direct its behavior in a global crisis situation. The global mindset helps leaders filter the global environment to manage complexity, ambiguity, and dynamism. The integrator is a holistic approach to framing a global crisis situation. It incorporates multiple perspectives to develop an awareness of geographical differences and the corresponding capabilities to lead a global crisis.
- Pay attention to the national cultural attributes of the various crisis stakeholders. Often the cultural attributes define the norms, beliefs, and practices that govern and differentiate behavior of a group of humans from one country to another. Cultural attributes to analyze when managing a global crisis include the distribution of power, values of individual or collective achievement, gender roles, tolerance level for uncertainty, and time orientation.
- Knowledge is power when dealing with the different stakeholders during a global crisis. This is because each group of stakeholders will try to contribute to or influence the decision-making process. To identify these various relationships create a map of stakeholders. This will help leaders analyze the relationships of key stakeholders and who controls essential resources for resolving the crisis. Also, a stakeholder map will enable leaders to identify the various interests of each stakeholder group.
- To prevent or resolve a global crisis, expand the organizational learning community by creating a megacommunity or rapid reflection force. The advantage of a megacommunity is it brings together the nonprofit, public, and corporate sectors because of interdependent mutual interests. Megacommunities facilitate the flow of human activities and resources within a formalized infrastructure. Similarly, rapid reflection forces can bring together collaborators from different countries, but the focus is on developing industry-specific knowledge for formulating crisis management strategies.
- Technology can be a source of advantage in the various phases of crisis management. This is especially the case when a crisis extends beyond domestic borders. Therefore, use technology to facilitate collaboration and coordination between various stakeholders. Also, design technological systems as a double-loop communication mechanism that enables the organizations to signal detect, sense-make of its environment, update stakeholders, and receive feedback on its actions. When double-loop communication is embedded in the organization's technological system, it will be more adaptable to its global environment (Figures 8.3 and 8.4).

How should I deal with the additional layer of complexity and uncertainty that globalization adds to leading during a crisis?

Leaders must broaden their mindset and actions to take in to account the socio-cultural, political, and economic, and demographic patterns beyond their domestic borders. Also, leading crises in a global environment calls for expanding your networks of stakeholders to include members from different geographical areas and sectors. By expanding the network to collaborate with a diversity of stakeholders, you enhance the potential for organizational learning, increase resources, create effective infrastructures for mobilizing action, and expedite the crisis resolution process.

What are some key points to remember when managing the global environment of a crisis?

Be cognizant of the organization global mindset.

Pay attention to the national cultural attributes of the various crisis stakeholders.

Knowledge is power when dealing with the different stakeholders during a global crisis.

To prevent or resolve a global crisis, expand the organization learning community by creating a mega-community or rapid reflection force.

Technology can be a source of advantage in the various phases of crisis management.

Figure 8.3   Leader's hot seat.

Figure 8.4   Leadership Links 8.1

- Creating Global a Mindset
  http://www.clomedia.com/features/2008/June/2235/index.php

- Leading Change with a Global Mindset: A Case Study
  http://knowledgenetwork.thunderbird.edu/research/2009/06/05/brazil/

- Center for Creative Leadership Discusses Megacommunities
  http://crisisleadership.blogspot.com/2008/08/megacommunity-harnessing-tri-sector-to.html

- World Health Organization Global Competency Model
  http://www.who.int/employment/competencies/WHO_competencies_EN.pdf

- Geert Hofstede home page
  http://stuwww.uvt.nl/~csmeets/index.html

Endnotes

1. Pinsdorf, *All crises are global.*
2. Rosenthal & Kouzmin, Globalizing an agenda for contingencies and crisis management, 1–12.
3. Farazmand, Learning from Katrina Crisis, 149–159.
4. Levy et al., What we talk about when we talk about "global mindset," 231–258.
5. Kedia & Muljerji, Global managers, 223–251.
6. Wooten, *Framing crisis management.*
7. Gutpa & Govindarajan, Cultivating a global mindset, 116–126.
8. Bolman & Deal, *Reframing organizations.*
9. Baird, *Meeting the global challenges.*
10. Kedia & Muljerji, Global managers, 223–251.
11. Gupta & Govindarajan, Cultivating a global mindset, 116–126.
12. Eimer, Chinese boycott Western chains over Olympics.
13. Hung, *Carrefour China and the Olympic torch relay.*
14. Leow, In China, citizens call for boycotts of their own, A10.
15. Hung, *Carrefour China and the Olympic torch relay.*
16. China Business, Thirteen days of crisis at Carrefour.
17. Hung, *Carrefour China and the Olympic torch relay.*
18. Kedia & Muljerji, Global managers, 223–251.
19. Moon & Herman, *McDonalds's Russia.*
20. Kenneth, McDonald's adds 22 locations to menu, 5.
21. Moon & Herman, *McDonalds's Russia,* 5.
22. Kedia & Muljerji, Global managers, 223–251.
23. Perlmutter, The tortuous evolution of the multi-national corporation, 9–18.
24. James & Wooten, Diversity crises, 1103–1118.
25. Barnett & Pratt, From threat rigidity to flexibility, 74–88.
26. Staw, Sandelands, & Dutton, Threat-rigidity effects in organizational behavior, 501–524.
27. Ibid.
28. Hart, Symbols, rituals, and power, 36–50.
29. Keida, Harveston, & Bhagat, Orienting curricula and teaching to produce international managers for global competition, 1–22.
30. Cray, Conducive to sexual harassment.
31. Powell, *How normal is normal?*
32. Peirce, Smolinksi, & Rosen, Why sexual harassment complaints fall on deaf ears, 41–54.
33. Pomerenke, Class action sexual harassment lawsuit, 207–219.
34. Cray, Conducive to sexual harassment.
35. Peirce, Smolinksi, & Rosen, Why sexual harassment complaints fall on deaf ears, 41–54.
36. Wokutch & Shepard, The maturing of the Japanese economy, 527–540.
37. Powell, *How normal is normal?*
38. Kounoupas, *A six-step process for effective crisis management in the port industy.*

39. Hensgen, Desouza, & Kraft, Games, signals, detection and processing in the context of crisis management.
40. Hagiwara, The eight characteristics of Japanese crisis-prone organizations, 253–270.
41. Simon, Scherer, & Rau, Sexual harassment in the heartland? 487–495.
42. Cray, Conducive to sexual harassment.
43. Keida, Harveston, & Bhagat, Orienting curricula and teaching to produce international managers for global competition, 1–22.
44. Wang, Developing organizational learning capacity in crisis management, 425–445.
45. Sen & Egelhoff, Six years and counting from crisis management at Bhopal, 69–83.
46. Haseley, Twenty years after Bhopal, 21–22.
47. Ayres & Rohatgi, Bhopal lessons for technological decision-makers, 1–15.
48. Browning, Union Carbide.
49. Ice, Corporate publics and rhetorical strategies, 341–361.
50. Browning, Union Carbide.
51. Preble, Handling international disasters, 550–560.
52. Smith, Bhopal aftermath, 500–553.
53. Farazmand, Learning from Katrina crisis, 149–159.
54. Levy et al., Global mindset, 11–47.
55. Ibid.
56. Vertovec & Cohen, Introduction.
57. Hannerz, Cosmopolitans and locals in world culture, 237–251.
58. Perlmutter, The tortuous evolution of the multinational corporation, 9–18.
59. Elliot & Smith, Cultural readjustment after crisis, 290–317.
60. Darling, Seristo, & Gabrielson, Anatomy of crisis management, 343–360.
61. Ibid.
62. Luthans, *Organizational behavior.*
63. Ake, Chrysler merger going smoothly, C3.
64. Hofstede, *Cultural consequences.*
65. Ibid.
66. Bond & Hofstede, The cash value of Confucian values, 195–200.
67. Haruta & Hallahan, Cultural issues in airline crisis communications, 122–150.
68. Schmidt & Berrell, *Western and Eastern approaches to crisis management for global tourism,* 66–80.
69. Ibid.
70. Acquier, Gand, & Szpirglas, From stakeholders to stakesholder management in crisis episodes, 101–114.
71. Freemen, *Strategic management.*
72. Savage, Dunkin, & Ford, Responding to a crisis, 383–413.
73. Tsang, Military doctrine in crisis management, 65–73.
74. Pfeffer & Salancik, *The external control of organizations.*
75. Charlebois & Labrecque, Processual learning, environmental pluralism, and inherent challenges of managing a socio-economic crisis, 115–125.
76. Pfeffer & Salancik, *The external control of organizations.*
77. Stephens, Malone, & Bailey, Communicating with stakeholders during a crisis, 391–419.

78. Savage, Dunkin, & Ford, Responding to a crisis, 383–413.
79. Gerencser, Van Lee, Napolitano, & Kelly, *Megacommunities*.
80. Stecklowe, How a web of activists gives Coke problems in India, 7.
81. Coplen, *Strategic bridge towards community building*.
82. Kelly, Gerenscer, Napolitano, & Van Lee, *The defining features of a megacommunity*.
83. Gerencser, Van Lee, Napolitano, & Kelly, *Megacommunities*.
84. FairRidge Group, *Water Wars*.
85. Gerencser, Van Lee, Napolitano, & Kelly, *Megacommunities*.
86. Kelly et al., *The defining features of a megacommunity*.
87. Coplen, *Strategic bridge towards community building*.
88. Benini & Badford-Benini, Ebola virus, 10–19.
89. Lagadec, Michel-Kerjan, & Ellis, Disaster via airmail, 99–117.
90. Ibid.
91. Ibid.
92. Hagenbourger, Lagadec, & Pouw, Postal security, anthrax and beyond Europe's posts and the critical network challenge, 105–107.
93. Ibid.
94. Pouw, Conclusions, 142–143.
95. Lagadec, Michel-Kerjan, & Ellis, Disaster via airmail, 99–117.
96. Dantas & Seville, Organizational issues in implementing and information sharing framework, 38.
97. Turoff, Chumer, Van de Walle, & Yao, The design of a dynamic emergency response management information system (DERMIS), 1–35.
98. Leidner, Pan, & Pan, The role of IT in crisis response, 80–99.
99. Yemen & James, *Exxon Valdez revisited*.
100. Teece, Pisano, & Shuen, Dynamic capabilities and strategic management, 509–533.
101. Collins, *Good to great*.
102. Wade & Hulland, The resource-based view and information systems research, 107–148.
103. Leidner, Pan, & Pan, The role of IT in crisis response, 80–99.
104. Barney, Firm resources and sustained competitive advantage, 99–120.
105. Winter, Understanding dynamic capabilities, 991–995.
106. Eisenhardt & Martin, Dynamic capabilities, 1105–1121.
107. Leidner, Pan, & Pan, The role of IT in crisis response, 80–99.
108. Schneider, Administrative breakdowns in the governmental response to Hurricane Katrina, 515–516.
109. Majchrzak, Jarvenpaa, & Holllingshead, Coordinating expertise among emergent groups responding to disasters, 147–161.
110. Leidner, Pan, & Pan, The role of IT in crisis response, 84.
111. Leidner, 80–99.
112. See Chapter 2 for more on these and other crisis leadership competencies.
113. Leidner, Pan, & Pan, The role of IT in crisis response, 87.
114. Ibid., 80–99.
115. Turoff, Past and future emergency response information systems, 29–32.
116. Leidner, Pan, & Pan, The role of IT in crisis response, 80–99.

117. Moynihan, Learning under uncertainty, 350–365.
118. Rosenthal & Kouzmin, Crises and crisis management, 277–304.
119. Lin, Zhao, Ismail, & Carley, Organizational design and restructuring in response to crises, 598–618.
120. Leidner, Pan, & Pan, The role of IT in crisis response, 80–99.

FROM SURVIVING TO THRIVING UNDER PRESSURE

Chapter 9

Crises as Sources of Opportunity and Change*

In 1993, a bacterial epidemic at a restaurant chain killed three toddlers, left 300 others with a severe case of food poisoning, contributed to the downgrading of the company's debt to junk bond status, and over the course of two years led to company losses in excess of $138 million. As a result, the Jack-in-the-Box chain of restaurants nearly collapsed. More than a decade later, however, the Jack-in-the-Box chain is at the top of its industry, having developed new systems and technologies in response to its crises that created opportunity for them to operate differently and better. How did this organization not only survive, but also thrive following this crisis? Quite simply, it was the beneficiary of effective crisis leadership.

Crises are often watershed events for organizations. As we have stated throughout this book, crises pose challenges in which much is at stake (economically, socially, and psychologically), for many constituencies (the organization, its members, and the parties who interact with the organization, such as customers, suppliers, and communities), in both the short and long term.

---

* Originally published in a slightly different form in Brockner, J., & James, E. H. (2008). Toward an understanding of when executives see crisis as opportunity. *Journal of Applied Behavioral Science, 44*(1), 94–115. Reprinted by permission of Joel Brockner and the publisher.

Furthermore, crisis management is extremely difficult. In the face of great uncertainty, and often with precious little time in which to respond, leaders have to take action; doing nothing is not an option in crisis situations. Given the stakes of crises and the challenges associated with their management, it is both theoretically and practically important to understand the conditions under which they are handled more versus less effectively. Whereas existing frameworks on crisis management have made some headway,[1] they have had relatively little to say about when executives come to perceive crises as sources of opportunity. Accordingly, this concluding chapter is designed to redress this deficiency. In it, we will bring key insights from previous chapters to bear specifically on the notion of crisis leadership.

Our working assumption is that crises have the potential to be a catalyst for positive organizational change. That is, if handled appropriately, crises may leave the organization or its constituents *better off* than they were beforehand. Of course, we are hardly the first to observe that crises are sources of opportunity. For example, expressions such as "when life gives you lemons, make lemonade" are a common part of the English vernacular. Similarly, in the Chinese language the identical characters are used to refer to crisis and to opportunity. Whereas the notion that crises provide opportunity is not new, much less is known about the factors that lead executives to be more versus less likely to perceive crises as opportunities.[2] And yet the ability to do so is to our mind what separates crisis management from crisis leadership.

Our general approach to crisis leadership, and the specific goal of this chapter to characterize the individual and organizational factors associated with the ability to perceive opportunity from crisis, is squarely embedded in the burgeoning research on positive organizational scholarship (POS). POS is "based on the premise that understanding how to enable human excellence in organizations will unlock potential, reveal possibilities, and facilitate a more positive course of human and organizational welfare."[3] One particularly important subarea of POS is positive organizational change, which to our mind is the epitome and ultimate consequence of crisis leadership. In other words, when confronted with a crisis, firm leaders may be more motivated than at any other time to change in ways they may have not previously considered. The changes may be procedural (how things are done in the organization), outcome based (what gets done in the organization), or both (new procedures yield new products or services). Consider the case of the Johnson & Johnson (J&J) Tylenol tampering case we discussed in Chapter 6. The crisis motivated J&J to consider alternative strategies for keeping their products and ultimately their customers safe. In the end, the firm led the industry in manufacturing tamper-resistant packaging, which included a glued box, a plastic seal over the neck of the bottle, and a foil seal over the mouth of the bottle. These industry-changing safety standards were introduced merely six months after the crisis occurred, but may never have been developed at all had it not been for the crisis that preceded them.

To be clear, we are not suggesting that crises are a necessary precondition for positive organizational change. After all, positive organizational change may even be engendered in the face of a satisfactory status quo, in which leaders proactively take steps to push their organizations to even greater heights. However, a well-handled crisis (e.g., in which leaders perceive the opportunity it affords) may be one way to bring about positive organizational change. Thus, by delineating the factors that lead crisis handlers to perceive opportunity in crisis, we aspire to contribute to a better understanding of one noteworthy form of positive organizational change.

In this chapter we build on prior research concerned with the framing and interpretation of strategic issues. Dutton and Jackson suggested that decision makers' cognitive processing of (and their organizations' responses to) strategic issues such as crises are affected by whether they frame them as threats or as opportunities.[4] Taylor and Milliken found, for example, that when decision makers framed strategic issues as opportunities, they felt more control and less uncertainty than when those same issues were framed as threats.[5] The opportunity frame also led to an enhanced likelihood that leaders would engage in strategic change initiatives, presumably because they felt more confident about the outcomes of their decisions.[6] In contrast, issues framed as threats resulted in actions associated with cost cutting, budget tightening, and other restrictive activities.[7] Thomas, Clark, and Gioia also demonstrated that the framing of strategic issues influences organizational performance.[8] In a study of sense-making processes within hospital settings, Thomas and colleagues found that when issues were framed positively, managers added products and services to their hospital's offerings, which, in turn, was associated with better hospital performance.

Whereas the above studies examined the *consequences* of executives' perceptions of strategic issues as threats or opportunities, there has been less emphasis on the factors that lead executives to perceive crises as threats or as opportunities. Research by Dutton and Jackson examined how characteristics of the issues influenced the likelihood of them being perceived as threats or as opportunities.[9] Our analysis also considers the characteristics of crises as one type of antecedent, but they are not the only type that we consider. As suggested below, factors residing in the organizational context and factors residing within leaders' dispositions also may influence their tendencies to perceive crises as sources of opportunity.

Moreover, our focus is on *when* leaders make the transition from perceiving crises as threats to perceiving them also as opportunities. The word *also* in the previous sentence is noteworthy. We do not view the framing of crises as threats and opportunities to be mutually exclusive. The threats associated with crises are very real and need to be dealt with, and to imply otherwise would be quite

Figure 9.1   Framing crisis events.

misleading. Thus, our framework has a dynamic flavor to it, in that we suggest that leaders are initially likely to focus on the threat(s) in crises; however, under certain conditions (elaborated upon below), they may come to perceive crises as sources of opportunity *and*, more important, eventually manifest those opportunities. In other words, crises leaders are those men and women who are able to maneuver through a set of challenging circumstances (and lead others to do the same) to steady the firm, and then leverage those circumstances to create positive change for themselves and for their organizations. See Figure 9.1 for a graphic depiction of the core set of ideas associated with crisis leadership.

Beneficiaries and Types of Opportunities

Individuals (e.g., those responsible for handling crises) and organizations may be the beneficiaries of the opportunities in crises. For the crisis handlers, opportunity may come in the form of an enhanced reputation and, with that, greater power and influence (e.g., former New York City mayor Rudolph Giuliani, for his handling of the 9/11 tragedy). For organizations, opportunity may manifest itself in the form of new systems or technologies that may not have come to fruition as quickly, or at all, in the absence of the crisis. As Intel's Andy Groves put it, "There is at least one point in the history of any company when you have to change dramatically to rise to the next performance level. Miss the moment and you begin to decline. . . . Emotionally, it's easier to change when you are hemorrhaging."[10]

Events at the Denny's restaurant chain show how crises may lead to positive organizational change. Following allegations of racial discrimination and a high-profile class action lawsuit, Denny's revamped its customer and employee service models, and in so doing made a number of cultural and structural changes. Subsequent to the implementation of these changes, Denny's has been ranked first in *Fortune*'s "Best Companies for Minorities." The Denny's example also shows how the same crisis may create opportunity for multiple beneficiaries, such as employees (who were subsequently treated more fairly), minority suppliers and vendors (who became more likely to be considered by the company), and the company as a whole (whose enhanced reputation led prospective employees to be more likely to select Denny's over its competitors for employment).[11]

Furthermore, opportunities emanating from crises fall into two broad types. On the one hand, opportunity may be realized if organizations can reduce the frequency, likelihood, or impact of a negative occurrence, for example, if, in managing the crisis, leaders eliminate conditions that detract from their firm's ability to compete, or if they make changes that make future crises less likely to recur. On the other hand, opportunity may be realized if organizations can enhance the frequency, likelihood, or impact of future positive events. For example, as Grove's comments imply, in managing a crisis, leaders may be able to introduce changes into the organization's systems, processes, products, or services that have the effect of enhancing firm performance.

An Overview of What Follows

Our analysis is based on the assumption that at the outset of crises leaders perceive them as threats. Indeed, much of the prescriptive writing on crisis management has focused on how companies may best deal with crises in the short term, in the form of various "damage control" activities.[12] As important as these short-term, damage control activities may be, however, they are not our primary concern. Rather, we focus on the factors that cause leaders to ultimately perceive the opportunity associated with crises, thereby setting the stage for positive organizational change.

We suggest that whether leaders make the transition from perceiving a crisis as a threat to perceiving it also as an opportunity is affected by two sets of variables. The first set pertains to whether executives exhibit a general tendency to engage in reflection and learning. These factors are general in the sense that they may influence learning in a variety of situations, including, but not limited to, crises. For example, we expect that executives with a reflection/learning mindset also will have a better understanding of the factors responsible for their organization's successes, thereby enabling them to build even further upon successful organizational outcomes. Furthermore, we believe that executives' tendencies to reflect and learn are jointly determined by organizational and individual factors.

The second set pertains to factors that are more specifically tied to crisis situations. Here, we draw on the expectancy theory of motivation to argue that leaders' beliefs about the value and attainability of the potential opportunities in a given crisis situation affect the likelihood that those opportunities will be perceived and manifested. We also identify a host of precursors of leaders' beliefs about the value and attainability of the opportunity in crises. These include not only organizational and individual factors, as in the case of reflection and learning, but also factors related to the crises themselves. Note that our two sets of variables (those pertaining to a general tendency to reflect and learn, and those pertaining specifically to crises) are consistent with well-established psychological principles that suggest people's beliefs and behaviors are a function of both general and specific factors associated with their motivation and ability.[13]

Another important purpose of the present analysis is to delineate leaders' behavioral manifestations of perceiving opportunity in crises. The perception of opportunity resides in leaders' minds. For both theoretical and practical reasons we need to discern whether they are acting on those perceptions. Thus, by delineating the behavioral manifestations of leaders perceiving opportunity in crises, we illustrate what positive organizational change entails, that is, what leaders who perceive crisis as opportunity actually do. It should also be noted that whereas our analysis throughout is at the individual level, in that we examine the psychological and behavioral tendencies of leaders who deal with crises, we consider how those tendencies may be affected by both individual- and organizational-level variables.

The remainder of the chapter consists of four sections. We begin by briefly reviewing previous research concerned with how people respond to threat, which is the overriding perception that managers maintain at the outset of a crisis. A common theme underlying the various reactions to threat is that they often (though not always) make crisis handlers unlikely to perceive the opportunity in crises. In the second section, we suggest that crisis handlers may make the transition from perceiving crises as threats to perceiving them also as opportunities, depending upon both situational and dispositional factors. In other words, both the context of the crisis situation and the characteristics of the crisis handlers matter. In the third section we offer a set of propositions on perceiving crisis as opportunity, and outline a potential future research agenda for scholars wanting to pursue this line of research. Also in this section we discuss research strategies (and challenges) for testing these propositions and for further exploration of the ideas presented throughout this book.

Because crisis leadership is a practical as well as theoretical matter, in the fourth section we attempt to answer the following question: How can it be determined whether executives have perceived a crisis as an opportunity? Here, we discuss some of the behavioral manifestations of organizational authorities adopting a "crisis as opportunity" mindset and thereby displaying crisis leadership. Last, we conclude with a final discussion of the fundamental ideas associated with crisis leadership as depicted in this chapter specifically and in the book overall. Here, we also distinguish crisis leadership from other related responses to crises, including marketing and public relations strategies and damage control.

Responses to Threat: A Brief Review
Emotional Reactions to Threat

Crises are initially likely to be perceived by leaders as threats to organizations and their stakeholders. Therefore, it may be instructive to draw on the vast psychological literature on how people respond to threatening circumstances, crisis induced or otherwise. Within this literature, several basic principles are relevant to our discussion. First, decision makers have a natural proclivity to think of external stimuli in relatively negative or positive ways. In organizational settings, for example, leaders generally frame stimuli as threats or opportunities.[14] Second, these stimuli elicit emotional and behavioral responses.[15] Stimuli that are appraised negatively (i.e., a crisis framed as a threat) elicit a different set of emotions than events that are appraised more positively (i.e., a crisis perceived to be an opportunity). Third, the emotions elicited by negatively appraised events include anger, anxiety, guilt, and depression,[16] depending upon the nature of the appraisal. For example, according to Smith and Ellsworth, threats perceived to be caused by other people elicit the emotion of anger,[17] which is the feeling that gripped many Americans in the aftermath of the tragedies of September 11, 2001. Alternatively, threats perceived to result from one's own behavior elicit guilt.[18] Finally, threats resulting from acts of nature (such as the tsunami that struck Asia in December 2004, or Hurricane Katrina that hit the Gulf Coast region of the United States in 2005) may elicit feelings of anxiety, hopelessness, and despair, as people contemplate the randomness of the event as well as the enormity (and perhaps the infeasibility) of the rebuilding effort.

Because the threat imposed by crises tends to be severe, the negative emotional reactions elicited by them may be quite pronounced. Furthermore, whereas the negative emotions elicited by severe threats such as crises may differ, they may have the common consequence of making decision makers less apt to perceive opportunity in crises. For example, guilt may cause leaders to become preoccupied with defending themselves or with protecting their self-esteem, whereas depression generally causes people to withdraw into themselves; both tendencies are hardly recipes for perceiving the opportunity in crises. Moreover, Staw, Sandelands, and Dutton described how organizations, and the people and groups that compose them, react to the stress and anxiety elicited by the interpretation of strategic issues as threats.[19] As we have described in earlier chapters, their influential threat-rigidity model asserts that stress and anxiety give rise to a restriction in the amount of information that is processed, and also to a restriction in how that information is processed. Thus, following a crisis organizational decision makers become less open to information that differs from traditional ways of thinking about problems. In addition, stress and anxiety lead to individuals adopting well-learned or habitual behaviors, not all of which are appropriate for the novelty that most crisis situations evoke. Given the prominent perception of threat in crises (which elicits a preoccupation with doing damage control), leaders may be unlikely to recognize crises as sources of opportunities.

Behavioral Responses to Threat

Impression management is the practice of manipulating the views that others have of you or of your organization so as to be judged favorably.[20] Impression management tactics are particularly relevant when people experience threats to their image as a result of accidents, mistakes, or failures. Examples of some of the most common forms of impression management include defenses of innocence,[21] denials,[22] excuses,[23] and apologies.[24] Early impression management researchers focused on identifying and categorizing individual-level impression management tactics.[25] Other scholars have examined organizational impression management tactics,[26] which represent tailored communications or other behaviors designed to respond to image-threatening events.[27] Often internal corporate communication and public relations professionals are formally tasked with managing a firm's image. Because crises pose a threat to the image (and hence to the effectiveness or even to the survival) of the organization as a whole, they lead to activity designed to minimize the negative effects of crises on how the organization and its members are seen by relevant audiences. To the extent that impression management tactics elicited by the perception of threat tend to be defensive in nature, they are also unlikely to foster in leaders' minds the belief that crises provide opportunity. In short, prior theory and research on people's emotional and behavioral responses to threat suggest that leaders often will be relatively unlikely to perceive opportunity in crises.

The Psychology of Crisis Response: Transitioning From Perception of Threat to Perception of Opportunity

Whereas leaders often may fail to perceive opportunity in crises, this is not always the case. In this section we delineate the factors that affect whether crisis handlers make the transition from perceiving crises as threats to seeing them also as opportunities. In it, we highlight a set of factors that facilitate a leader's transition from fear and panic (and the subsequent damage control behaviors such feelings evoke) following the onset of a crisis, to the realization of opportunities from that crisis. Given that the ability to perceive and manifest opportunity from crisis is so central to our conception of crisis leadership, we also introduce the formal model alluded to at the outset of this book. Figure 9.1 outlines the core elements from this and preceding chapters to capture the individual, group, and organizational characteristics that allow crisis handlers to move from a crisis management mindset (with an emphasis on damage control) to a crisis leadership mindset (in which one strives to create a better organization following a crisis).

Note that decision makers' emotional and behavioral responses to crises set forth above tend to be antithetical to those needed for learning and ensuing creativity to occur.[28] Put differently (and more optimistically), crises are more apt to be seen as sources of opportunity when organizational decision makers, and the firm overall, adopt a learning orientation.[29] As we described in detail in Chapter 7, organizational learning is an adaptive process in which individuals and firms use prior experience to develop new routines or behaviors that create opportunities for enhanced performance.[30] We believe that crises can serve as the kinds of experiences from which learning and the subsequent potential for opportunity are generated.[31]

Whereas conventional wisdom suggests that failures (such as crises) are to be avoided, Sitkin posited that the absence of failures might present a number of challenges to organizations.[32] Among these are complacency and the perpetuation of the status quo,[33] along with homogeneity among organizational members, and rigidity in the routines and processes through which organizations seek to achieve their goals. Inherent in these liabilities is a shortfall in organizational learning. Like Sitkin, we believe that executives' capacity to engage in reflection and learning is critical to an organization's growth and development. More specific to the present context, leaders who engage in reflection and learning subsequent to their initial threat-induced reactions are more likely to perceive opportunity in crisis.

Beyond Damage Control: Getting to Reflection and Learning

If the presence of a learning orientation affects whether organizational leaders make the transition from perceiving crisis as threat to perceiving it also as opportunity, then it is important to delineate the factors needed to produce a learning orientation. We suggest that both organizational characteristics (e.g., shared values and beliefs) and individual characteristics (e.g., dispositional factors) affect leaders' learning orientation in the face of crises.

Organizational Characteristics

Under certain conditions organizational failures (including, but not limited to, crises) elicit a variety of learning-based benefits to organizations, such as increased resilience and a heightened understanding of the reasons for their poor performance.[34] For example, Sitkin argued that "intelligent failures" are more likely to occur when organizations are outcome focused *and* process focused. Moreover, learning is more likely to occur in organizations that legitimate organizational failure. Such organizations (1) encourage individuals to engage in thoughtful experimentation and risk taking, and (2) publicize intelligent failure. Organizational systems are a key component of their learning orientations. To this point, Pham and Swierczek found that an organizational incentive system that provided rewards for employee engagement in learning and knowledge-related activities was positively related to an organization's learning climate.[35]

Individual Characteristics

In addition to organizational characteristics, leaders' dispositions (i.e., their nature or temperament) may influence their learning orientations. Carol Dweck, a leading authority on learning, has suggested that people differ in their orientation toward achievement.[36] Those with a learning orientation strive to develop competence by acquiring new skills and mastering new situations.[37] They are motivated by the learning process and by the opportunities for growth and development that it provides. Alternatively, performance-oriented people are motivated to learn primarily to gain favorable judgments of their competence or to avoid unfavorable judgments.[38] Learning orientations versus performance orientations have been found to predict different patterns of emotional and behavioral responses to threats.[39] One study found, for example, that having a learning orientation elicited more adaptive responses to adverse conditions.[40] In this case, learning-oriented people were not easily discouraged by challenges, and setbacks and failure did not keep them from the pursuit of new knowledge. Such findings may be particularly relevant to whether leaders will engage in reflection and learning subsequent to the initial responses to crisis, and thereby make the transition from perceiving crisis as threat to perceiving it also as an opportunity.

Whereas there may be separate and direct effects of organizational and dispositional sources of learning orientation on leaders' tendencies to perceive opportunity in crises, we also believe that it would be worthwhile to examine whether organizational and dispositional sources of learning interact with one another. Research has shown that people are more energized and engaged when their work environments support problem-solving orientations that are congruent rather than incongruent with their own.[41] It is entirely possible that conceptually similar findings may emerge for people's learning orientations.

The Jack-in-the-Box case provides an example of how the learning process (whether situationally or dispositionally produced) may manifest itself in response to crisis. After the deaths and illnesses at Jack-in-the-Box, the company called in an outside expert (a microbiologist) to specify every point in its workflow in which bacterial contamination could occur. The analysis began with the company's suppliers. If a supplier's products were contaminated on more than one occasion, the supplier was dropped. Furthermore, daily tests were conducted on cooking systems and on cooking sample products. They even went as far as checking every cooked patty before removing it from the cooking grill. As the microbiologist put it, "Laws do not make food safe. Companies make it happen with extra focus and effort."[42] The company buttressed its hard-nosed analysis of its workflows with a symbolic gesture indicating a radical change in its corporate culture, in advertisements in which "Jack" was shown blowing up the company headquarters. The company could have merely adopted a damage control stance by, for example, implementing a public relations strategy to convince prospective customers of its food safety. Instead, company leaders adopted a learning orientation that resulted in technological innovations in food handling.

Perceiving the Opportunity in Crises: A Multifactor Approach

Whereas having a learning orientation generally makes leaders more likely to perceive opportunity in crises, other factors more specifically related to crises also will affect their likelihood of doing so. Drawing on motivation theory, which suggests that beliefs and behavior are a function of what people value and what they expect,[43] we hypothesize that perceiving the opportunity in crises is a function of decision makers' perceptions of the value of the opportunity in crises as well as their expectations for success (i.e., the perceived likelihood that the opportunity will be attained). The greater the perceived value and the greater the expectations for success, the more likely are leaders to perceive the opportunity in crises.[44]

The value assigned to the opportunity in crises, and the expectations about being able to realize the opportunity, in turn, may be influenced by a host of factors, some pertaining to characteristics of the leaders, some pertaining to properties of the crises, and others pertaining to the organizational context in which the crises occur. For example, properties of the crises and of the organizational context (in conjunction with one another, as we will argue below) may affect the value that leaders assign to a particular opportunity. Recall that the opportunities in crises fall into two distinct categories. In some instances the opportunity is to reduce the likelihood, frequency, or severity of events that may affect organizations negatively. For example, in responding to allegations of widespread racial discrimination and harassment, Georgia Power implemented a series of measures to prevent subsequent charges, including working with experts and diversity advocates external to their organization to make changes in their human resources and compensation practices.

In other instances the opportunity is to increase the likelihood or impact of events that affect organizations positively. Hence, a crisis may be used by leaders as an impetus for creativity and innovation. Indeed, the ability to take this opportunity for change is central to separating people with a crisis leadership mindset from those with a crisis management mindset. Clearly, crises must be managed in order to bring about resolution, but crisis leaders are those individuals who see beyond the resolution of crisis. Presumably, creativity and innovation should be ongoing organizational practices and outcomes. However, without the sense of urgency elicited by a crisis, organization members may not be sufficiently motivated to think and act creatively. In this instance, the changes made by the organization do more than reduce the likelihood of negative outcomes. They may actually enable the organization to reap additional benefits, such as enhancing their reputation or increasing the profitability of their existing lines of business, or gaining traction in hitherto untapped markets and customers. The positive organizational changes that can result from crises are akin to episodic changes as described by Weick and Quinn.[45] In fact, according to these authors, episodic organizational changes routinely occur in the context of some form of event that threatens the organization (e.g., crises).

Perhaps no organization embodies the notion of having seized the positive form of opportunity from crisis more than Johnson & Johnson (J&J). Clearly the product-tampering case threatened not only J&J's financial standing but also its reputation. However, because of extraordinary crisis handling, and a crisis leadership mindset, the company was able to reintroduce Tylenol in the form of caplets, and to pioneer tamper-resistant packaging. In essence, the firm introduced positive changes following a significant jolt, and was rewarded by becoming the market leader in the sale of analgesics and consistently winning awards such as "Most Admired Pharmaceutical Company" and "Best Corporate Reputation."

Leaders are more likely to perceive opportunities in crises when the opportunities are perceived to have value for the organization. Yet, how much they covet a particular opportunity may also depend upon their own or their organization's values. Recent motivation theory suggests that people engage in self-regulation (the process of trying to match behaviors and self-conceptions with appropriate goals and standards) in two very distinct ways: with a promotion focus or with a prevention focus.[46] Promotion and prevention foci differ along three dimensions: (1) the needs that people are seeking to satisfy, (2) the nature of the goal or standard that people are trying to achieve or match, and (3) the type of outcome that is meaningful to them. When promotion focused, people are motivated to try to bring themselves into alignment with their ideal selves (hopes, wishes, and aspirations), thereby heightening the importance of positive outcomes to be attained. When prevention focused, people's security needs prompt them to attempt to bring themselves into alignment with the side of themselves that emphasizes duty, obligation, and responsibility, thereby increasing the prominence of negative outcomes to be avoided. Put differently, promotion focus induces a self-regulatory process characterized by "playing to win," whereas prevention focus elicits a self-regulatory process described as "playing to not lose." Higgins has convincingly demonstrated that promotion and prevention foci are stable traits within people, but can also be influenced by situational factors.[47] Therefore, dispositional differences between leaders, as well as factors residing within organizations, may influence the extent to which leaders value promotion and prevention.

To put the implications of regulatory focus into perspective and tie it into the concept of crisis leadership we offer the following metaphor. Consider a championship basketball game in its final minute of play. Team A is ahead by 2 points and Team B has the ball. If Team A is composed of players that are largely prevention focused and whose goal is to run down the clock, and if they have a prevention-focused and possibly risk-averse coach, then chances are Team A will begin to play fairly conservatively in that final minute. Defense will take priority (along with a strategy to run down the clock), but in so doing the team fails to play aggressive offense (as they probably have been doing up to this point). No doubt Team B will shoot and score to tie (or perhaps lead if it is a 3-point shot) the game. In this case, by playing not to lose, Team A misses opportunities to continue to score and give themselves a better chance of winning. Team B, on the other hand, recognizes that in order to win they *must* continue to play aggressive offense. Not shooting is typically not an option. So by playing to win, Team B is in a better position to continue to score, whereas playing not to lose means Team A is unlikely to score and, moreover, puts their fate much more in the hands of their opponents.

We see the same phenomenon occur in business settings. A prevention-focused executive operating in an organization that also values and rewards prevention focus (avoid bad things) is unlikely to perceive, much less strive toward, achieving opportunity when an organizational threat arises. There is simply no incentive or motivation to do so. Yet there is every incentive to play it safe. The prevention-focused leader in this context may make conservative decisions that prevent or minimize some threats. More than likely, the leader will seek to use standard responses (play it safe) to a situation that requires unconventional thinking. Although doing so can result in effective damage control, such an approach is unlikely to generate the creative thinking that is often required for handling unconventional occurrences, and is certainly unlikely to spawn any motivation to learn, change, or innovate as a result of the crisis. To the contrary, when both the executive and the organization in which he or she works value promotion focus, the likelihood that the leader will perceive opportunity from threat and act in ways that will bring about those opportunities increases.

Promotion and prevention foci are as relevant to organizational cultures as they are to individuals. To this point, one study considered how organizations differ in the extent to which they value promotion versus prevention.[48] Some organizations have more of a promotion-focused mission (e.g., entrepreneurial start-ups, which often reflect the vision, dreams, and ideals of their founders), whereas others have more of a prevention-focused purpose (e.g., utility companies whose goal is to "keep the meters running" by preventing power outages). Whether organizational decision makers value promotion or prevention lends greater specificity to the possible relationship between the value of the opportunity associated with a crisis and leaders' tendencies to perceive the opportunity.

Perceived Attainability

Leaders' tendencies to perceive opportunity in crises also depend upon their beliefs about the attainability of the opportunity. At the individual level, a variety of factors have been shown to influence people's expectations for success at their endeavors, including self-efficacy,[49] optimism,[50] and outcome expectancy.[51] For example, self-efficacy (which refers to people's beliefs about their capabilities to perform needed behaviors) determines how people feel, think, and motivate themselves.[52] People with a strong sense of self-efficacy are more confident of their abilities to handle difficult situations and tend to view these situations as challenges to be overcome rather than as threats to be avoided. In this way, self-efficacy may play an important role in whether leaders believe they can attain the opportunity inherent to a crisis.

Beliefs about attainability also may be affected by attributes of the crisis and by the organizational context in which the crisis occurs. Certain crises have such a wide scope that it is difficult to see the potential for opportunity, let alone work toward trying to achieve it, at least in the short term. For example, the likelihood of successfully building a new infrastructure in tsunami-ravaged Asia seems remote, given the amount of territory and the number of people that were devastated by it. This is especially true in the weeks or even months following the devastating storm. Likewise, organizations in the Gulf Coast region of the United States have encountered difficulty in the task of business continuity or rebuilding in light of the devastation caused by Hurricane Katrina. In contrast, the rebuilding effort at Jack-in-the-Box, while heroic in its own way, was far more attainable, even in the short term, given the more limited scope of the crisis. Yet we fundamentally believe that over a period of time people with a crisis leadership mindset will be more inclined to see the ways in which, for example, the rebuilding efforts could create a better, safer, more economically viable, and more attractive region than even what existed before the tsunami or the hurricane hit. In other words, perceived attainability of an opportunity can play a significant role in whether or when crisis handlers perceive opportunity from crisis. That said, crisis handlers who approach threats with a crisis leadership frame of mind are more likely to eventually see and manifest the opportunity.

Leaders' beliefs that they can attain opportunity from crisis may also be affected by the source of the crisis, that is, whether the organization was responsible for the crisis or whether the organization was the victim of unfortunate events. One study found that the more the organization was seen as responsible for a crisis situation, the more damage was done to its reputation.[53] Similarly, research shows that organizations with a history of related crises elicit more negative perceptions of their reputations.[54] The more organizations are seen as responsible for their crises, the less likely are leaders to perceive a possibility of attaining opportunity from crisis. In this regard, J&J, as a victim rather than the source of product tampering, was in a better position to realize opportunity from the incident.

Finally, beliefs about the attainability of opportunity also may depend upon the organization's culture (i.e., its shared values or beliefs). Organizational cultures differ along efficacy dimensions in much the same sense that individuals differ. For example, Bandura defined collective efficacy as "a group's shared belief in its conjoint capabilities to organize and execute the courses of action required to produce given levels of attainments."[55] Just as individual self-efficacy may influence people's beliefs about the attainability of difficult challenges (such as perceiving the opportunity in crises), so too may the collective efficacy residing within the culture of the group or organization (Figure 9.2).

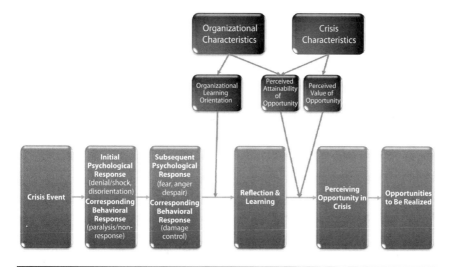

Figure 9.2   The process of perceiving crises as opportunities.

What Leaders Do: Behavioral Manifestations of Perceiving Crisis as Opportunity

Whereas in the previous section we considered factors that make executives more versus less likely to perceive the opportunity in crises, here we consider the behaviors reflective of leaders having adopted a crisis leadership mindset. In other words, this is what crisis leaders *do*. Delineating the behavioral manifestations of a "crisis as opportunity" mindset is a matter of theoretical and practical importance. Although prior research on crisis management has theorized about the importance of learning from crisis,[56] it has not identified exactly what people do when they perceive opportunity in crisis. If crisis handlers (or those advising them) wish to evaluate the extent to which they perceive opportunity in crises, it would be useful to have a set of criteria against which to compare their behavior. Below, we offer one such set of criteria.

Treat Causes, Not Merely Symptoms

One behavioral manifestation of perceiving opportunity in crisis is a willingness to "drill down" to the root cause(s) of the crisis. Informed root cause analyses may help organizations seize opportunity by reducing the recurrence of crises. The utility company Florida Power and Light (FP&L) provides an example of a clever root cause analysis:[57]

> Florida Power and Light often had to deal with power outages that occurred when a tree fell on a power line and severed it . . . FP&L organized a unit to trim all the trees in sites where damage had occurred, and thus prevent future outages. However, . . . the procedure . . . prevented problems only in areas that had already experienced a crisis. They searched for a solution at a deeper level, and asked managers a number of questions about . . . forestry! What kinds of trees grow in the region? Do palms grow faster or slower than oaks? Managers at FP&L realized that they did not know the answers to these questions, and that they had not searched deeply enough to solve their problems. . . . FP&L managers consulted with foresters and developed a regular maintenance procedure to trim trees based on their growth rates and [did so] across the entire region, not just in areas where trees had previously severed lines.[58]

Thus, one indicator of whether organizational authorities have perceived the opportunity in crises is the extent to which they engage in an information search that provides a solid understanding of why the crises occurred. Moreover, to do so organizations may need to draw on sources of expertise that reside external to the organization. It could be argued that the FP&L example above refers less to an organizational crisis and more to a (simpler) threat to their day-to-day operations. Nevertheless, the principle of seeking expertise from nonobvious sources, including those residing outside of the organization, would seem to be highly applicable to crises as well. Thus, Jack-in-the-Box consulted with microbiologists and Georgia Power contracted with prominent diversity experts in the public and private sector to help them diagnose and resolve their respective crises. The fact that crises elicit threat, which in turn engenders rigidity,[59] may help to explain why such outside-the-box thinking in crisis situations is relatively unusual.

Seek the Views of Multiple and Diverse Stakeholders

One manifestation of the threat-induced, damage control activities engendered by crises is that its handlers focus on the needs of a small number of stakeholders,[60] for example, those that have power over the organization, or those that have been severely harmed by the crisis. Taking a multiple stakeholder perspective, however, will expose leaders to an array of internal and external constituents with differing perspectives of the organization and of the crisis. These stakeholders may offer a range of solutions, which could broaden leaders' views on how best to manage the crisis. Even if the multiple stakeholders do not make suggestions, the fact that leaders are taking a multiple stakeholder perspective may enable them to generate more robust solutions to the problems introduced by the crises. For example, when the views of multiple stakeholders are considered, leaders may be more open-minded about the potential ways in which various parts of the organization can learn from each other. Such was the case with the J&J product-tampering crisis. Although the cyanide-laced Tylenol was primarily a marketing and sales concern, it provided the opportunity for the research and development unit to design a new and safer packaging system that has subsequently been adopted throughout the industry.

Emphasize Short- and Long-Term Outcomes, Not Merely Short-Term Outcomes

Many of the opportunities in crises are likely to materialize over the long term rather than in the short term. Thus, an additional way to determine whether organizational authorities are positioned to bring about the opportunity in crises is by evaluating the relative emphasis they place on short-term versus long-term outcomes. Our hunch is that when organizational authorities predominantly focus on short-term results, they and their firms will be less likely to come to see the opportunity in crises, relative to when authorities try to strike a balance between short- and long-term results. To test this reasoning, it may be useful to examine various indicators of the time frame of senior managers' thinking, such as information appearing in annual reports, internal memos, and public speeches. Another indicator of time frame may be how much the firm invests in research and development (with greater investments reflecting more of a long-term orientation). Hiring practices may also be reflective of senior management's thinking. If one or a small number of key leaders resign as "sacrificial lambs" and no other changes are made, it may indicate more of a short-term orientation. If, however, the organization is willing to revamp its hiring practices or other human resource policies (as in the case of Denny's), it is likely to reflect more of a long-term orientation. Finally, another way to evaluate senior managers' time horizons is by asking various organizational constituents who are familiar with how senior managers think, such as employees, customers, and suppliers. The more that these various indicators suggest that senior managers care about short- and long-term outcomes, the more likely they and their firms are to be positioned to seize opportunity in crises.

Establish Norms for Divergent Thinking

Related to the notions of treating cause, not merely symptoms, seeking the views of multiple and diverse stakeholders, and emphasizing short- and long-term outcomes is the need to elicit divergent thinking among employees. Divergent thinking, or the ability to generate a variety of differing ideas, opinions, or arguments, is an integral part of the creative problem-solving process for individuals and teams,[61] and the link between divergent thinking and creativity has been demonstrated in a variety of contexts.[62] A reasonable inference from prior research is that organizations with norms for divergent thinking are more likely to inspire creativity in employees and, in turn, develop fruitful ways to transform crisis into opportunity than those organizations that emphasize more uniform perspectives and approaches to decision making. Specifically, to the extent that multiple and differing views can be represented in decision-making processes (which include diagnosing root causes, identifying the relevant stakeholders, and prioritizing short- and long-term outcomes), higher-quality decisions and more creative problem solving are likely to ensue, which may better enable leaders to bring about the opportunity in crises. Without divergent thinking, employees may be less able to generate different or unique solutions to crises or to think about crises in different or unique ways. Unfortunately, leaders all too often feel threatened by crises[63] and become rigid in their response to them. This rigidity is reflected in the restriction of information flow, the centralization of authority and decision making, and the reliance on standardized procedures, all of which inhibit divergent thinking.

To counteract these tendencies, Janis's prescriptions for avoiding groupthink may be helpful.[64] For example, once the acute stage of the crisis has passed and leaders are in a position to adopt more of a long-term perspective, they may be well served to refrain from making their preferences known at the outset of a discussion about the possible opportunity in crises. Allowing others to voice their opinions first may reduce the likelihood of anchoring them to the leader's position, with which they may feel uncomfortable disagreeing. Breaking the leadership or crisis management team into smaller subgroups before reconvening as one, calling in outside experts to offer advice (as seen in the Texaco, Jack-in-the-Box, and Florida Power & Light examples), and assigning someone to play the role of devil's advocate, whose job it is to be skeptical about any emerging plans on how to transform crisis into opportunity, are other ways of encouraging divergent thinking. Brainstorming techniques may also be indicative of divergent thinking. After all, how to identify and how to seize the opportunity in crises are complex problems, which are much more likely to be solved when approached from diverging points of view.

Perceiving Crisis as Opportunity: A Research Agenda

Before moving on to our final section, it makes sense to pause and reflect on the ideas that have been inspired by our discussion in this and previous chapters. Below, we articulate the way in which a number of factors relate to one another in order to contribute to the capability of organizations, and the leaders that run them, to perceive and manifest positive organizational change. We offer the following research propositions in Figure 9.3.

We have offered these propositions in the course of specifying factors expected to affect whether leaders come to perceive opportunity in crises and ultimately display crisis leadership behavior (the details of which will be articulated below). An empirical examination of these propositions is likely to require a longitudinal research design. In addition to the inherent difficulties of studying people and organizations over time, there are related challenges with which researchers must contend. Because crises are rare and often unforeseen, it may be difficult to capture the psychological mindset and behavioral responses of organizational leaders at various stages in the process. Moreover, assessing some of the factors described here may be no easy matter. For example, it is hard to imagine leaders completing a self-report instrument or taking part in an interview when they are in the midst of dealing with crises, especially during the relatively early stages. Perhaps even more difficult to overcome may be their unwillingness to talk about issues that are potentially sensitive, have legal ramifications, and threaten their organizations' reputations.

Proposition 1	•Leaders will be more likely to make the transition from perceiving crises as threats to perceiving them also as opportunities when their organizational context supports reflection and learning.
Proposition 2	•Leaders who are more inclined to have a learning orientation are more likely to perceive crisis as opportunity, relative to leaders who are more inclined to have a performance orientation.
Proposition 3	•When the type of opportunity in a crisis is congruent with the type of regulatory focus (i.e., promotion or prevention) favored by leaders, leaders are likely to assign greater value to the opportunity, which, will make them more likely to perceive the opportunity.
Proposition 4	•When the opportunity type entails *decreasing* the likelihood or impact of events that affect organizations negatively, the opportunity is more likely to be perceived by those leaders who are inclined to be prevention focused.
Proposition 5	•When the opportunity type entails *increasing* the likelihood or impact of events that affect organizations positively, the opportunity is more likely to be perceived by leaders who are inclined to be promotion focused.
Proposition 6	•The greater the perceived attainability of the opportunity in crises, the more likely are leaders to perceive the opportunity.
Proposition 7	•The greater the leaders' self-efficacy, the more likely they are to perceive the opportunity in crises as attainable.
Proposition 8	•The narrower the scope of the crisis (e.g., crises that are less severe or less public), the more likely are leaders to perceive the opportunity as attainable.
Proposition 9	•The less an organization is perceived to be responsible for a crisis, the more likely are leaders to perceive the opportunity in crises as attainable.
Proposition 10	•The more that the organization's belief system fosters an optimistic ("can-do") attitude on the part of its employees, the more likely are leaders to perceive the opportunity in crises as attainable.

Figure 9.3 Perceiving crisis as opportunity propositions.

Nevertheless, there may be ways to overcome these challenges. Whereas researchers may be unlikely to procure firsthand information from leaders dealing with crises, it may be possible to obtain documentation, such as written minutes or audio recordings from meetings, and memos or other communiqués to and from employees and other stakeholders (e.g., the wording in annual reports or other official statements of strategies and goals). These forms of information may be quite revealing of many variables that affect crisis leadership. Evidence from customer and employee surveys may also be informative. Moreover, after the acute stage of the crisis has passed, it may be more feasible to measure the relatively stable attributes of the executives involved as well as those of the organization (e.g., their respective learning orientations), in that stable dimensions measured after the fact are likely to be reasonably good proxies for what was true before (Figure 9.3).

Summary

As stated at the outset of this book, our goal was to bring forth the research and practical implications associated with leading under pressure. We focused almost exclusively on the pressure that comes with managing crises. In so doing, we speak to both the academic and practitioner audiences and offer a comprehensive examination of what crisis leadership entails, including the individual, organizational, and situational characteristics described throughout the book. Namely, leading under pressure is about confronting threats and taking appropriate risk at precisely the moment at which one's natural human tendency would be to retreat and become defensive and risk averse. It is about being open to learning, especially learning from failure, whether one's own or others'. It is about making consequential decisions under enormous pressure for circumstances never before experienced. It is about leading teams and inspiring the capabilities of crisis leadership in them and throughout the organization. It is about fostering trust with stakeholders so that they devote their full energy to work with leaders and not against them. It is about fostering a global mindset so that organizations can work across borders and share information that will facilitate crisis handling. Finally, it is about doing all of the above in full view of every possible stakeholder, each of whom has different needs to be met and will pull leaders in different directions.

Previous approaches to crisis management as "damage control" place heavy emphasis on marketing savvy, in which the organization tries to present itself in the most favorable or least unfavorable light, vis-à-vis the crisis. While marketing savvy may play an important role in doing damage control, it falls well short of the considerable work required to reach the point in which crises may be perceived as opportunities. The changes at Denny's provide a case in point. Although Denny's *initial* response to wide-scale allegations of discrimination may have been a skilled effort in public relations, the extensive changes made to its hiring and customer services practices *over a sustained period of time* suggest that a fundamental organizational transformation rather than mere marketing savvy was responsible for its turnaround. As we have suggested in some of our earlier research (much of which is captured in this book), when crisis management focuses on redressing the organizational systems that are the root causes of the problem, leaders are more likely to be in learning mode, and as a result, perceive opportunity in crises.[65] The fact that more than a decade after the discrimination allegations Denny's is still considered a top employer and continues to receive accolades for its diversity and employment practices suggests that its positive organizational change was not merely the result of a high-quality marketing effort.

This is not to say that marketing savvy and effective public relations are irrelevant to effective crisis handling. To the extent that leaders come to perceive opportunity in crises, engage in the behavioral manifestations of having done so, and also artfully publicize the positive changes they were able to bring about, they and their organizations are likely to reap reputational benefits. However, marketing savvy alone is highly unlikely to lead to the positive organizational changes that have been the focus of this book.

In summary, we join with other scholars who have suggested that in addition to experiencing crises as threats, effectively leading under pressure requires that crisis handlers also view them through the lens of opportunity. Doing so, in our minds, epitomizes crisis leadership.[66] A key question is when leaders may be more versus less likely to do so. Throughout this book we have attempted to provide an organizing framework to better understand leadership amidst crisis, and a central component of that leadership is the ability to seize and manifest opportunity from crisis. There are numerous examples of people and organizations that have adopted a more optimistic frame of mind in response to threat. Consequently, what these individuals and organizations do in response to crisis is worth examining. It is possible that the ideas set forth in these chapters, and this one in particular, will combine interactively (and not simply additively), such that each of the events in the chain may need to occur for leaders to perceive crisis as opportunity. In other words, in the absence of any one of these events, perceiving crisis as opportunity may be unlikely to happen. For example,

What is crisis leadership?

The ability to lead under pressure. To confront threats and take appropriate risk at precisely the moment in which one's natural human tendency would be to retreat, become defensive, or risk averse. It is about being open to learning, especially learning from failure whether it is one's own or others'. It is about making consequential decisions under enormous pressure for circumstances never before experienced. It is about leading teams and inspiring the capabilities of crisis leadership in them and throughout the organization. It is about fostering trust with stakeholders so that they devote their full energy to work with leaders and not against them. It is about fostering global mindset so that organizations can work across borders and share information that will facilitate crisis handling. Finally it is about doing all of the above in full view of every possible stakeholder each of whom has different needs to be met and will pull leaders in different directions.

What factors make it more likely that a leader will see the opportunity in crisis?

Leaders will be most likely to perceive the opportunity in crisis, rather than the threat, when the following conditions are met: (1) the leader is inclined to engage in reflection and learning; (2) s/he believes that there is a high payoff in perceiving opportunity in crises; (3) s/he perceives the attainability of the opportunity as high, and; (4) s/he exhibits behavioral manifestations of perceiving crisis in opportunity. In other words, in the absence of any one of these events, perceiving crisis as opportunity may be unlikely to happen.

Figure 9.4 Leader's hot seat.

Figure 9.5   Leadership Links 9.1

* Turning Crisis Into Opportunity: An Example
  http://gmj.gallup.com/content/28609/turningcrisis-into-opportunity.aspx
* How Great Companies Turn Crisis Into Opportunity
  http://money.cnn.com/2009/01/15/news/companies/Jim_Collins_Crisis
  .fortune/
* Adaptive Responses to Crisis
  http://www.bus.umich.edu/Positive/POS-Teaching-and-Learning/POS-
  Cases.htm

even if leaders are inclined to engage in reflection and learning, and even if they believe that there is high payoff in perceiving opportunity in crises, they may be unlikely to do so if the perceived attainability of the opportunity is low. The lack of either high value or high expectations may be sufficient to prevent certain actions from happening (in this case, for leaders to perceive the opportunity in crises). We share this realization not to be pessimistic per se, but rather to help explain why it can be so challenging for leaders to perceive opportunity in crisis. Nevertheless, given the potential benefits for both theory and practice served by better understanding the factors that contribute to leaders perceiving opportunity in crises, it is our hope that this book stimulates future research and enables organizations to develop leadership capabilities in this vitally important area (Figures 9.4 and 9.5).

Endnotes

1. Mitroff, Pauchant, & Shrivastava, Conceptual and empirical issues in the development of a general theory of crisis management, 83–107; Pearson & Clair, Reframing crisis management, 59–76; Shrivastava, Crisis theory/practice, 23–42.
2. Elsbach, Managing organizational legitimacy in the California cattle industry, 57–88; Elsbach, Members' responses to organizational identity threats, 442–476. Somewhat related to our analysis is Elsbach's work on how threats to a firm's image motivate organizations and its members to maintain positive perceptions of their organizations and their own social identities. However, our analysis differs from that of Elsbach in at least two respects. First, our focus is on crisis situations rather than on situations that merely threaten an organization's image. In other words, whereas crises obviously threaten an organization's image, not all threats to organizational image reach crisis proportions. Second, our focus is on the determinants of executives perceiving crises as opportunities and the behavioral manifestations of them having done so. In contrast, Elsbach drew on impression management theory to describe how organizational members reframe image-threatening events in ways

that preserve positive identities. That is, we explore *what* factors induce executives to perceive opportunity in crises, whereas Elsbach delineates *how* (or the ways in which) executives reconceptualize threat in a positive way.

3. Cameron, Dutton, Quinn, & Spreitzer, What is positive organizational scholarship?
4. Dutton & Jackson, Categorizing strategic issues, 76–90.
5. Taylor, *Positive illusions*; Milliken, Perceiving and interpreting environmental change, 42–63.
6. Milliken, Three types of uncertainty about the environment, 133–143.
7. Starbuck & Hedberg, Saving an organization from a stagnating environment, 45–80.
8. Thomas, Clark, & Gioia, Strategic sensemaking and organizational performance, 239–270.
9. Dutton & Jackson, Categorizing strategic issues, 76–90.
10. Groves, The ambidextrous organization, 43.
11. James & Wooten, Leadership as (un)usual, 141–152.
12. Coombs, Impact of past crises on current crisis communication, 265–289. Coombs & Holladay, Helping crisis managers protect reputational assets, 165–186. Fombrun, *Reputation*.
13. For example, Spielberger, *Manual for the State-Trait Anxiety Inventory (STAI)*.
14. Dutton & Jackson, Categorizing strategic issues, 76–90; Jackson & Dutton, Discerning threats and opportunities, 370–387.
15. Janis, *Psychological stress*; Smith, Haynes, Lazarus, & Pope, In search of the "hot" cognitions, 916–929.
16. Smith & Ellsworth, Patterns of cognitive appraisal in emotion, 813–838.
17. Ibid.
18. Ibid.
19. Staw, Sandelands, & Dutton, Threat-rigidity effects in organizational behavior, 501–524.
20. Goffman, *The presentation of self in everyday life*; Leary & Kowalski, Impression management, 34–47; Rosenberg, *Conceiving of the self*.
21. Schlenker, *Impression management*.
22. Higgins & Snyder, The business of excuses, 73–86.
23. Schlenker, Translating actions into attitudes, 193–247.
24. Benoit, *Accounts, excuses, and apologies*; Goffman, Remedial interchanges, 95–187.
25. See Schlenker & Weingold, Interpersonal processes involving impression regulation and management, 133–168, for a review.
26. For example, Elsbach, Managing organizational legitimacy in the California cattle industry (pp. 57–88); Elsbach & Sutton, Acquiring organizational legitimacy through illegitimate actions, (699–738); Sutton & Callahan, The stigma of bankruptcy, 405–436.
27. Schlenker, *Impression management*.
28. Amabile, *Creativity in context*.
29. Wooten & James, When firms fail to learn, 23–33.
30. For example, Levinthal & March, A model of adaptive organizational search, 187–218; Glynn, Lant, & Milliken, Mapping learning processes in organizations, 43–83.

31. Sitkin, Learning through failure, 231–266.
32. Ibid.
33. Kahneman & Tversky, Prospect theory, 263–291; Sitkin & Pablo, Reconceptualizing the determinants of risk behavior, 9–38.
34. Sitkin, Learning through failure, 231–266.
35. Pham & Swierczek, Facilitators of organizational learning in design, 186–201.
36. Dweck, *Self-theories*; Dweck & Leggett, A social-cognitive approach to motivation and personality, 256–273.
37. Dweck, Motivation.
38. Diener & Dweck, An analysis of learned helplessness, 451–462; Diener & Dweck, An analysis of learned helplessness II, 940–952.
39. Dweck, *Self-theories*.
40. Cron, Slocum, VandeWalle, & Fu, The role of goal orientation, negative emotions, and goal setting when initial performance falls short of one's performance, 55–80.
41. For example, Higgins, Making a good decision, 1217–1230.
42. Entine, The ethical edge, 1.
43. For example, Vroom, *Work and motivation*.
44. Whereas we discuss the more general learning orientation factors prior to considering the more specific expectancy-theory-based factors of valence and likelihood, we are not implying that these two sets of factors exert influence on executives in the same order in the real world. Thus, future research should examine not only whether the factors we identify influence executives' perceptions of opportunity in crises, but also whether certain factors may be more versus less likely to do so at different points in time.
45. Weick & Quinn, Organizational change and development, 361–386.
46. Higgins, Promotion and prevention, 1–46.
47. Ibid.
48. Brockner & Higgins, Regulatory focus theory, 35–66.
49. Bandura, *Self-efficacy*.
50. Seligman, *Learned optimism*.
51. Scheier & Carver, Optimism, coping, and health, 219–247.
52. Bandura, Self-efficacy, 71–81.
53. Coombs & Holladay, Helping crisis managers protect reputational assets, 165–186; Coombs & Schmidt, An empirical analysis of image restoration, 163–178.
54. Coombs, Impact of past crises on current crisis communication, 265–276; James & Wooten, Leadership as (un)usual, 141–152.
55. Bandura, *Self-efficacy*, 477.
56. For example, Pearson & Claire, Reframing crisis management, 59–76.
57. Heath, Larrick, & Klayman, Cognitive repairs, 1–37.
58. Ibid., 9.
59. Staw, Sandelands, & Dutton, Threat-rigidity effects in organizational behavior, 501–524.
60. James & Wooten, Leadership as (un)usual, 141–152.
61. Janis, *Groupthink;* Williams, Personality, attitude and leader influences on divergent thinking and creativity in organizations, 187–201.

62. Eisenberger, Armeli, & Pretz, Can the promise of reward increase creativity? 704–715; McGlynn et al., Brainstorming and task performance in groups constrained by evidence, 75–88; McCrae, Creativity, divergent thinking, and openness to experience, 1258–1271.
63. Staw, Sandelands, & Dutton, Threat-rigidity effects in organizational behavior, 501–524.
64. Janis, *Victims of groupthink;* Janis, *Groupthink.*
65. Wooten & James, When firms fail to learn, 23–33.
66. For example, Chattapadhyay, Glick, & Huber, Organizational actions in response to threats and opportunities, 937–955; Dutton & Jackson, Categorizing strategic issues, 76–90; Mitroff, Crisis management and environmentalism, 101–114; Pearson & Mitroff, From crisis prone to crisis prepared, 48–59.

References

Acquier, A., Gand, S., & Szpirglas, M. (2008). From stakeholders to stakeholder management in crisis episodes: A case study of a public transportation company. *Journal of Contingencies and Crisis Management, 16*(2), 101–114.

Adair, J. 1987. *Effective Team Building*. Vermont: Gower Publishing.

Aguilera, D. C. (1990). *Crisis intervention: Theory and methodology* (6th ed.). St. Louis, MO: Mosby.

Akre, B. S. (1998, August 6). Chrysler merger going smoothly. *Denver Post*, p. C3.

Aldwin, C. M. (1994). *Stress, coping, and development: An integrative perspective*. New York: Guilford Press.

Algorta, P. (2008). Notes from a survivor of the Andean air crash. Stepping into the void, http://crisisleadership.blogspot.com/2008/04/notes-from-survivor-of-andean-aircrash.html.

Allen, M. W., & Caillouet, R. H. (1994). Legitimation endeavors: Impression management strategies used by an organization in crisis. *Communication Monographs, 61*(1), 44–63.

Amabile, T. (1982). Social psychology of creativity: A consensual assessment technique. *Journal of Personality and Social Psychology, 43*(5), 997–1013.

Amabile, T. (1983). The social psychology of creativity: A componential conceptualization. *Journal of Personality and Social Psychology, 45*(2), 357–376.

Amabile, T. (1996). *Creativity in context*. Boulder, CO: Westview Press.

Ancona, D. & Backman, E. & Bresman, H. (2008). X-Teams: New ways of leading in a new world. *Ivey Business Journal Online, 72*(5), Retrieved March 2009, from http://www.iveybusinessjournal.com/article.asp?intArticle_ID=755.

Annual ICM Crisis Report (2004). *Institute for Crisis Management, 14*(1).

Argyris, C. (1977). Double loop learning in organizations. *Harvard Business Review, 55*(5), 115–125.

Argyris, C. (1990). *Overcoming organizational defenses: Facilitating organizational learning*. Boston: Allyn and Bacon.

Argyris, C. (1991). Teaching smart people how to learn. *Harvard Business Review, 69*(3), 99–109.

Argyris, C., & Schon, D. A. (1978). *Organizational learning: A theory of action perspective*. Reading, MA: Addison-Wesley.

Arnold, M. B. (1960). *Emotion and personality* (Vols. I and II). New York: Columbia University Press.

Arrow, K. J. (1985). The economics of agency. In J. W. Pratt & R. J. Zeckhauser (Eds.), *Principals and agents: The structure of business* (pp. 37–51). Boston: Harvard Business School Press.

Arthur, W. B. (1994). Inductive reasoning and bounded rationality. *American Economic Review, 84*(2), 406–411.

Ayres, R. U., II, & Rohatgi, P. K. (1987). Bhopal lessons for technological decision-makers. *Technology in Society, 9*(1), 1–15.

Baird, L. (1994). *Meeting the global challenges: The executive perspective.* Unpublished working paper, Boston University, Boston.

Baker, W., & Sinkula, J. (1999). The synergistic effect of market orientation and learning orientation on organizational performance. *Journal of Academy of Marketing Science, 27*, 411–427.

Baltimore & Ohio Museum (2004). Baltimore & Ohio Museum 2004 Annual Report. Baltimore, Maryland.

Bandura, A. (1977a). Self efficacy: Toward a unifying theory of behavioral change. *Psychological Review, 84*(2), 191–215.

Bandura, A. (1977b). *Social learning theory.* Englewood Cliffs, NJ: Prentice Hall.

Bandura, A. (1994). Self-efficacy. In V. S. Ramachandran (Ed.), *Encyclopedia of human behavior* (Vol. 4, pp. 71–81). San Diego, CA: Academic Press.

Bandura, A. (1997). *Self-efficacy: The exercise of control.* New York: W. H. Freeman.

Barber, B. (1983). *The logic and limits of trust.* New Brunswick, NJ: Rutgers University Press.

Barnett, C., & Pratt, M. (2000). From threat rigidity to flexibility: Toward a learning model of autogenic crisis in organizations. *Journal of Organizational Change Management, 13*(1), 74–88.

Barney, J. B. (1991). Firm resources and sustained competitive advantage. *Journal of Management, 17*(1), 99–120.

Bass, B. (1985). *Leadership and performance beyond expectations.* New York: The Free Press.

Batson, C. D. (1991). *The altruism question: Toward a social-psychological answer.* Hillsdale, NJ: Erlbaum.

Baumeister, R. F., Bratslavsky, E., Finkenauer, C., & Vohs, K. D. (2001). Bad is stronger than good. *Review of General Psychology, 5*(4), 323–370.

Baumeister, R. F., Heatherton, T. F., & Tice, D. M. (1993). When ego threats lead to self-regulation failure: Negative consequences of high self-esteem. *Journal of Personality and Social Psychology, 64*(1), 141–156.

Bazerman, M. H. (1998). *Judgment in managerial decision making* (4th ed.). New York: John Wiley & Sons.

Bazerman, M. H., & Chugh, D. (2006a). Bounded awareness: Focusing failures in negotiation. In L. Thompson (Ed.), *Negotiation theory and research.* New York: Psychological Press.

Bazerman, M. H., & Chugh, D. (2006b). Decisions without blinders. *Harvard Business Review, 84*(1), 88–97.

Bazerman, M. H., & Watkins, M. D. (2008). *Predictable surprises*. Boston: Harvard Business School Press.

Beauchamp, T., & Bowie, N. E. (1979). *Ethical theory and business*. New York: Prentice Hall.

Benini, A., & Badford-Benini, J. (1996). Ebola virus: From medical emergency to complex disaster. *Journal of Contingencies and Crisis Management, 4*(1), 10–19.

Benoit, W. L. (1992). *Accounts, excuses, and apologies*. Albany, NY: State University of New York Press.

Benoit, W. L. (1995). *Accounts, excuses, and apologies: A theory of image restoration strategies*. Albany, NY: State University of New York Press.

Berry, E. (1996) How did they do it? Conative talents in crisis. *Journal of Management Inquiry, 5*(4); 407-417.

Bettman, J. R., & Weitz, B. A. (1983). Attributions in the board room: Causal reasoning in corporate annual reports. *Administrative Science Quarterly, 28*(2), 165–183.

Billings, R. S., Milburn, T. W., & Schaalman, M. L. (1980). A model of crisis perception: A theoretical and empirical analysis. *Administrative Science Quarterly, 25*, 300–316.

Blackmon, D. A. & Harris, N. (2001, April 2,). Suit alleges pattern of bias at a southern co. Unit. Retrieved June 2, 2009, from http://www.slaverybyanothername.com/other-writings/racial-bind-black-utility-workers-in-georgia-see-nooses-as-sign-of-harassment/

Blasi, A. (1980). Bridging moral cognition and moral action: A critical review of the literature. *Psychological Bulletin, 88*(1), 1–45.

Bobocel, D. R., Son Hing, L. S., Davey, L. M., Stanley, D. J., & Zanna, M. P. (1998). Justice-based opposition to social policies: Is it genuine? *Journal of Personality and Social Psychology, 75*(3), 653–669.

Bolman, L. G., & Deal, T. E. (2008). *Reframing organizations* (4th ed.). San Francisco: Jossey-Bass.

Bond, M. H., & Hofstede, G. (1989). The cash value of Confucian values. *Human Systems Management, 8*, 195–200.

Boone, S. D., & Holmes, J. G. (1991). The dynamics of interpersonal trust: Resolving uncertainty in the face of risk. In R. A. Hinde & J. Groebel (Eds.), *Cooperation and prosocial behavior* (pp. 190–211). New York: Cambridge University Press.

Braden, V., Cooper, J., Klingele, M. Powell, J. & Robbins, M. (2005). Crisis—A leadership opportunity. Working Paper. John F. Kennedy School of Government, Harvard University.

Brenner, S. N., & Molander, E. A. (1977). Is the ethics of business changing? *Harvard Business Review, 55*(1), 57–71.

Brief, A. P., & Hayes, E. (1998). The continuing "American dilemma": Studying racism in organizations. In C. L. Cooper & D. M. Rousseau (Eds.), *Trends in organizational behavior* (Vol. 4, pp. 89–105). New York: John Wiley & Sons.

Brockner, J., & Higgins, E. T. (2001). Regulatory focus theory: Its implications for the study of emotions at work. *Organizational Behavior and Human Decision Processes, 86*, 35–66.

Brockner, J. B., & James, E. H. (2008). Toward an understanding of when executives see crisis as opportunity. *Journal of Applied Behavioral Science, 44*(1), 94–115.

Bromiley, P., & Cummings, L. (1993). *Organizations with trust: Theory and management.* Unpublished manuscript, University of Minnesota.

Brommer, M., Gratto, C., Gravander, J., & Tuttle, M. (1987). A behavioral model of ethical and unethical decisionmaking. *Journal of Business Ethics, 6*(4), 265–280.

Broom, G., Center, A., & Cutlip, S. (1994). *Effective public relations* (7th ed.). Englewood Cliffs, NJ: Prentice Hall.

Browning, J. (1993). Union Carbide: Disaster at Bhopal. In J. Gottschalk (Ed.), *Crisis response: Inside stories on managing image under siege* (pp. 1–15). Detroit, MI: Visible Ink Press, a division of Gale Research.

Bueno, J. (1997, September 22). Home Depot's agreement to settle suit could cut 3rd quarter earnings by 21%. *Wall Street Journal,* p. B18.

Bunderson, J. S., & Sutcliffe, K. M. (2002). Why some teams emphasize learning more than others: Evidence from business unit management teams. In M. Neal, E. Mannix, & H. Sondak (Eds.), *Research on managing groups and teams* (Vol. 4, pp. 49–84). New York: Elsevier Science.

Cacioppo, J. T., & Gardner, W. L. (1999). Emotion. *Annual Review of Psychology, 50,* 191–214.

Cameron, K., Dutton, J., Quinn, R., & Spreitzer, G. (2006). What is positive organizational scholarship? Retrieved November 23, 2006, from http://www.bus.umich.edu/Positive/WhatisPOS/

Cannon, M. D & Edmonson, A. C. (2001). Confronting failure: antecedents and consequences of shared beliefs about failure in organizational work groups. *Journal of Organizational Behavior, 22,* 161–177.

Cannon, M. D., & Edmonson, A. C. (2005). Failing to learn and learning to fail (intelligently): How great organizations put failure to work to innovate and improve. *Long Range Planning, 38*(3), 299–319.

Caponigro, J. R. (2000). *The crisis counselor.* Chicago, IL: Contemporary Books.

Carr, S. (2009). *Dynamic interpretations of strategic issues: The effects of cognitive processing demands on bounded awareness.* Unpublished manuscript.

Carver, C. S. (1998). Resilience and thriving: Issues, models, and linkages. *Journal of Social Issues, 54*(2), 245–266.

Castka, P., Bamba, C.J., Sharp, J. M., & Belohoubeck, J. (2001). Factors affecting successful implementation of high performance teams. *Team Performance Management, 7,* 123–134.

Caudron, S. (1997). Don't make Texaco's $175 million mistake. *Workforce, 76,* 58–66.

Cavanagh, G. F., Moberg, D. J., & Velasquez, M. (1981). The ethics of organizational politics. *Academy of Management Review, 6*(3), 363–374.

CBS News Interactive. (2007, February 15). JetBlue attempts to calm passenger furor. Retrieved July 1, 2008, from http://cbs2.com/national/jetblue.tarmac.JFK.2.279800.html

Charlebois, S., & Labrecque, J. (2007). Processual learning, environmental pluralism, and inherent challenges of managing a socio-economic crisis: The case of the Canadian mad cow crisis. *Journal of Macromarketing, 27*(2), 115–125.

Chattopadhyay, P., Glick, W. H., & Huber, G. P. (2001). Organizational actions in response to threats and opportunities. *Academy of Management Journal, 44*(5), 937–955.

Chen, C. C., & Meindl, J. R. (1991). The construction of leadership images in the popular press: The case of Donald Burr and People Express. *Administrative Science Quarterly, 36*, 521–551.

Chelariu, C., Jonhston, W. & Young, L. (2002). Learning to improvise, improvising to learn: A process of responding to complex environments. *Journal of Business Research, 55*, 141–147.

China Business. (2008, April 26). Thirteen days of crisis at Carrefour. Retrieved July 27, 2009, from http://www.zonaeuropa.com/20080428_1.htm

Choi, J. (2002). External activities and team effectiveness: Review and theoretical development. *Small Group Research, 33*(2), 181–208.

Chugh, D., & Bazerman, M. H. (2007). Bounded awareness: What you fail to see can hurt you. *Mind & Society, 6*(1), 20–25.

Cisco (2009). Health & Safety Crisis Management. Retrieved June 2009, from http://www.cisco.com/web/about/ac227/ac222/employees/health_safety/crisis_management.html.

Clarkson, M. B. E. (1991). Defining, evaluating, and managing corporate social performance: The stakeholder management model. In L. E. Preston (Ed.), *Research in corporate social performance and policy* (Vol. 12, pp. 331–358). Greenwich, CT: JAI Press.

Cohen, J. (2008, December 1). Kodak's image is picture perfect. Retrieved April 8, 2008, from http://www.salesandmarketing.com/msg/content_display/marketing/e3i2dd2f2ead332946a2a47d6839edf3e2c#

Collins, J. C. (2001). *Good to great: Why some companies make the leap and others don't.* New York: Harper Business.

Cook, S. D. N., & Yanow, D. (1993). Culture and organizational learning. *Journal of Management Inquiry, 2*(4), 373–390.

Coombs, W. T. (1999). *Ongoing crisis communication: Planning, managing and responding.* Thousand Oaks, CA: Sage Publications.

Coombs, W. T. (2004). Impact of past crises on current crisis communication: Insights from situational crisis communication theory. *Journal of Business Communication, 41*(3), 141–152.

Coombs, W. T., & Holladay, S. J. (1996). Communication and attributions in a crisis: An experimental study in crisis communication. *Journal of Public Relations Research, 8*(4), 279–295.

Coombs, W. T., & Holladay, S. J. (2002). Helping crisis managers protect reputational assets: Initial tests of the situational crisis communication theory. *Management Communication Quarterly, 16*(2), 165–186.

Coombs, W. T., & Schmidt, L. (2000). An empirical analysis of image restoration: Texaco's racism crisis. *Journal of Public Relations Research, 12*(2), 163–178.

Coplen, L. (2008). *Strategic bridge towards community building: The military's role.* Strategy Research Project. Carlisle, PA: Army War College, Carlisle Barracks.

Cowan, D. A. (1986). Developing a process model of problem recognition. *Academy of Management Review, 11*(4), 763–776.

Cox, T. H., Lobel, S., & McLeod, P. (1991). Effects of ethnic group cultural difference on cooperative and competitive behavior on a group task. *Academy of Management Journal, 34*(4), 827–847.

Cray, C. (1997). Conducive to sexual harassment: The EEOC's case against Mitsubishi. *The Multinational Monitor, 18*(10). Retrieved September 2008, from http://multi-nationalmonitor.org/hyper/mm1097.09.html

Crittenden, A. (1984, August 19). The age of "me-first" management. *New York Times,* p. 1.

Crocitto, M., & Youssef, M. (2003). The human side of organizational agility. *Industrial Management + Data Systems, 103*(6), 388–397.

Cron, W., Slocum, J., VandeWalle, D., & Fu, Q. (2005). The role of goal orientation, negative emotions, and goal setting when initial performance falls short of one's performance goal. *Human Performance, 18*(1), 55–80.

Crosby, F., Bromley, S., & Saxe, L. (1980). Recent unobtrusive studies of black and white discrimination and prejudice: A literature review. *Psychological Bulletin, 87,* 546–563.

Curtin, T., Hayman, D., & Husein, N. (2005). *Managing a crisis: A practical guide.* New York: Palgrave Macmillan.

Cyert, R., & March, J. (1963). *A behavioral theory of the firm.* Englewood Cliffs, NJ: Prentice Hall.

Daft, R. L., & Weick, K. E. (1984). Toward a model of organizations as interpretation systems. *Academy of Management Review, 9*(2), 284–295.

Dantas, A., & Seville, E. (2006). Organizational issues in implementing and informa-tion sharing framework: Lessons from the Matata flooding events in New Zealand. *Journal of Contingencies and Crisis Managements, 14*(1), 38–52.

Darling, J., Seristo, H., & Gabrielson, M. (2005). Anatomy of crisis management: A case focusing on a major cross-cultural clash within DaimlerChrysler. *Finnish Journal of Business Economics, 3*(5), 343–360.

D'Aveni, R. (1989). The aftermath of organizational decline: A longitudinal study of the strategic and managerial characteristics of declining firms. *Academy of Management Journal, 32*(3), 577–605.

Davis, M. H. (1983). Measuring individual differences in empathy: Evidence for a multidimensional approach. *Journal of Personality and Social Psychology, 44*(1), 113–126.

Davis, S., & Lawrence, P. (1977). *Matrix.* Reading, MA: Addison-Wesley.

Denis, J., Lamothe, L., & Langley, A. (2001). The dynamics of collective leadership and strategic change in pluralistic organizations. *Academy of Management Journal, 44*(4), 809–837.

Deogun, N. (1999, May 3). Coke was told in '95 of need for diversity. *Wall Street Journal,* p. A3.

Department of Defense. (2009). *Joint course in communications.* Retrieved March 12, 2009, from http://www.ou.edu/deptcomm/dodjcc/groups/02C2/Johnson%20 &%20Johnson.htm

Deutch, M. (1962). Cooperation and trust: Some theoretical notes. In M. R. Jones (Ed.), *Nebraska symposium on motivation* (No. 10, pp. 275–319). Lincoln, NE: University of Nebraska Press.

Devitt, K. & Borodzicz (2008). Interwoven leadership: The missing link in multi-agency major incident response. *Journal of Contingencies and Crisis Management, 16*(4), 208–216.

Diener, C., & Dweck, C. S. (1978). An analysis of learned helplessness: Continuous changes in performance, strategy, and achievement cognitions following failure. *Journal of Personality and Social Psychology, 36*(5), 451–462.

Diener, C., & Dweck, C. S. (1980). An analysis of learned helplessness. II. The processing of success. *Journal of Personality and Social Psychology, 39*, 940–952.

Donaldson, L. (1990). A rational basis for criticism of organizational economics: A reply to Barney. *Academy of Management Review, 15*(3), 394–401.

Donaldson, T., & Preston, L. E. (1995). The stakeholder theory of the corporation: Concepts, evidence, and implications. *Academy of Management Review, 20*(1), 65–91.

Dubrovski, D. (2007). Management mistakes as causes of corporate crises: Countries in transition. *Managing Global Transitions, 5*(4), 333–354.

Dutton, J. E. (1986). The processing of crisis and non-crisis strategic issues. *Journal of Management Studies, 23*(5), 501–517.

Dutton, J. E., & Ashford, S. I. (1993). Selling issues to top management. *Academy of Management Review, 18*(3), 397–428.

Dutton, J. E., Ashford, S. I., O'Neil, R., Hayes, E., & Wierba, E. (1997). Reading the wind: How middle managers assess the context for selling issues to top managers. *Strategic Management Journal, 18*(5), 407–423.

Dutton, J. E., & Jackson, S. E. (1987). Categorizing strategic issues: Links to organizational action. *Academy of Management Review, 12*(1), 76–90.

Dweck, C. (1990a). Motivation. In R. Glaser & A. Lesgold (Eds.), *Foundations for a cognitive psychology of education.* Hillsdale, NJ: Erlbaum.

Dweck, C. (1990b). Self-theories and goals: Their role in motivation, personality and development. In R. A. Dienstbier (Ed.), *Nebraska symposium on motivation. Perspectives on motivation* (No. 38, pp. 199–235). Lincoln, NE: University of Nebraska Press.

Dweck, C. (2000). *Self-theories: Their role in motivation, personality, and development.* Florence, KY: Psychology Press, Taylor & Francis Group.

Dweck, C. S., & Leggett, E. L. (1988). A social-cognitive approach to motivation and personality. *Psychological Review, 95*(2), 256–273.

Eagly, A., & Carli, L. L. (2007). *Through the labyrinth: The truth about how women become leaders.* Cambridge, MA: Harvard Business School Press.

Edmonson, A. (1999). Psychological safety and learning behavior in work teams. *Administrative Science Quarterly, 44*, 350–383.

Edmonson, A. (2002). Managing the risk of learning. Psychological safety in teams. In M. West (Ed.) *International Handbook of Organizational Teamwork.* London: Blackwell.

Edmonson, A. (2003). Speaking up in the operating room: How team leaders promote learning in interdisciplinary action teams. *Journal of Management Studies, 40*(6), 1420–1452.

Eimer, D. (2008, April 20). Chinese boycott Western chains over Olympics. Retrieved July 2009 from http://www.telegraph.co.uk/news/worldnews/1896175/Chinese-boycott-Western-chains-over-Olympics.html

Eisenberger, R., Armeli, S., & Pretz, J. (1998). Can the promise of reward increase creativity? *Journal of Personality and Social Psychology, 74*(3), 704–714.

Eisenhardt, K. (1989). Building theories from case study research. *Academy of Management Review, 14*(4), 532–550.

Eisenhardt, K. M., & Martin, J. A. (2000). Dynamic capabilities: What are they? *Strategic Management Journal 21*(10–11), 1105–1121.

Elliot, D., & Smith, D. (2006). Cultural readjustment after crisis: Regulation and learning from crisis within the UK soccer industry. *Journal of Management Studies, 43*(2), 289–317.

Elsbach, K. D. (1994). Managing organizational legitimacy in the California cattle industry: The construction and effectiveness of verbal accounts. *Administrative Science Quarterly, 39*(1), 57–88.

Elsbach, K. D. (2000). The architecture of legitimacy: Constructing accounts of organizational controversies. In J. T. Jost & B. Major (Eds.), *The psychology of legitimacy: Emerging perspectives on ideology, justice and intergroup relations.* New York: Cambridge University Press.

Elsbach, K. D., & Kramer, R. M. (1996). Members' responses to organizational identity threats: Encountering and countering the *Business Week* rankings. *Administrative Science Quarterly, 41*(3), 442–476.

Elsbach, K. D., & Sutton, R. I. (1992). Acquiring organizational legitimacy through illegitimate actions: A marriage of institutional and impression management theories. *Academy of Management Journal, 35*(4), 699–738.

Ely, R. & Thomas, D. A. (2001). Cultural diversity at work: The effects of diversity perspectives on work group processes and outcomes. *Administrative Science Quarterly, 46*(2), 229–273.

Entine, J. (1999). The ethical edge: How "Jack" turned crisis into opportunity. Retrieved April 4, 1999, from *Business Digest*: http://www.jonentine.com/ethical_edge/jack_crisis.htm

Essed, P., & Stanfield, J. (1991). *Understanding everyday racism: An interdisciplinary theory.* Newbury Park, CA: Sage.

Evans, C., Hammersley, G. O., & Robertson, M. (2001). Assessing the role and efficacy of communication strategies in times of crisis. *Journal of European Industrial Training, 25,* 297–309.

FairRidge Group. (2009). *Water wars—The beverage industry as a canary or future innovation leader?* Retrieved October 12, 2009, from http://www.triplepundit.com/2009/10/water-wars-the-beverage-industry-as-a-canary-or-future-innovation-leader/

Farazmand, A. (2007). Learning from Katrina crisis: A global and international perspective with implications for future crisis management. *Public Administration Review, 67*(1), 149–159.

Ferrell, O. C., & Gresham, L. G. (1985, Summer). A contingency framework for understanding ethical decision making in marketing. *Journal of Marketing, 49,* 87–96.

Fiol, M., & Lyles, M. (1985). Organizational learning. *Academy of Management Review, 10,* 803–813.

Fiske, S. T. & Taylor, S. T. (1984). *Social cognition.* New York: Random House.

Fombrun, C. (1996). *Reputation: Realizing value from the corporate image.* Boston: Harvard Business School Press.

Freeman, R. E. (1984). *Strategic management: A stakeholder approach.* Boston: Pitman.

Gabarro, J. (1987). *The dynamics of taking charge*. Boston: Harvard Business School Press.

Gaertner, S. L., & Dovidio, J. F. (1981). Racism among the well intentioned. In J. Bermingham & E. Claussen (Eds.), *Racism, pluralism and public policy: A search for equality*. Boston: G. K. Hall.

Galinsky, A. D., & Moskowitz, G. B. (2000). Perspective-taking: Decreasing stereotype expression, stereotype accessibility, and in-group favoritism. *Journal of Personality and Social Psychology, 78*(4), 708–724.

Gambetta, D. (Ed.). (1988). *Trust: Making and breaking cooperative relations*. Oxford, UK: Basil Blackwell.

Gand, S. Acquier, A. & Szpirglas, M. (2005). Understanding organizational crisis management processes: An analytical framework drawn from a case study in a public company. Presented at the Communication at Euram 2005, Munich Germany.

Gardiner, W. L., & Martinko, M. J. (1988). Impression management in organizations. *Journal of Management, 14*(2), 321–338.

Garvin, D. & Roberto, M. (2001). What you don't know about making decisions. *Harvard Business Review, 79*(8), 108–116.

Gerencser, M., Van Lee, R., Napolitano, F., & Kelly, C. (2008). *Megacommunities: How leaders of government, business and non-profits can tackle today's global challenge together*. New York: Palgrave Macmillan.

Ginzel, L. E., Kramer R. M., & Sutton, R. I. (1993). Organizational impression management as a reciprocal influence process: The neglected role of the organizational audience. In B. M. Staw & L. L. Cummings (Eds.), *Research on organizational behavior* (Vol. 15). Greenwich, CT: JAI.

Gladwell, M. (2008). *Outliers: The story of success*. New York: Little Brown and Company.

Glynn, M. A., Lant, T. K., & Milliken, F. J. (1994). Mapping learning processes in organizations: A multilevel framework linking learning and organizing. *Advances in Managerial Cognition and Organizational Information Processing, 5*, 43–83.

Goffman, E. (1959). *The presentation of self in everyday life*. New York: Doubleday.

Goffman, E. (1971). Remedial interchanges. In E. Goffman (Ed.), *Relations in public: Microstudies of the public order* (pp. 95–187). New York: Basic Books.

Goodman, R. A. (1981). *Temporary systems: Professional development, manpower utilization, task effectiveness, and innovation*. New York: Praeger.

Goodman, R. A., & Goodman, L. P. (1976). Some management issues in temporary systems: A study of professional development and manpower—The theater case. *Administrative Science Quarterly, 21*(3), 494–501.

Goodpaster, K. E. (1991). Business ethics and stakeholder analysis. *Business Ethics Quarterly, 1*(1), 53–73.

Groves, A. (1997). The ambidextrous organization. *Journal of Business Strategy, 18*, 42–46.

Gundel, S. (2005). Towards a new typology of crises. *Journal of Contingencies and Crisis Management, 13*(3), 106–115.

Gupta, A., & Govindarajan, V. (2002). Cultivating a global mindset. *Academy of Management Executive, 16*(1), 116–126.

Hackman, M. & Johnson, C. (1996). *Leadership: A communication perspective*. Prospect Heights, IL: Waveland Press.

Hadley, C. N., Pittinsky, T. L., & Zhu, W. (2007). *Measuring the efficacy of leaders to assess information and make decisions in a crisis: The C-LEAD scale*. Faculty Research Working Paper Series RWP07-035.

Hagenbourger, M., Lagadec, P., & Pouw, M. (2003). Postal security, anthrax and beyond Europe's posts and the critical network challenge: Lessons from the anthrax case to meet future challenges. *Journal of Contingencies and Crisis Management, 11*(3), 105–107.

Hagiwara, T. (2007). The eight characteristics of Japanese crisis-prone organizations. In C. Pearson, C. Roux-Dufort, & J. Clair (Eds.), *International handbook of organizational crisis management* (pp. 253–270). Thousand Oaks, CA: Sage Publications.

Hammond, J. S., Keeney, R. L., & Raiffa, H. (1998a, March–April). Even swaps: A rational method for making tradeoffs. *Harvard Business Review, 76*(5), 137–150.

Hammond, J. S., Keeney, R. L., & Raiffa, H. (1998b, September–October). The hidden traps in decision making. *Harvard Business Review, 76*(5), 47–58.

Hannerz, U. (1996). Cosmopolitans and locals in world culture. In U. Hannerz (Ed.), *Transnational connections: Culture, people, places* (pp. 102–111). London: Routledge.

Hargadon, A., & Sutton, R. (1997). Technology brokering and innovation in a product development firm. *Administrative Science Quarterly, 42*(4), 716–749.

Harris, N. (1996, April 1). Revolt at the deli counter: A sex discrimination suit against Publix may galvanize unions. *Business Week*, p. 32.

Hart, P. (1993). Symbols, rituals, and power: The lost dimensions of crisis management. *Journal of Contingencies and Crisis Management, 1*(1), 36–50.

Haruta, A., & Hallahan, K. (2003). Cultural issues in airline crisis communications: A Japan–US comparative study. *Asian Journal of Communication, 13*(2), 122–150.

Haseley, K. (2004, November 22). Twenty years after Bhopal: What you need to know about managing today's crisis. *Chemical Market Reporter, 266*(18), 21–22.

Heath, C., Larrick, R. P., & Klayman, J. (1998). Cognitive repairs: How organizational practices can compensate for shortcomings of individual learners. In B. M. Staw & L. L. Cummings (Eds.), *Research in organizational behavior* (Vol. 20, pp. 1–37). Greenwich, CT: JAI Press.

Hedberg, B. (1981). How organizations learn and unlearn. In P. C. Nystrom & W. H. Starbuck (Eds.), *Handbook of organizational design: Adapting organizations to their environments* (Vol. 1, pp. 3–27). Oxford, UK: Oxford University Press.

Heilman, M. E., Simon, M. C., & Repper, D. P. (1987). Intentionally favored, unintentionally harmed? The impact of sex-based preferential selection on self-perceptions and self-evaluations. *Journal of Applied Psychology, 72*(1), 62–68.

Heller, J., & White, J. (2000, August 3). Ford Motor Co. is investigating reports about failures of Firestone truck tires. *Wall Street Journal* (Eastern Edition), p. A6.

Hemphill, H., & Haines, R. (1997). *Discrimination, harassment, and the failure of diversity training: What to do now*. Westport, CT: Quorum Books.

Hensgen, T., Desouza, K. C., & Kraft, G. D. (2003). Games, signals, detection and processing in the context of crisis management. *Journal of Contingencies and Crisis Management, 11*(2), 67–77.

Herman, C. (1963). Some consequences of crisis which limit the viability of organizations. *Administrative Science Quarterly, 8*(1), 61–82.

Herriott, S., Levinthal, D., & March, J. G. (1988). Learning from experience in organizations. Reprinted in J. G. March, *Decisions and organizations* (pp. 219–227). New York: Basil Blackwell.

Higgins, E. T. (1998). Promotion and prevention: Regulatory focus as a motivational principle. In M. P. Zanna (Ed.), *Advances in experimental social psychology* (Vol. 30, pp. 1–46). New York: Academic Press.

Higgins, E. T. (2000). Making a good decision: Value from fit. *American Psychologist, 55*(11), 1217–1230.

Higgins, R. L., & Snyder, C. R. (1989). The business of excuses. In R. A. Giacalone & P. Rosenfeld (Eds.), *Impression management in the organization* (pp. 73–86). Hillsdale, NJ: Lawrence Erlbaum Associates.

Hill, L. (1995). *Managing your team* (Case: 9-494-081). Cambridge, MA: Harvard Business School Publishing.

Hilton, J., & von Hippel, W. (1996). Stereotypes. *Annual Review of Psychology, 47*, 237–271.

Hmelo, C., Nagarajan, A. Day, R., (2000). Effects of high and low prior knowledge on construction of a joint problem space. *Journal of Experimental Education, 69*, 36–56.

Hobbs, J. D. (1995). Treachery by any other name: A case study of the Toshiba public relations crisis. *Management Communication Quarterly, 8*, 323–346.

Hofstede, G. (1980). *Cultural consequences: International differences in work-related values.* Newbury Park, CA: Sage Publications.

Huber, G. (1991). Organizational learning: The contributing processes and the literature. *Organization Science, 2*(1), 88–115.

Huber, G. P. (1980). *Managerial decision making.* Glenview, IL: Scott, Foresman.

Hung, K., & Wai, C. (2009). *Carrefour China and the Olympic torch relay: Managing corporate crisis amid evolving expectations of multinational firms.* Case 09/425C. Hong Kong: Asian Case Research Centre, University of Hong Kong.

Ibarra, H. (1992). Homophily and differential returns: Sex differences in network structure and access in an advertising firm. *Administrative Science Quarterly, 37*(3), 422–447.

Ibarra, H. (1993). Personal networks of women and minorities in management: A conceptual framework. *Academy of Management Review, 18*(1), 56–87.

Ibarra, H. (1995). Race, opportunity, and diversity of social circles in managerial networks. *Academy of Management Journal, 38*(3), 673–703.

Ice, R. (1991). Corporate publics and rhetorical strategies: The case of Union Carbide's Bhopal crisis. *Management Communication Quarterly, 4*(3), 341–362.

Jackson, S. E., & Dutton, J. E. (1987). Categorizing strategic issues: Links to organizational action. *Academy of Management Review, 12*(1), 76–90.

Jackson, S. E., & Dutton, J. E. (1988). Discerning threats and opportunities. *Administrative Science Quarterly, 33*, 370–387.

Jacobs, K. (2000, July 28). Georgia Power hit with bias suit. *Wall Street Journal*, p. A1.

James, E. H. (2000). Race-related differences in promotions and support: Underlying effects of human and social capital. *Organization Science, 11*(5), 493–508.

James, E. H., Brief, A. P., Dietz, J., & Cohen, R. (2001). Prejudice matters: Understanding the reactions of whites to affirmative action programs targeted to benefit blacks. *Journal of Applied Psychology, 86*(6), 1120–1128.

James, E. H., & Wooten, L. P. (2000). *Being in the spotlight: How firms respond to public diversity crises*. Paper presented at the Academy of Management meeting, Toronto, Canada.

James, E. H., & Wooten, L. P. (2002). *Actions speak louder than words: Impression management techniques for managing discrimination lawsuits*. Unpublished manuscript.

James, E. H., & Wooten, L. P. (2005). Leadership as (un)usual: How to display competence in times of crisis. *Organizational Dynamics, 34*, 141–152.

James, E. H., & Wooten, L. P. (2006). Diversity crises: How firms manage discrimination lawsuits. *Academy of Management Journal, 49*(6), 1103–1118.

Janis, I. (1958). *Psychological stress*. New York: Wiley.

Janis, I. (1972). *Victims of groupthink*. Boston: Houghton-Mifflin.

Janis, I. (1982). *Groupthink* (2nd ed.). Boston: Houghton-Mifflin.

Janis, I. and Mann, L. (1977). *Decision making: A psychological analysis of conflict, choice, and commitment*. New York: Free Press.

Johnson, A. (2007, April 17). *College gunman disturbed teachers, classmates*. Retrieved from http://www.msnbc.msn.com/id/18148802/?GT1=9246

Jones, T. M. (1991). Ethical decision making by individuals in organizations: An issue contingent model. *Academy of Management Review, 16*, 366–395.

Kahneman, D., Slovic, P., & Tversky, A. (1982). *Judgment under uncertainty: Heuristics and biases*. Cambridge, UK: Cambridge University Press.

Kahneman, D., & Tversky, A. (1979). Prospect theory: An analysis of decision under risk. *Econometrica, XLVII*, 263–291.

Kanter, R. M. (1977). *Men and women of the corporation*. New York: Basic Books.

Kanter, R. M. (1983). *Change masters: Innovation and entrepreneurship in the American corporation*. New York: Simon & Schuster.

Katzenbach, J. R., & Smith, D. S. (1993). *The wisdom of teams*. Boston, MA: Harvard Business School Press.

Katzenbach, J., & Smith, D. (1992). Why teams matter. *McKinsey Quarterly, 3*, 3–27.

Katzenbach, J., & Smith, D. (1993). The discipline of teams. *Harvard Business Review, 71*(2), 111–120.

Keida, B., Harveston, P., & Bhagat, R. (2001). Orienting curricula and teaching to produce international managers for global competition. *Journal of Teaching in International Business, 13*(1), 1–22.

Kedia, B., & Muljerji, A. (1999). Global managers: Developing a mindset for global competitiveness. *Journal of World Business, 34*(3), 223–251.

Kelly, C., Gerencser, M., Napolitano, F., & Van Lee, R. (2007). *The defining features of a megacommunity*. Retrieved October 12, 2009, from Booz & Company: http://www.boozallen.com/media/file/Defining_Features_Megacommunity.pdf

Kenneth, C. (2002, April 26). McDonald's adds 22 locations to menu. *The Russia Journal, 158*, 5.

King, G. (2002). Crisis management and team effectiveness: A closer examination. *Journal of Business Ethics, 41*, 235–249.

Kipnis, D., Schmidt, S. M., & Wilkinson, I. (1980). Intraorganizational influence tactics: Explorations in getting one's way. *Journal of Applied Psychology*, 65(4), 440–452.

Kirkpatrick, S., & Lock, E. (1991). Leadership: Do traits matter? *Academy of Management Executive*, 5(2), 48–60.

Kohlberg, L. (1976). Moral stages and moralization: The cognitive-developmental approach. In T. Lickona (Ed.), *Moral development and behavior* (pp. 31–53). New York: Holt, Rinehart & Winston.

Kohlberg, L., & Turiel, E. (Eds.). (1973). *Moralization research: The cognitive-developmental approach.* Unpublished manuscript, Harvard University, Boston.

Kotter, J., & Schlesinger, L. (1979). Choosing strategies for change. *Harvard Business Review*, 57, 106–114.

Kounoupas, E. (2006). *A six-step process for effective crisis management in the port industy.* Paper presented at the international conference Shipping in the Era of Social Responsibility, Argostoli, Cephalonia, Greece.

Kransdorff, A. (1997). Fight organizational memory lapse. *Workforce*, 76, 34–40.

Kravitz, D. A., & Platania, J. (1993). Attitudes and beliefs about affirmative action: Effects of target and of respondent sex and ethnicity. *Journal of Applied Psychology*, 78, 928–938.

Kuchinke, K. (1995). Managing learning for performance. *Human Resource Development Quarterly*, 6, 307–316.

Lagadec, P., Michel-Kerjan, E., & Ellis, R. (2006, Summer). Disaster via airmail: The launching of a global reaction capacity after the 2001 anthrax attacks. *Technology/Governance/Globalization*, 99–117.

Larson, J. R., Jr., Foster-Fishman, P. G., & Keys, C. B. (1994). Information sharing in decision-making groups. *Journal of Personality and Social Psychology*, 67, 446–461.

Leary, M. R., & Kowalski, R. M. (1990). Impression management: A literature review and two-component model. *Psychological Bulletin*, 107, 34–47.

Lefkowitz, J. (1994). Race as a factor in job placement: Serendipitous findings of "ethnic drift." *Personnel Psychology*, 47, 497–514.

Legal Information Center. (2000). Overview of the recall. Retrieved January 28, 2009, from http://www.firestone-tire-recall.com/pages/overview.html

Leidner, D. E., Pan, G., & Pan, S. L. (2009). The role of IT in crisis response: Lessons from the SARS and Asian Tsunami disasters. *Journal of Strategic Information Systems*, 18, 80–99.

Leow, J. (2008, April 14). World news: In China, citizens call for boycotts of their own; campaigns target retailers supportive of the Dalai Lama. *Wall Street Journal* (Eastern Edition), p. A10. Retrieved July 30, 2009, from ABI/INFORM Global (Document ID: 1461496001).

Levinthal, D., & March, J. G. (1988). A model of adaptive organizational search. In J. G. March (Ed.), *Decisions and organizations* (pp. 187–218). New York: Basil Blackwell.

Levitt, B., & March, J. (1988). Organizational learning. *Annual Review of Sociology*, 14, 319–340.

Levy, O., Beechler, S., Taylor, S., & Boyacigiller, N. (2007). What we talk about when we talk about "global mindset": Managerial cognition in multinational corporations. *Journal of International Business Studies*, 38, 231–258.

Levy, O., Taylor, S., Boyacugiller, N. A., & Beechler, S. (2007). Global mindset: A review and proposed extensions. In M. Javidan, R. M. Steers, & M. A. Hitt (Eds.), *Advances in international management: The global mindset* (pp. 11–47). Oxford, UK: Elsevier.

Levy, P. F. (2001). The Nut Island effect: When good teams go wrong. *Harvard Business Review, 79*(3), 51–59.

Lewicki, R. J., & Bunker, B. B. (1995). Trust in relationships: A model of trust development and decline. In B. B. Bunker & J. Z. Rubin (Eds.), *Conflict, cooperation, and justice* (pp. 133–174). San Francisco: Jossey-Bass.

Lewicki, R. J., & Bunker, B. B. (1996). Developing and maintaining trust in work relationships. In R. M. Kramer & T. R. Tyler (Eds.), *Trust in organizations: Frontiers of theory and research* (pp. 114–139). Thousand Oaks, CA: Sage.

Lin, Z., Zhao, X., Ismail, K. M., & Carley, K. M. (2006). Organizational design and restructuring in response to crises: Lessons from computational modeling and real-world cases. *Organization Science, 17*(5), 598–618.

Lincoln, D. J., Pressley, M. M., & Little, T. (1982). Ethical beliefs and personal values of top level executives. *Journal of Business Research, 10*, 475–487.

Littlejohn, R. (1983). *Crisis management: A team approach.* New York: American Management Association.

Locke, E., & Latham, G. (1990). *A theory of goal setting and task performance.* Englewood Cliffs, NJ: Prentice Hall.

Loe, T. W., Ferrell, L., & Mansfield, P. (2000). A review of empirical studies assessing ethical decision making in business. *Journal of Business Ethics, 25*(3), 185–204.

Luhmann, N. (2001). Familiarity, confidence, trust: Problems and alternatives. In D. Gambetta (Ed.), *Trust: Making and breaking cooperative relations* (pp. 94–107). Oxford, UK: University of Oxford. Electronic edition.

Luthans, F. (1998). *Organizational behavior* (8th ed.). New York: Irwin McGraw-Hill.

Luthar, S. S., Cicchetti, D., & Becker, B. (2000). The construct of resilience: A critical evaluation and guidelines for future work. *Child Development, 71*(3), 543–562.

MacCrimmon, K.R. (1973). An overview of multiple objective decision making. In J.L. Cochrane & M. Zelany (Eds.), *Multiple criteria decision making* (pp. 18–43). Columbia: The University of South Carolina Press.

Maier, N. R. F. (1970). *Problem solving and creativity in individual and groups.* Belmont, CA: Brooks/Cole.

Majchrzak, A., Jarvenpaa, S., & Holllingshead, A. 2007. Coordinating expertise among emergent groups responding to disasters. *Organization Science, 18*(1), 147–161.

Mandell, B., & Kohler-Grey, S. (1990). Management development that values diversity. *Personnel, 67*, 42–47.

March, J. G. (1994). *A primer on decision making: How decisions happen.* New York: The Free Press.

March, J. G., & Olsen, J. (1989). *Rediscovering institutions: The organizational basis of politics.* New York: The Free Press.

March, J. G., & Simon, H. A. (1958). *Organizations.* New York: Wiley.

Marcus, A. A., & Goodman, R. S. (1991). Victims and shareholders: The dilemmas of presenting corporate policy during a crisis. *Academy of Management Journal, 34*, 281–305.

Marks, M., Mathieu, J., & Zaccaro, S, (2001). A temporarily based framework and taxonomy of team processes. *Academy of Management Review, 26*(3), 356–376.

Marlys, C., Farkas, M., Sutcliffe, K., Weick, K. (2008). Learning through rare events: Significant interruptions at the Baltimore & Ohio railroad museum. *Organization Science, 20*(5), 846–860.

Masten, A. S. (1994). Resilience in individual development: Successful adaptation despite risk and adversity. In M. C. Want & E. W. Gordon (Eds.), *Educational resilience in inner city America: Challenges and prospects* (pp. 3–25). Hillsdale, NJ: Erlbaum.

Matthews, J. (1996). Organizational foundations of economic learning. *Human Sysems Management, 15*, 113–124.

McAuley, E., Duncan, T. E., & Russell, D. W. (1992). Measuring causal attributions: The revised causal dimension scale (CDSII). *Personality and Social Psychology Bulletin, 18*(5), 566–573.

McCartney, S. (2009). Crash courses for the crew. *The Wall Street Journal,* D1 & D8.

McCrae, R. (1987). Creativity, divergent thinking, and openness to experience. *Journal of Personality and Social Psychology, 52*(6), 1258–1271.

McGlynn, R. P., McGurck, D., Effland, V. S., Johll, N. L., & Harding, D. J. (2004). Brainstorming and task performance in groups constrained by evidence. *Organization Behavior and Human Decision Processes, 93,* 75–88.

McGregor, D. (1967). *The professional manager.* New York: McGraw-Hill.

McLean, B., & Elkind, P. (2003). *The smartest guys in the room: The amazing rise and fall of Enron.* New York: Portfolio.

Menu Foods. (2008, May 15). *Menu Foods income fund announces 2008 first quarter results.* Retrieved June 30, 2008, from http://menufoods.com/ir/financial_reports.html

Meyer, A. (1982). Adapting to environmental jolts. *Administrative Science Quarterly, 27,* 515–537.

Meyer, J., & Rowan, E. (1977). Institutionalized organizations: Formal structure as myth and ceremony. *American Journal of Sociology, 83,* 340–363.

Meyerson, D., Weick, K. E., & Kramer, R. M. (1996). Swift trust and temporary groups. In R. M. Kramer & T. R. Tyler (Eds.), *Trust in organizations* (p. 167). Thousand Oaks, CA: Sage.

Milgram, S. (1974). *Obedience to authority: An experimental view.* New York: Harpercollins.

Milliken, F. J. (1987). Three types of uncertainty about the environment: State, effect, and response uncertainty. *Academy of Management Review, 12,* 133–143.

Milliken, F. J. (1990). Perceiving and interpreting environmental change: An examination of college administrators' interpretation of changing demographics. *Academy of Management Journal, 33,* 42–63.

Miner, A., Bassoff, P., & Moorman, C. (2001). Organizational improvisation and learning: A field study. *Administrative Science Quarterly, 46*(2), 304–337.

Mintzberg, H. (1975). *The nature of managerial work.* New York: Harper and Row.

Mintzberg, H., Raisinghani, D., & Theoret, A. (1976). The structure of "unstructured" decision making. *Administrative Science Quarterly, 21,* 246–275.

Mishra, A. (1996). Organizational responses to crisis: The centrality of trust. In R. Kramer & T. Thomas (Eds.), *Trust in organizations* (pp. 261–287). Newbury Park, CA: Sage.

Mitroff, I. I. (1994). Crisis management and environmentalism: A natural fit. *California Management Review, 36,* 101–114.

Mitroff, I. I. (2004). Think like a sociopath, act like a saint. *Journal of Business Strategy, 25*(4), 42–53.

Mitroff, I. I., & Aspaslan, M. C. (2003). Preparing for evil. *Harvard Business Review, 81*(4), 109–115.

Mitroff, I., Pauchant, T., & Shrivastava, P. (1988). Conceptual and empirical issues in the development of a general theory of crisis management. *Technological Forecasting and Social Change, 33,* 83–107.

Mitroff, I. I., Pearson, C. M., & Harrington, L. K. (1996). *The essential guide to managing corporate crises: A step-by-step handbook for surviving major catastrophes.* New York: Oxford University Press.

Mohammed, S. & Brad, D. (2001). Team mental models in a team knowledge framework: Expanding theory and measurement across disciplinary boundaries. *Journal of Organizational Behavior, 22*(2), 89–106.

Mohammed, S. & Dumville, B. (2001). Team mental models in a team knowledge framework: Expanding theory and measurement across disciplinary boundaries. *Journal of Organizational Behavior, 22,* 89–106.

Moon, Y., & Herman, K. (2002). *McDonald's Russia: Managing a crisis.* Case 9-503-020. Cambridge, MA: Harvard Business School Publishing.

Moorman, C., Zaltman, G., & Deshpande, R. (1994). Factors affecting trust in market research relationships. *Journal of Marketing Research, 57*(1), 81–101.

Morgan, G. (1993). *Imaginization: The art of creative management.* Newbury Park, CA: Sage.

Morris, B., Seller, P., & Tarpley, N. (2000). *What really happened at Coke?* Retrieved October 28, 2008, from http://money.cnn.com/magazines/fortune/fortune_archive/2000/01/10/271736/index.htm

Moynihan, D. P. (2008). Learning under uncertainty: Networks in crisis management. *Public Administration Review, 68*(2), 350–365.

Nacoste, R. W. (1985). Selection procedure and responses to affirmative action: The case of favorable treatment. *Law and Human Behavior, 9,* 225–242.

Nelson, S., & Winter, R. (1982). *An evolutionary theory of economic change.* Cambridge, MA: Harvard University Press.

Nembhard, I., & Edmonson, A. (2006). Making it safe: The effects of leader inclusiveness and professional status on psychological safety and improvement efforts in health care teams. *Journal of Organizational Behavior, 27,* 941–966.

Ocasio, W. (1995). The enactment of economic diversity: A reconciliation of theories of failure-induced change and threat-rigidity. In L. Cummings & B. Staw (Eds.), *Research in organizational behavior* (Vol. 17, pp. 287–331). Greenwich, CT: JAI Press.

Oliver, C. (1991). Strategic responses to institutional processes. *Academy of Management Review, 16*(1), 145–179.

Orlando Sentinel. (2008). Maker of contaminated pet food settles with pet owners. Retrieved June 30, 2008, from http://blogs.orlandosentinel.com/features_lifestyle_animal/2008/04/maker-of-contam.html

Ouchi, W. G. (1981). *Theory Z: How American business can meet the Japanese challenge.* Reading, MA: Addison-Wesley.

Pearson, C., & Claire, J. (1998). Reframing crisis management. *Academy of Management Review, 23*, 59–76.

Pearson, C., & Mitroff, I. (1993). From crisis prone to crisis prepared: A framework for crisis management. *Academy of Management Executive, 7*, 48–59.

Peirce, E., Smolinksi, C., & Rosen, B. (1998). Why sexual harassment complaints fall on deaf ears. *Academy of Management Executive, 12*(3), 41–54.

Perlmutter, H. (1969). The tortuous evolution of the multi-national corporation. *Columbia Journal of Business, 4*(1), 9–18.

Perrow, C. (1984). *Normal accidents.* New York: Basic Books.

Pfeffer, J. (1981). *Power in organizations.* Marshfield, MA: Pitman.

Pfeffer, J., & Salancik, G. (1978). *The external control of organizations: A resource dependence perspective.* New York: Harper and Row.

Pham, N. T., & Swierczek, F. W. (2006). Facilitators of organizational learning in design. *The Learning Organization, 13*, 186–201.

Piaget, J. (1932). *The moral judgment of the child.* London, UK: Kegan, Paul, Trench & Trubner.

Pinsdorf, M. (2004). *All crises are global: Managing to escape chaos.* New York: Fordham University Press.

Poe, J. (2000, September 30). Making sure diversity gets a chance: Upclose Harriett Watkins, external manager of Georgia Power. *The Atlanta Journal-Constitution*, p. H2.

Pollard, D., & Hotho, S. (2006). Crises, scenarios and the strategic management process. *Management Decision, 44*(6), 721–736.

Pomerenke, P. J. (1998). Class action sexual harassment lawsuit: A study in crisis communication. *Human Resource Management, 37*(3), 207–219.

Post, J. E., Preston, L. E., & Sachs, S. (2002). *Redefining the corporation.* Stanford, CA: Stanford University Press.

Pouw, M. (2003). Conclusions: Operational perspectives. *Journal of Contingencies and Crisis Management, 11*(3), 142–143.

Powell, E. (1998). *How normal is normal? The Mitsubishi Motors sexual harassment case.* Case UVA-BC-0128. Charlottesville, VA: University of Virginia, Darden School Foundation.

Preble, J. (1994). Handling international disasters. *Lessons for Management, 11*(1), 550–560.

Pruitt, S. W., & Nethercutt, L. L. (2002). The Texaco racial discrimination case and shareholder wealth. *Journal of Labor Research, 23*(4), 685–693.

Quarantelli, E. L. (1988). Disaster crisis management: A summary of research findings. *Journal of Management Studies, 25*, 373–385.

Quinn, M. (2000a, July 29). Ga. Power learns from Coca-Cola bias suit cases similar: Utility's response shows lessons gleaned from soft drink giant's actions. *The Atlanta Journal-Constitution*, p. F1.

Quinn, M. (2000b, August 30). Ga. Power says five nooses displayed. *The Atlanta Journal-Constitution*, p. F1.

Rahim, M. (1997). Managing organizational learning. *International Journal of Organizational Analysis, 5,* 5–8.

Rego, L. (2009). Crisis leadership lessons from the "Miracle on the Hudson." Stepping into the void, Retrieved March 2009, from http://crisisleadership.blogspot.com/search?updated-min=2009-01-01T00%3A00%3A00-08%3A00&updated-max=2010-01-01T00%3A00%3A00-08%3A00&max-results=12.

Reina, D. S., & Reina, M. L. (1999). *Trust and betrayal in the workplace.* San Francisco: Berrett-Koehler Publishers.

Rest, J. R. (1986). *Moral development: Advances in research and theory.* New York: Praeger Publishers.

Ribbens, B. (1997). Organizational learning styles: Categorizing strategic predisposition from learning. *International Journal of Organizational Analysis, 5,* 59–73.

Rice, F. (1996, May 13). Denny's changes its spots. *Fortune,* 133–142.

Richard, O. (2000). Racial diversity, business strategy, and firm performance: A resource-based view. *Academy of Management Journal, 43,* 164–177.

Richardson, D. R., Hammock, G. S., Smith, S. M., Gardner, W., & Signo, M. (1994). Empathy as a cognitive inhibitor of interpersonal aggression. *Aggressive Behavior, 20,* 275–289.

Rike, B. (2003). "Preared or not … That is the vital question." *Information Management Journal, 37*(3), 25–32.

Roberto M., Bohmer R., Edmondson A. (2006). Facing ambiguous threats. *Harvard Business Review, 84,* 106–113, 157.

Robinson, G., & Dechant, K. (1997). Building a business case for diversity. *Academy of Management Executive, 11,* 21–31.

Rosenberg, M. (1979). *Conceiving of the self.* New York: Basic Books.

Rosenthal, U., & Kouzmin, A. (1993a). Crises and crisis management: Toward comprehensive government decision making. *Journal of Public Administration Research and Theory, 2,* 277–304.

Rosenthal, U., & Kouzmin, A. (1993b). Globalizing an agenda for contingencies and crisis management: An editorial statement. *Journal of Contingencies and Crisis Management, 1*(1), 1–12.

Rosenthal, U., & Kouzmin, A. (1997). Crises and crisis management: Toward comprehensive government decision making. *J-PART: Journal of Public Administration Research and Theory, 7*(2), 277–304.

Ross, L., & Anderson, C. A. (1982). Shortcomings in the attribution process: On the origins and maintenance of erroneous social assessments. In D. Kahneman, P. Slovic, & A. Tversky (Eds.), *Judgment under uncertainty: Heuristics and biases* (pp. 129–152). New York: Oxford University Press.

Roux, Dufort, C., & Vidaillet, B. (2003). The difficulties of improvising in a crisis situation: A case study. *Int. Studies of Management & Organization, 33*(1), 86–115.

Russell Sage Foundation. Retrieved from http://www.russellsage.org/publications/books/subjects/TRUST.

Savage, G., Dunkin, J., & Ford, D. (2003/2004). Responding to a crisis: A stakeholder analysis of community health organizations. *Journal of Health and Human Services Administration, 26*(3/4), 383–413.

Savage, G. T., Nix, T. W., Whitehead, C. J., & Blair, J. D. (1991). Strategies for assessing and managing organizational stakeholders. *Academy of Management Executive, 5*(2), 61–75.

Scheier, M. F., & Carver, C. S. (1985). Optimism, coping, and health: Assessment and implications of generalized outcome expectancies. *Health Psychology, 4*, 219–247.

Schein, E. (1996). Three cultures of management: The key to organizational learning. *Sloan Management Review, 38*, 9–20.

Schlenker, B. R. (1980). *Impression management: The self-concept, social identity, and interpersonal relations*. Monterey, CA: Brooks/Cole.

Schlenker, B. R. (1982). Translating actions into attitudes: An identity-analytic approach to the explanation of social conduct. In L. Berkowitz (Ed.), *Advances in experimental and social psychology* (Vol. 15, pp. 193–247). New York: Academic Press.

Schlenker, B. R., & Weingold, M. F. (1992). Interpersonal processes involving impression regulation and management. *Annual Review of Psychology, 43*, 133–168.

Schmidt, P., & Berrell, M. (2007). *Western and Eastern approaches to crisis management for global tourism: Some differences* (E. Laws, B. Prideaux, & K. Chon, Eds., pp. 66–80). Wallingford, UK: CABI (CAB International).

Schneider, K. (2005). Administrative breakdowns in the governmental response to Hurricane Katrina. *Public Administration Review, 65*(5), 515–516.

Scholtes, P., Joiner, B., & Steibel, B.H. (1996). *The team handbook*. Madison, WI: Oriel Incorporated.

Schonbach, P. (1980). A category system for account phases. *European Journal of Social Psychology, 10*, 195–200.

Scott, M. H., & Lyman, S. M. (1968). Accounts. *American Sociological Review, 33*, 46–62.

Scott, R. (2008). Jindal takes full command in crisis. *New Orleans Time-Picayune*, September 7.

Scott, W. R. (1987). The adolescence of institutional theory. *Administrative Science Quarterly, 32*, 493–511.

Seligman, M. E. P. (1990). *Learned optimism*. New York: Pocket Books.

Sen, F., & Egelhoff, G. (1991). Six years and counting from crisis management at Bhopal. *Public Relations Review, 17*(1), 69–83.

Senge, P. (1990). *The fifth discipline*. New York: Doubleday.

Shafer, R. A., Dyer, L., Kilty, J., Amos, J., & Ericksen, J. (2001). Crafting a human resource strategy to foster organizational agility: A case study. *Human Resource Management, 40*(3), 197–208.

Shrivastava, P. (1983). A typology of organizational learning systems. *Journal of Management Studies, 20*, 7–27.

Shrivastava, P. (1993). Crisis theory/practice: Towards a sustainable future. *Industrial and Environmental Crisis Quarterly, 7*, 23–42.

Shrivastava, P., Mitroff, I. I., Miller, D., & Miglani, A. (1988). Understanding industrial crises. *Journal of Management Studies, 25*(4), 285–303.

Simision, R., Lundegaard, K., Shirouzu, N., & Heller, J. (2000, August 10). Blowout: How the tire problem turned into a crisis for Firestone and Ford—Lack of a database masked the pattern that led to yesterday's recall—The heat and the pressure. *Wall Street Journal*, p. A1.

Simon, H. A. (1957). *Administrative Behavior* (2nd ed.). New York: Macmillan.

Simon, H. A. (1959). Theories of decision-making in economics and behavioral science. *American Economic Review, 49*, 253–283.

Simon, H. A. (1976). *Administrative behavior* (3rd ed.). New York: The Free Press.

Simon, H. A. (1991). Bounded rationality and organizational learning. *Organization Science, 2*, 125–134.

Simon, R., Scherer, J., & Rau, W. (1999). Sexual harassment in the heartland? Community opinion on the EEOC suit against Mitsubishi Motor Manufacturing of America. *Social Science Journal, 36*(3), 487–495.

Simons, D. J., & Chabris, C. F. (1999). Gorillas in our midst: Sustained inattentional blindness for dynamic events. *Perception, 28*, 1059–1074.

Simpson, C. (1998, May 21). Suit accuses Gingiss of race bias. *Chicago Sun-Times*, p. 22.

Sitkin, S. (1992). Learning through failure: The strategy of small losses. In B. M. Staw & L. L. Cummings (Eds.), *Research in organizational behavior* (pp. 231–266). Greenwich, CT: JAI.

Sitkin, S. B., & Pablo, A. L. (1992). Reconceptualizing the determinants of risk behavior. *Academy of Management Review, 17*, 9–38.

Skinner, B. F. (1971). *Contingencies of reinforcement*. East Norwalk, CT: Appleton-Century-Crofts.

Slater, S., & Narver, J. (1995). Market orientation and the learning organization. *Journal of Marketing, 58*, 63–74.

Slovic, P., Fischoff, B., & Lichtenstein, S. (1980). Facts and fears: Understanding perceived risk. In R. Schwing & W. Albers (Eds.), *Societal risk assessment* (pp. 67–93). New York: Plenum.

Smith, C. A., & Ellsworth, P. (1985). Patterns of cognitive appraisal in emotion. *Journal of Personality and Social Psychology, 48*, 813–838.

Smith, C. A., Haynes, K. N., Lazarus, R. S., & Pope, L. K. (1993). In search of the "hot" cognitions: Attributions, appraisals, and their relation to emotion. *Journal of Personality and Social Psychology, 65*, 916–929.

Smith, C. C. (1990). Bhopal aftermath: Union Carbide rethinks safety. *Business and Society Review, 75*, 500–553.

Smith, H. R. & Carroll, A. B. (1984). Organizational ethics: A stacked deck. *Journal of Business Ethics, 3*, 95–100.

Smith, (2000). Crisis management teams: Issues in the management of operational crisis. *Risk Management, 2*(3), 61–78.

Souza, D. (1997). The diversity trap. *Forbes, 159*(2), 83.

Spielberger, C. D. (1983). *Manual for the State-Trait Anxiety Inventory (STAI)*. Palo Alto, CA: Consulting Psychologists Press.

Spreitzer, G., & Quinn, R. (2001). *A company of leaders: Five disciplines for unleashing the power of your workforce*. San Francisco: Jossey-Bass.

Starbuck, W., & Hedberg, B. L. (1977). Saving an organization from a stagnating environment. In H. Thorelli (Ed.), *Strategy + structure = performance* (Vol. 2, pp. 45–80). Greenwich, CT: JAI Press.

Starkey, K. (Ed.). (1996). *How organizations learn*. London, UK: International Thomson Business Press.

Staw, B. M., Sandelands, L. E., & Dutton, J. E. (1981). Threat-rigidity effects in orga-nizational behavior: A multilevel analysis. *Administrative Science Quarterly, 26,* 501–524.

Stecklowe, S. (2005, June 7). How a web of activists gives Coke problems in India. *Wall Street Journal,* 7.

Stephens, K., Malone, P., & Bailey, C. (2005). Communicating with stakeholders during a crisis: Evaluating message strategies. *Journal of Business Communication, 42*(4), 391–419.

Suburban Emergency Management Project. (2008, November 27). *Wal-Mart way in disaster preparedness/response: Policy implications.* Retrieved November 1, 2009, from http://www.semp.us/publications/biot_reader.php?BiotID=569

Sundaram, A. K., & Inkpen, A. C. (2004). The corporate objective revisited. *Organization Science, 15*(3), 350–363.

Sutcliffe, K. M., & Vogus, T. J. (2003). Organizing for resilience. In K. S. Cameron, J. E. Dutton, & R. E. Quinn (Eds.), *Positive organizational scholarship* (pp. 94–110). San Francisco: Berrett-Koehler.

Sutton, R., & Callahan, A. (1987). The stigma of bankruptcy: Spoiled organizational image and its management. *Academy of Management Journal, 30,* 405–436.

Taylor, S. (1989). *Positive illusions.* New York: Basic Books.

Teece, D. J., Pisano, G., & Shuen, A. (1997). Dynamic capabilities and strategic manage-ment. *Strategic Management Journal, 18,* 509–533.

Terpstra, D. E., & Kethley, B. R. (2002). Organizations' relative degree of exposure to selection discrimination litigation. *Public Personnel Management, 3,* 277–292.

Thomas, D. A. (1993). Racial dynamics in cross-race developmental relationships. *Administrative Science Quarterly, 38,* 169–194.

Thomas, D., & Ely, R. (1996). Making differences matter: A new paradigm for managing diversity. *Harvard Business Review, 74,* 79–81.

Thomas, J., Clark, S., & Gioia, D. (1993). Strategic sensemaking and organizational performance: Linkages among scanning, interpretation, action, and outcomes. *Academy of Management Journal, 36,* 239–270.

Trevino, L. K. (1986). Ethical decision making in organizations: A person–situation interactionist model. *Academy of Management Review, 11*(3), 601–617.

Trice, H., & Beyer, J. (1993). *The culture of work organizations.* Englewood Cliffs, NJ: Prentice Hall.

Tsang, A. (2000). Military doctrine in crisis management: Three beverages contamination cases. *Business Horizons, 43*(5), 65–73.

Tsang, E. (1997). Organizational learning and the learning organization: A dichotomy between descriptive and prescriptive research. *Human Relations, 50,* 73–89.

Turner, M. E., & Pratkanis, A. R. (1994). Affirmative action as help: A review of recipient reactions to preferential selection and affirmative action. *Basic and Applied Social Psychology, 15,* 43–69.

Turoff, M. (2002). Past and future emergency response information systems. *Communications of the ACM, 45*(4), 29–32.

Turoff, M., Chumer, M., Van de Walle, B., & Yao, X. (2004). The design of a dynamic emergency response management information system (DERMIS). *JITTA: Journal of Information Technology Theory and Application, 5*(4), 1–35.

Tversky, A., & Kahneman, D. (1974). Judgment under uncertainty: Heuristics and biases. *Science, 211*, 453–463.

Tversky, A., & Kahneman, D. (1992). Advances in prospect theory: Cumulative representation of uncertainty. *Journal of Risk and Uncertainty, 5*, 297–323.

Unger, H. (1999, April 24). Discrimination lawsuit: Coca-Cola accused of company-wide patterns. *Atlantic Journal-Constitution,* p. H1.

Vardi, Y., & Wiener, Y. (1996). Misbehavior in organizations: A motivational framework. *Organization Science, 7*(2), 151–165.

Velasquez, M., & Rostankowski, C. (1985). *Ethics: Theory and practice.* Englewood Cliffs, NJ: Prentice Hall.

Vertovec, S., & Cohen, R. (2002). Introduction: Conceiving cosmopolitanism. In S. Vertovec & R. Cohen (Eds.), *Conceiving cosmopolitanism: Theory, context and practice* (pp. 1–22). Oxford, UK: Oxford University Press.

Vroom, V. (1964). *Work and motivation.* New York: Wiley.

Wade, M., & Hulland, J. (2004). The resource-based view and information systems research: Review, extension, and suggestions for future research. *MIS Quarterly, 28*(1), 107–148.

Wal-Mart: Beyond Business. Retrieved from http://www.sendwordnow.com/walmart Release2.aspx.

Walsh, J., & Ungson, J. (1991). Organizational memory. *Academy of Management Review, 16*, 57–93.

Wang, J. (2008). Developing organizational learning capacity in crisis management. *Advances in Developing Human Resources, 10*(3), 425–445.

Webb, E. J. (1996). Trust in crisis. In R. M. Kramer & T. R. Tyler (Eds.), *Trust in organizations* (pp. 288–301). Thousand Oaks, CA: Sage.

Webb, G. (2004). Role improvising during crisis situations. *International Journal of Emergency Management, 2*(1–2), 47–61.

Weber, J. (1990). Managers' moral reasoning: Assessing their responses to three moral dilemmas. *Human Relations, 43*(7), 687–702.

Weick, K. E. (1988). Enacted sensemaking in crisis situations. *Journal of Management Studies, 25*(4), 305–317.

Weick, K. E. (1991). The nontraditional quality of organizational learning. *Organization Science, 2*, 116–124.

Weick, K. E. (1993). The collapse of sensemaking in organizations: The Mann Gulch disaster. *Administrative Science Quarterly, 38*(4), 628–652.

Weick, K. E., & Quinn, R. E. (1999). Organizational change and development. *Annual Review of Psychology, 50*, 361–386.

Weick, K. E., Sutcliffe, K. M., & Obstfeld, D. (2005). Organizing and the process of sense making. *Organization Science, 14*(4), 409–421.

Weiner, B. (1985). An attributional theory of achievement motivation and emotion. *Psychological Review, 92*(4), 548–573.

Wentling, R. M., & Palma-Rivas, N. (2000). Current status of diversity initiatives in selected multinational corporations. *Human Resource Development Quarterly, 11*, 35–60.

Whetten, D., & Cameron, K. (1991). *Developing management skills* (2nd ed.). New York: Harper-Collins.

Whoriskey, P. (2008). Jindal presents a face of calm during the storm. *Washington Post,* September 3: A6.

Wildavesky, A. (1988). *Searching for safety.* New Brunswick, NJ: Transaction Books.

William Davidson Institute (Producer) (2008). Presentation by Courtney Wilson, Executive Director of Baltimore & Ohio Museum. Ann Arbor, Michigan: Ross School of Business.

Williams, S. D. (2004). Personality, attitude and leader influences on divergent thinking and creativity in organizations. *European Journal of Innovation Management, 7,* 187–201.

Winter, G. (2000). Coca-Cola settles racial bias case. Retrieved March 2004, from http://www.nytimes.com/2000/11/17/business/coca-cola-settles-racial-bias-case.html?pagewanted=1

Winter, S. (2003). Understanding dynamic capabilities. *Strategic Management Journal, 24*(10), 991–995.

Witzel, D. (Moderator). (2008, March 27). Interview with C. Kelly & M. Gerencser on megacommunities. Retrieved October 10, 2009, from http://interviews.forumone.com/content/interview/detail/971/

Wokutch, R., & Shepard, J. (1999). The maturing of the Japanese economy: Corporate social responsibility implications. *Business Quarterly, 9*(3), 527–540.

Wood, R., & Bandura, A. (1989). Social cognitive theory of organizational management. *Academy of Management Review, 14,* 361–384.

Wooten, L. P. (2006). *Framing crisis management: A multiple lens perspective.* Darden Executive Briefing Series on Crisis Management. Charlottesville, VA: Darden Press, Batten Institute.

Wooten, L. P., & James, E. H. (2004). When firms fail to learn: Perpetuation of discrimination in the workplace. *Journal of Management Inquiry, 13*(1), 23–33.

Wooten, L. P., & James, E. H. (2008). Linking crisis management and leadership competencies: The role of human resource development. *Advances in Developing Human Resources, 10*(3), 352–379.

Ybarra, O., Chan, C., Park, H., Burnstein, E., & Monin, B. (2008). *The primitive templates of the mind (PToM), the ubiquity and different stability of the sociomoral and taskability dimensions.* Unpublished manuscript.

Yemen, G., & James, E. (2006, January 24). *Exxon Valdez revisited: The untold story.* UVA-OB-0867 and UVA-OB-0868. Darden Business Publishing.

Yukl, G., & Falbe, C. M. (1990). Influence tactics and objectives in upward, downward, and lateral influence attempts. *Journal of Applied Psychology, 75*(2), 132–140.

Zacarro, S. J. (2007). Trait-based perspectives of leadership. *American Psychologist, 62,* 6–16.

Zimmerman, A. (2008, August 30). Wal-Mart's emergency-relief team girds for Hurricane Gustav. *The Wall Street Journal,* A3.

Author Index

Subject Index

Hooters, 170
Hurricane Gustav, 46, 48, 113
Hurricane Katrina, 50, 109, 137, 202, 228
Imclone, 16
Jack-in-the-Box, 215, 224
Japanese Airlines, 193
JetBlue Airways, 18
Johnson & Johnson, 131, 133, 143, 216,
    226
JPMorgan Chase, 3
Kodak, 90
Lehman Brothers, 3
Mann Gulch forest fires, 29
Martha Stewart Omnimedia, 58
Mattel, 121
McDonald's, 186
Menu Foods, 19
Merrill Lynch, 3
Mitsubishi, 188
Morgan Stanley, 109
Northern Natural Gas Company, 15
Nut Island disaster, 120
Publix, 164
SARS crisis (China), 110, 203
Texaco Corporation, 157, 172
Tyco, 63
Tylenol crisis, 131, 133, 143, 216, 226
Union Carbide, 190
US Airways, 69, 120
Virginia Tech massacre, 41
Wal-Mart, 46, 48, 109
Washington Mutual, 3
Worldcom, 16
World Trade Center attacks, 24, 30
CEO apology, 53
Cerberus Capital Management, 192
Chernobyl disaster, 20
Chrysler, 192
Cisco, 108
Civil Rights Act of 1991, 158
Class action lawsuit, 172
Coalition building, 47
Coca-Cola, 7, 64, 155, 168, 172, 197
Cognitive limits, 76
Cognitive moral development, model of, 94
Collective efficacy, 62, 229
Communication
    culture of, 150
    damage control and, 51
    double-loop, 190, 206

to shareholders, 19
strategy, 82
visionary style, 113
Competence trust, 135
Concern, description of, 136
Consumer Product Safety Commission, 121
Conventional crises, 28
Corporate Crisis Management Team, 108
Corporate culture
    decision making and, 77
    efficacy dimensions, 229
    indications, 94
    post-scandal, 63
    promotion-focused mission, 228
    readiness mentality, 33
    reflective learning process and, 174
    trusting, 12, 148
Creativity, definition of, 50
Crises
    definition of, 17
    handling teams, vulnerability of, 145
    internally derived, 27
    leadership, see Leadership, importance of
    smoldering, 25
Crises and crisis management, 15–36
    abnormal crises, 27
    accidents, definition of, 27
    assigning responsibility for crisis, 29–31
    Bhopal industrial disaster, 16
    business crisis, definition of, 17
    business problem versus crisis, 18
    categorizing crisis types, 23–24
    Chernobyl disaster, 20
    conventional crises, 28
    crisis phase questions, 33–34
    crisis types, 26
    crisis typologies, 24–29
    defining crisis, 17–23
        publicity, 22–23
        rarity, 18–19
        significance, 19
        stakeholders, 20–22
    fundamental crises, 29
    influence possibility, 28
    internally derived crises, 27
    intractable crises, 29
    negative influence, 21
    normal crises, 27
    phases of crisis management, 31–32
        business recovery, 32